Contemporary Feminism and Women's Short Stories

Dedicated to the memory of Joan Young,
always a strong woman

The short story is a great painting, a perfect photograph. The single image that allows the viewer in, not just to see what is there, within the frame, but to dream into what has not been painted.

Stella Duffy (2014)

Contemporary Feminism and Women's Short Stories

Emma Young

EDINBURGH
University Press

Edinburgh University Press is one of the leading university presses in the UK. We publish academic books and journals in our selected subject areas across the humanities and social sciences, combining cutting-edge scholarship with high editorial and production values to produce academic works of lasting importance. For more information visit our website: edinburghuniversitypress.com

Edinburgh University Press Ltd
The Tun – Holyrood Road, 12(2f) Jackson's Entry, Edinburgh EH8 8PJ

First published in hardback by Edinburgh University Press 2018

Typeset in 11/13 Adobe Sabon by
IDSUK (DataConnection) Ltd, and
printed and bound in Great Britain by
CPI Group (UK) Ltd, Croydon CR0 4YY

A CIP record for this book is available from the British Library

ISBN 978 1 4744 2773 9 (hardback)
ISBN 978 1 4744 2774 6 (paperback)
ISBN 978 1 4744 2775 3 (webready PDF)
ISBN 978 1 4744 2776 0 (epub)

Contents

Acknowledgements

From its inception, many people have been influential in shaping this work. First and foremost, I am indebted to Professor Lucie Armitt, who has been a wonderful mentor – without her support and guidance during the earlier stages of this project, this book would not be what it is today. A wholehearted thank you goes to Dr Claire O'Callaghan. Her wonderful friendship, the inspiration she provides as an academic and her never-ending support throughout have been more valuable than she can know. I would like to thank Dr Claudia Capancioni for her words of kindness and feedback during the early stages of this project. I am indebted to the readers who have provided insightful comments, all in the spirit of development. Thanks are also due to Jackie Jones at Edinburgh University Press for her belief in this project and for her ongoing support for publishing in the field of women's writing. Sections of Chapter 2 originally appeared in my chapter 'Feminist F(r)iction: Short Stories and Postfeminist Politics at the Millennial Moment', in *British Women Short Story Writers: The New Woman to Now* (2015); thank you to Edinburgh University Press and my co-editor James Bailey for allowing me to reproduce elements of this work in my book.

Thanks are due to all my family, and most especially of all to my parents. Their enduring support and faith have never wavered and I am eternally grateful for all they have done to enable me to pursue an academic path. I would like to thank Steve for encouraging me to persevere with this project, even when it seemed like a challenge too large. And finally, to my grandparents: their desire to see this book published has been the ultimate motivation.

Introduction: Contexts, Politics and Genre

The contemporary moment appears to be *the moment* for women short story writers, who have received increased critical attention and popular acclaim. Indeed, in surveying this literary field and attending to the reoccurring tropes and discourses in this body of work, it seems reasonable to argue that this is an opportune moment for considering the ways in which shifting feminist sensibilities and gendered subjectivities are revealed through women's short story writing. A prevailing tendency in the short stories of many contemporary British women writers is a preoccupation with issues of gender and sexuality that, in turn, signals a wider engagement with feminist politics. In such narratives, the short story is used as an intentionally feminist literary vehicle in which to explore the issues and debates at the heart of feminist politics today. By framing the discussion in this way, 'the moment' brings together the short story and feminist politics and offers a means of conceptualising their independent status in the twenty-first century; as well as offering a new perspective on their interrelationship in the context of British women's short story writing. The focus on the moment, then, bridges the formal features of the short story, the momentary experience of reading short fiction, and the 'of the moment' nature of feminist politics.

In discussing the all-women shortlist for the BBC National Short Story Award 2013 the chair of the judging panel, Mariella Frostrup, heralded this event as evidence that 'the short story is a form much suited to the innovative brilliance of women writers' (Bury 2013: n. p.), a statement that signals the timeliness of discussing contemporary British women writers and their relationship with the short story. By 2016, when K. J. Orr won the BBC National Short Story Award, it was the fourth time since 2009 that the award celebrated an all-female shortlist.[1] Furthermore, in recent years there has been increasing speculation about the so-called renaissance of the short story. In 'The Irresistible Rise of the Short Story' (2014), Sam Baker considers why the short story is the 'perfect literary form for the 21st century' and highlights the importance of 'the moment': 'there's no doubt about it, the short story is having "a moment"' (n. p.). Similarly, numerous authors make anecdotal reference to the momentary nature of the short story. Stella Duffy notes how 'the short story has a freedom to take one moment and explode it' (as cited in Baker 2014: n. p.); while in her 'Foreword' to *The Mistletoe Bride and Other Haunting Tales* (2013) Kate Mosse celebrates 'the need to capture a moment of experience, rather than creating a whole world and everything in it' (xiv). Such diverse understandings of 'the moment' provide a conceptual framework through which to scrutinise the relationship between British women writers and the short story and to interrogate what this literary medium provides for writers in creatively contributing to critical feminist debates.

The relationship between women writers and the short story has re-emerged in literary criticism over the years, with Clare Hanson asserting that it 'has offered itself to losers and loners, exiles, women, blacks – writers who for one reason or another have not been part of the ruling "narrative" or epistemological/experiential framework of their society' (1989a: 1). Equally, Kasia Boddy (1996) proposes that a 'more fruitful way of examining the relationship between women writers and the short story would be to look at the characteristics of the genre itself and to consider what advantages the short story form holds' (80). Undoubtedly, the short story is a useful literary vehicle for women writers, not because of the short story's marginalised or renegade status, but because it is a genre with certain formal features that all contribute to its 'momentariness', naturally conducive to engaging, mapping and reflecting feminist politics.[2] As such, I develop the approach first outlined by Dominic Head (1994), which proposes 'a connection between the generic capacities of the short story and the way in which writers have depicted their social world, a connection which stems from a special kind of literary experience relevant to readers, as well as to writers, of short stories' (1). While Head's analysis focuses on the politics of Modernism, here, in a similar vein, I scrutinise how the short story's formal features facilitate nuanced negotiations with contemporary feminisms.

The chapters that follow are moments in their own right, as they all focus on a particular theme or issue that has been central to contemporary feminisms. In fact, each of these chapters can be viewed as forming a short story of its own about contemporary feminisms. By structuring the chapters around these issues, which stimulate ongoing feminist debate, I illuminate some of the ways in which feminisms 'speak' across different cultural and temporal moments. The analysis is reader-orientated in its approach due to the politicising of feminisms that occurs through the social dialogue between reader and text. Accordingly, the question of the reader re-emerges throughout the chapters: fundamentally, does the political potential of the narrative always rely on the reader's subjective, personal politics or, indeed, is it possible for the short story to act as a literary vehicle for feminisms regardless of the reader's political orientation? Consequently, the importance of experience and affect reoccurs in many of the textual discussions with the immediacy of reading short fiction, 'in the moment', offering a further appendage to this motif.

A particularly significant 'moment' in literary history was the writing of Angela Carter, who is a notable predecessor in the context of contemporary women's short story writing. In an 'Afterword' to her collection *Fireworks* (1987) she draws an important line between the short story and the 'tales' that she produces. For Carter, it was important to return to the oral roots of short fiction and to tell tales of women's experiences, with the tropes of femininity and sexuality being especially pertinent to her politics. While *The Bloody Chamber* (1995) is Carter's most notorious and widely discussed contribution to the field of short story writing, she also played an important role in exploiting the potential of the anthology for championing women's voices. As editor of *The Virago Book of Fairy Tales* (1990), *The Second Virago Book of Fairy Tales* (1992) and *Angela Carter's Book of Wayward Girls and Wicked Women* (2004), Carter offers stories 'in a valedictory spirit, as a reminder of how wise, clever, perceptive, occasionally lyrical, eccentric, sometimes downright crazy our great-grandmothers were' ('Introduction', 1990, p. xxiv). Carter's short fiction, therefore, was acutely attuned to history, to the acts of reclaiming, revising and rewriting the stories of women's lives. This political engagement with myth and fairytale continues beyond Carter in contemporary short story rewriting by authors such as A. S. Byatt, Emma Donoghue and Fay Weldon. Thus, while Carter does not feature throughout the chapters that follow, she remains an important foremother and path-maker for many of the writers that come after. Moreover, this book seeks to progress the conversation, to understand better how Carter's legacy, as a champion of the short story form, lives on in more recent (feminist) contributions to the literary field.

Across the chapters I discuss a body of post-1980 British women's short story writing, including: Kate Atkinson, Nicola Barker,

A. S. Byatt, Aminatta Forna, Janice Galloway, Sarah Hall, Victoria Hislop, Jackie Kay, Andrea Levy, Hilary Mantel, Kate Mosse, Michèle Roberts, Jane Rogers, Helen Simpson, Ali Smith, Zadie Smith and Rose Tremain. While this is by no means an exhaustive selection, all of these writers have either published short story collections, been nominated for short story prizes, or published in anthologies and/ or magazines and, therefore, in some way notably contributed to the field of short story writing in recent years. In keeping with the desire to recognise the multiplicity of contemporary feminisms, the discussion of each writer's work articulates their engagement with feminisms and aims to acknowledge their unique significance, while also investigating how the work contributes to a wider literary trend. The stories by these women writers all engage, explicitly or subtly, with the themes that shape this book. By recognising the diverse, sometimes contradictory and ever-shifting terrain of feminist politics, the multi-vocal and heterogeneous nature of writing in contemporary Britain today is foreground and, throughout, the chapters continually reflect on how gender and sexuality debates intersect with issues of race, migration and ethnicity, as well as the politics of ageing. By scrutinising how literature explores the everyday lived realities and experiences of gender, sexuality and feminist theories, the short stories of these women writers are considered to be both creative *and* critical literary contributions.

A series of questions runs throughout this book, all of which illuminate the relationship between contemporary British women's short story writing and feminist politics. The first of these questions is: how do notions of first-, second- and third-wave feminism, and post(-)feminisms, inform and influence women's short story writing and, subsequently, how are these differing political moments represented within women's short story narratives? In reflecting on issues of genre, a question to reoccur across all five chapters is: what are the specific aesthetic qualities of the short story that make it a viable literary vehicle for contemporary women writers' negotiation of feminist politics and how do these formal features shape the fictional negotiation of feminisms? Furthermore, how does the short story as a genre position the reader and what are the implications of this positioning for the feminist potential of these narratives? The politics of race, ethnicity, migration, class and ageing are all important features of contemporary British life: how do writers acknowledge and engage with these discourses and what does this mean for feminist politics? Finally, in the context of 'differing versions of feminism', Lynne Segal (2001: 57) suggests that part of the ongoing project of feminism involves 'attempting to map out and assess which different pieces in the jigsaw of feminism get picked up' (ibid.). Segal suggests that there is also a need to think critically and to question 'who is selecting the fragments, and whose particular interests their delivery serves' (ibid.). An alternative means of phrasing Segal's assertion would be to consider which key *moments* of feminist thought are being represented; how and why are these strands being depicted and what does this say about contemporary feminisms? This is the final question considered as I reflect on how short stories (the pieces) contribute to the literary jigsaw of feminisms today.

The story of contemporary feminisms

Before outlining the theoretical position underpinning this book, firstly it seems useful to contextualise the terminology and concepts used throughout the analysis in relation to contemporary feminisms. In order to do this it is necessary to engage in an act of retelling by outlining the broad narrative of contemporary feminisms, in which sequential waves are located and indeed defined by specific temporal parameters and political paradigms. As a movement emerging in the late 1960s, second-wave feminism embodied divergent voices and ideas that united around one political goal: women's equality. The second wave is therefore most readily associated with the 1970s and 1980s. In her introduction to *Once a Feminist: Stories of a Generation* (1990), Michelene Wandor positions the Ruskin Women's Weekend as a pivotal point in the 'realisation that, marginal as I very often felt, I was objectively a part of the historical process' (2).[3] For Wandor, women's 'consciousness raising' and formation as a political group are a crucial part of second-wave feminism. There were four key demands formulated at the Ruskin weekend: equal pay, equal education and opportunity, twenty-four-hour nurseries, and free contraception and abortion on demand (Wandor 1990: 242–3). These demands are often positioned as indicative of the broader focus of the movement during this time, with the emphasis on the materiality of women's bodies, including questions about sexual choice and agency, motherhood and women's employment, being taken as *the* hallmarks of the second wave.

Academic feminism developed in tandem with this political activism. Simone de Beauvoir's *The Second Sex* (first published 1949) and Betty Friedan's *The Feminine Mystique* (first published 1963) are viewed as the cornerstones of second-wave feminist theory. However, as Sue Thornham (2001) contends, by 1970 there was an explosion of feminist theoretical writing (34), most notably with the publication of Kate Millett's *Sexual Politics* (first published 1970), Shulamith Firestone's *The Dialectic of Sex* (first published 1970) and Germaine Greer's *The Female Eunuch* (first published 1970). These texts all tackle the concept of 'patriarchy' and its (previously) socially invisible ideology and cultural manifestations. From Millett's argument that women have come to internalise the idea or ideology of femininity, through to Firestone's assertion that women's oppression is based on their reproductive abilities, these writers reveal the political bias of *all* culture and how this affects women's bodies and lives.

While second-wave feminism is firmly located in the 1970s and early 1980s, by the mid-1980s unease started to develop amongst feminists as to the direction of the movement. The question mark in the title of *What is Feminism?* (1986), edited by Juliet Mitchell and Ann Oakley, illustrates that atmosphere of uncertainty, and Susan Faludi's *Backlash: The Undeclared War Against Women* (1991) captures this milieu. In using the term 'post-feminism' it is important to differentiate it from 'postfeminism', a label with which it is often amalgamated. Sarah Gamble (2001) notes that the 'postfeminist debate tends to crystallise around issues of victimisation, autonomy and responsibility' (43). Because of this stance, Gamble asserts, post-feminism is often unwilling to condemn pornography and is sceptical of the date-rape phenomenon (44). Gamble's outline concludes that, 'because it tends to be implicitly heterosexist in orientation, post-feminism commonly seeks to develop an agenda which can find a place for men' (ibid.). Crucially, like third-wave feminism, postfeminism is an attempt to develop earlier feminist thought while taking into account postmodernism and post-structuralism, thus signalling where the 'post' aspect of its name originates.

Conversely, post-feminism is a notably media-driven notion which results in the discourse often being manipulated to produce provocative headlines. Female celebrities are heralded for their iconic status and deployed as symbols of women 'having it all'. In *Backlash*, Faludi argues that post-feminism *is the backlash* and that women are told (particularly by the media) that, 'you may be free and equal now, . . . but you have never been more miserable' (1993: 1). The subtext of Faludi's claim is that feminism is blamed for the woes of women *and* men today. In *The Morning After: Sex, Fear and Feminism* (1993) Kate Roiphe claims that the second-wave movement fuelled the backlash against feminism. Equally, in *Fire with Fire: The New Female Power and How it Will Change the 21st Century* (1993), Naomi Wolf argues that feminism has failed to recognise and capitalise on its gains. In the late 1980s and1990s feminism becomes seen as a problematic term and an ideology troubled by fissures. The narrative of feminisms during this period emphasises the breaks and conflict between the differing waves, as exemplified by the usage of 'post'.

Finally, in this story of contemporary feminisms, the third wave tends to be celebrated for its resonantly personal politics; a point seemingly emphasised by the proliferation of early third-wave anthologies and academic scholarship's tendency towards anecdotal accounts of individuals' personal experiences.[4] In part, the prevalence of these collections is a result of third-wavers' 'preference for defining feminism in their own terms – that is, for each individual feminist to define feminism *for herself individually*' (Henry 2004: 43). Of course, one consequence of this emphasis on individuality, and the embracing of embodied politics that 'aims to provoke change by exercising and resisting power in everyday life' (Fixmer and Wood 2005: 237), is that the movement is frequently critiqued for not progressing beyond 'individual assertions of identity to a larger, collective political identity' (Henry 2004: 44). Consequently, this aspect of the third wave is positioned in direct conflict with second-wave feminism's more 'sisterly' approach. While third-wavers are consciously attempting to avoid the monolithic generalisation of the category 'woman' often assumed by the 'sisterhood' discourse, their scepticism entraps the third wave in a further critique, and this often results in the second and third waves of feminism being discussed simultaneously in terms of difference and rejection, development and progress.

Third-wave feminism's focus on individuality means it 'addresses the subject's experience of having fragmented and conflicting selves that do not constitute a seamless and coherent whole' (Genz and Brabon 2009: 159). Like the focus on an individual woman's personal life choices, this is a recognition that individual identities are also heterogenic discourses that are not always easily unified. In the context of gender equality and sexual liberation, the turn to individual choice can be problematic. As Claire Snyder-Hall remarks, the third wave 'sometimes seems to uncritically endorse behaviours that appear problematic' (2010: 255). However, in defending this critique, Snyder-Hall argues that the movement 'actually exhibits not a thoughtless endorsement of "choice", but rather a deep respect for pluralism and self-determination' (ibid.). Third-wave feminism requires exponents and critics to scrutinise intently its politics and read both with and against its surface narrative. After all, third-wave feminism navigates an entangled ground of personal and theoretical politics as it attempts to learn from and build on the work of its second-wave foremothers, while outlining its own agenda. Suggestively, there is a need for a more nuanced recognition of the relationship between these two waves in feminist criticism in order to understand how, as is the case with waves, one overlaps with and into the other.

The conscious recovery of women's history has been a vital element of contemporary feminism. Moreover, such consciousness raising is also, in part, the reason that the narrative of feminism, as outlined here, exists today. While literary critics Elaine Showalter, Sandra Gilbert and Susan Gubar sought to rectify the critical neglect of women writers and to give voice to a specifically female literary tradition, feminist historians also worked to bring to light forgotten histories. Most notably, Sheila Rowbotham published profusely on women's and feminist histories throughout the latter decades of the twentieth century. Interestingly, in the 'Preface' to *Hidden from History* (1973), Rowbotham notes that this work started as a pamphlet 'and it is still a kind of pamphlet, or perhaps a bundle of pamphlets, bursting out of their binding with unfinished problems' (x). Likewise, she suggests that *Women in Movement: Feminism and Social Action* (1992) can be read in the traditional manner, from the beginning to the end, or 'it could even be read backward by those who prefer to approach the past from the present' (4). Both of these statements signal the importance of moving beyond traditional, linear understandings of narrative and focusing instead on the momentary, the experiential, and therefore unsettling the certainty which is naturally affiliated with history's linear tradition.

Theorising feminist moments

In recent years there has been a proliferation in scholarship which reconsiders the ways in which feminist history has been theorised. In 'Telling Feminist Stories' (2005) Clare Hemmings questions how Western feminist theory tells the story of its own recent past, and suggests that the dominant narrative to emerge is one of 'relentless progress or loss, proliferation or homogenization', which is ultimately a 'developmental narrative' (115). Hemmings rightly takes issue with this narrative because it oversimplifies different areas of feminist thought and forces 'others' outside of this narrative either to conform to the dominant position or to be seen as transcendent of it (116). Interrogating whether we can do feminist theory differently (130), Hemmings concludes by advocating an approach that 'stresses the links rather than the discontinuities between different theoretical frameworks, as a way of challenging the linear "displacement" of one approach by another' (131). By focusing on different moments of feminism, and by structuring the book by themes that have emerged across a range of contemporary British women's short story writing, rather than on the overarching frameworks that have come to define feminist history, the aim of this book is to engage with stories about feminism and feminist stories without being confined to the dominant narrative of feminisms.

In *Feminism's Queer Temporalities* (2016), Sam McBean declares an interest 'in encountering feminism's unruly temporalities, in complicating the linear and the generational' (3). By drawing on an archive of feminist literary and cultural material, McBean moves beyond the generational model of feminist history and repeatedly articulates the ways in which so-called feminist pasts 'might not be left for dead but might instead travel into various feminist presents' (17). While acknowledging the impossibility of ever fully extricating oneself from the dominant discourse (as already illuminated by my usage of wave-based terminology in this Introduction), through the focus and approach of this study I hope to offer readings which in some way frustrate the traditional linearity applied to feminisms and instead engage with the diverse, multifaceted, contradictory and overlapping nature of contemporary feminisms through thematic readings of short stories.

The concept of the moment is used in feminist theory but it remains undertheorised, and I propose that this concept resonates with current tendencies in literary and feminist scholarship to unsettle the dominant narrative of feminism, to draw on Hemmings' phrase. Imelda Whelehan structures the chapters of *Overloaded: Popular Culture and the Future of Feminism* (2000) to 'reflect on various cultural moments in an attempt to offer in miniature an anatomy of the backlash against feminism in Britain' (12). Jane Gallop in *Around 1981* (1992) identifies the year in her title as a resonant moment for academic feminism, and uses the unique approach of structuring her work around a specific moment to interrogate the mainstreaming of academic feminism before and after its general acceptance as a part of literary studies. The subsequent discussion is framed as both a personal narrative on Gallop's part and an analysis of the shifts in the wider academic arena. By focusing her inquiry on critical scholarship that has subsequently influenced the shape of feminist literary criticism, Gallop's study usefully pinpoints the anthology as an important medium for feminist analysis.

Deborah Siegel challenges the notion of waves and simultaneously validates the concept of the moment in 'Reading Between the Waves: Feminist Historiography in a "Postfeminist" Moment' (1997b). She argues that because 'feminism speaks itself differently at different times and in different locations, narrative chronologies that say "in this wave" tend to erase the heterogeneity of feminisms at any given moment' (61). Siegel's preference for thinking about moments in order to accommodate the heterogeneity of contemporary feminisms also helps to negotiate the generational tensions that have emerged because of the increasing distortion surrounding the wave metaphor. As Barbara Christian et al. (1990) argue, the generational wave metaphor creates 'an illusory unity for feminism, taking as representative of feminism whatever discourse seems dominant at a particular moment' (83). Firstly, the first-, second- and third-wave labels imply a cohesive generational unit that negates any difference or contradiction within them. This assertion implies an almost patriarchal impetus, as a singular vision of feminism emerges as the dominant model to the detriment of the rest. Secondly, the generational wave metaphor invokes the familial relationship between mothers and daughters and thereby nurtures a binary understanding of feminisms. As Astrid Henry suggests in *Not My Mother's Sister: Generational Conflict and Third-Wave Feminism* (2004) 'when we remain stuck in feminism's imagined family, we lose sight of the myriad relations feminists have with one another as well as the possibility of cross-generational identification and similarities' (182).

The generational tension within feminisms arises partially because of the sweeping conceptualisations of 'waves' that purport to speak of and for a much more diverse range of issues, voices and individuals than the notion ever conveys. Moreover, the temporal division, signalled in the labelling of the waves numerically and sequentially, is often construed as fractious. However, instead of focusing on these issues, I suggest, we need to scrutinise the potential overlap and continuity that exist within feminisms, a description that appropriately describes the movement of waves. It is in focusing on the various moments that arise within and across these various 'waves' that the potential to illuminate diverse strands of feminist thought emerges. While accepting the usefulness of the wave metaphor for conceptualising the peaks and troughs and framing the overarching narrative of feminisms, it is in recognising the need to think more specifically about the significance of multiplicity, subtleties and nuance within these larger narratives that the rise of *feminisms* as opposed to the more cohesive first-wave *feminism* (which centred upon demands for suffrage) can be accommodated.

Such a conceptualisation of feminisms also resists some of the problems outlined in recent twenty-first-century debates about the linear, generational approach to feminist history by propagating a more nuanced understanding of contemporary feminist discourse. As Hemmings writes in *Why Stories Matter: The Political Grammar of Feminist Theory* (2011): 'The moment, that snapshot of the discursive dissonance that makes up feminist history, might operate instead as a reminder that all histories are selective and motivated histories' (16). Accordingly, as a work of literary criticism, a pivotal aim of this study is to respond in one small way to Hemmings' call to experiment 'with how we might tell stories differently rather than telling different stories' (ibid.).

The short story's moment: formal features

Certain specific formal characteristics of the short story make the genre hospitable to, or suitable for, the engagement with and representation of feminist politics by the women writers discussed here. Hitherto, the concept of 'the moment' is visible, yet surprisingly opaque in short story criticism, as the phrase is repeatedly used in passing observations while never being fully interrogated for its expediency in discussing the short story. For example, Adrienne Gavin (2003) asserts that 'the short story's momentariness is reflective of dreamtime' and that the genre is therefore well suited to exploring female fantasy and identity (122). Similarly, Hanson notes that the 'short stories of the 1880s and 1890s were written in a period of emphasis on the moment and on the ephemeral' (1996: 135). Respectively, Gavin and Hanson acknowledge the interior and momentary formal feature of the genre as well as the external and contextual moment in their analysis. It is by interrogating how the internal momentariness of the short story and the external context of the moment of publication both inform the final textual artefact that we can fully interrogate the relationship between genre and political contexts.

The particular formal features of the short story that resonate significantly in the writings of these contemporary authors, and that facilitate much of the feminist critique these writers offer, are open endings, ambiguity, voice, time and brevity. Although autonomous, these features also overlap significantly and are often interdependently connected within and across stories in collections. Hanson (1989b) talks about these features in a chapter that seeks to outline the poetics of short fiction. She acknowledges the '"open" quality of the short story' (23), as well as the prevalence of ellipsis and gaps in narratives that create 'a degree of mystery, elision, uncertainty' and invite the reader 'to enter the text' (25). In a contribution to the same collection, Jean Pickering (1989) explores the importance of time in the short story and how the brevity and immediacy stand 'at the heart of the short story' (53). Thus, in identifying these formal features as important for women writers' textual engagement with feminist politics I do not suggest these are features unique to this political purpose. Instead, it is these well-established features of the short story that are creatively exploited by women writers in order to facilitate engagement, reflection and critique of contemporary feminisms.

In general, short stories tend to utilise two types of narrative ending that can be categorised as conclusive and therefore revealing, or open-ended and subsequently ambiguous. The origins of the conclusive model can be traced back to the fourth century BC and Aristotle's *Rhetoric*. For Aristotle, the end provides closure, ensures narrative resolution and in turn ensures compliance with the unity of action. Damon Knight argues that 'here if anywhere, the author has a chance to make the reader understand what the whole meaning of the story is' (1997: 174) and thus advocates the short story's ending as a moment of closure and revelation. Conversely, the open-ended or ambiguous narrative 'closure' is often associated with the modernist short story writer Anton Chekhov and, as Helen Simpson explains, '*Chekhovian* gets used when you're not doing that sort of party-trick twist-in-the-tale ending' (Gharraie 2012: n. p.). In an interview with Boddy (2010), Ali Smith surmises, 'the thing about the short story form is that it is completely wide open. Its end is never an end, it's always some kind of middle or beginning' (68). The ending, then, is responsible for either the short story's resolution of narrative tension or ongoing ambiguity. Regardless of which critical approach is upheld in a story, both of these endings entice the reader towards this narrative moment with high expectations, as either the story's 'meaning' is uncovered or the reader is left to imagine it for herself.

In interrogating the function of the short story's ending and its generic specificities Ursula Hurley suggests, 'reader autonomy is a gift of the genre' but requires 'imaginative and intellectual engagement [by the reader]; it does not tolerate passivity' (2011: 29). However, the idea of 'reader autonomy' is problematic because it implies a reader is unconstrained, when in fact the reader always functions within the confines of a narrative: no matter how ambiguous a narrative, the notion of reader engagement is crucial. It is the reader's investment in the story which gives epiphany and narrative resolution their power. In instances in which the ending is left open or is ambiguous, this structure also encourages the reader to think beyond the ending. Finally, by extending this relationship between the reader and the ending, the significance of literal and narrative death is brought into play. Valerie Shaw argues that the 'short story's pressure to move resolutely towards a climax makes it an ideal form in which to juxtapose life and death in striking ways' (1983: 201). After all, following Edgar Allan Poe's assertion that a good short story should be able to be consumed in one sitting (as cited in Shaw 1983: 61), the reader is always aware that the story will end soon. As such, the short story's ending 'is the moment that restores the reader to [their] own mortality' (Brown 2003: 40).

A further important characteristic of a short story is ambiguity. While one of the means by which narrative ambiguity can be achieved is through open endings, it can also be generated via characterisation. As Michael Trussler (1996) suggests, 'a short story's brevity creates a compression that renders context opaque' (564). This means the reader is often asked to make the connections between characters, events and settings. Further, in this shorter space the characters within a short story can remain nameless throughout, with minimal information being disclosed to the reader. It is through suggestion and implication that short stories develop their narratives and consequently dispel much of the material upon which the reader depends for continuity, coherence and context. Indeed, a central contention of this book is that contemporary women writers have utilised the short story's capacity for narrative and character ambiguity to challenge representations of gendered identity and the boundaries of sexuality; this feature can also perpetuate a more subtle and less militant engagement with feminist politics.

Voice is a vital component of the stories discussed in subsequent chapters. In narratives where context is sparse and the ending is often open, the narrative voice is an essential means by which the reader understands both the characters and the story. In the conclusion to the edited collection *Cross-Gendered Literary Voices* (2012), Claire Westall theorises voice as a dynamic force that carries a sense of agency and is of, but also outside, the body (222). She argues that

> the voice is suggestive of a forward moving potentiality – that even when silent it carries the potential for speech – and it is indicative of a backward orientated gesture of delay, or a time lag, because the sounds of the voice can only be received by a listener after the moment of vocalization. (ibid.)

According to Westall's definition, voice is produced at the moment of articulation, but it also has the ability to transcend time as it contains both a 'forward' and a 'backward' potentiality. Furthermore, the voice stands between self and 'Other' as it originates within one body but is received by that of another, a listener. Voice, then, creates a dynamic between people and therefore can nurture narrative tension. Developing Westall's proposition in the context of the short story and short story collection, there exist multiple ways in which voice is used in the projection of narrative moments.

The voice's origins in the body's organs and its subsequent reception *at that moment* by a listener imply it exists and can articulate the immediate, the present moment. Given the acknowledged historical origins of the short story's orality in myth and fairytale, this element is significant. However, importantly, there is always a time lag between the moment of articulation and the moment of reception which opens the potential for a troubling of voice and knowledge within narratives through this temporal delay. This immediacy of voice can also exist in stories that are set across different historical periods and it can therefore function to trouble history as the past is brought to life in the present. Of course, narrative voice is not just an act of speech but can be delivered through the representation of thought and memory, thus destabilising the speaker/listener dynamic as the only 'listener' in this context becomes the reader. Perhaps most crucial of all, given the importance of the reader's engagement with the short story's narrative development and meaning, is the implication of the voice in relation to individual agency and identity. While, on the one hand, the act of speaking instils the story's character(s) with a sense of selfhood it is also the means through which the reader interprets for herself that very same character. In this respect, voice is ambivalent in that it can simultaneously contribute to the telling of a story, facilitate the reader's ability 'to know' a character *and* be the cause of misdirection or temporal transience.

The concept of time is a significant aspect of the short story, and narratives often deal with, or are structured by, the phenomenological experience of immediacy. As the short story writer Nadine Gordimer (1968) phrases it, the short story is like 'the flash of fireflies' because the short story writer 'sees by the light of the flash; theirs is the art of the only thing that one can be sure of – the present moment' (459). In dealing with an often limited or isolated period of time, short story narratives have a tendency to move vertically, not just horizontally. The issue of temporality plays a vital role in shaping the short story's ability to engage with contemporary issues. It is because of this trait that the short story often works against the grain of a totalising narrative of history, subjectivity and knowledge, marking it out as a potentially subversive genre. After all, with a differing set of expectations and demands, compared to other forms of literature, the short story can resist expectations of linear plot progression that are often associated with the 'traditional' novel.

Brevity is undoubtedly a catalyst in the short story's emphasis upon the ending, its ambiguity and the prevalence of time, and it is strongly affiliated with the short story's interrogation of the present. Adrian Hunter (2007) suggests that narrative shortness should be viewed 'as a "positive" quality, in the sense that the form, handled right, is able to embody an experiential condition of modernity – a sense of chronic uncertainty, historical sequestration and social isolation' (3). For Hunter, brevity allows writers to engage with social modernity in the twentieth century. Further, Hunter positions narrative brevity alongside narrative complexity and suggests that both of these features of the short story emerge out of the avant-garde dictum of saying less but meaning more (2). Transposing this relationship from the modernist period and placing it in a contemporary context reveals the short story's relevance in capturing the passing moment. As Viorica Patea (2012) claims, 'compactness and conciseness are responsible for the short story's proclivity to fragmentariness, its tendency to describe moments instead of processes' (13).

Curating a moment: the short story anthology and feminist politics

The anthology is particularly significant in the context of women's short story writing, most notably in the context of the 1960s and 1970s when consciousness raising and the affiliated notion of 'sisterhood' caused the anthology to become not only a viable medium but, I would argue, a desirable mode of publication. The first important example of a fictional anthology to emerge out of the Women's Liberation Movement was *Tales I Tell My Mother: A Collection of Feminist Short Stories* (1978), edited by a collective of women (Zoë Fairbairns, Sara Maitland, Valerie Miner, Michèle Roberts and Michelene Wandor).[5] The strong links between the women's movement and this publication are discussed by Valerie Miner in her introduction to section two of the book, 'Feminist Fiction and Politics'. She states that 'these stories are part of our work within the women's movement' (1978: 63). In the introduction, Zoë Fairbairns demonstrates how the self-proclaimed 'collective' of editors and authors have worked as 'a group of equals' in publishing this title, and she makes their feminist and socialist objectives abundantly clear (1978: 3). This is a point emphasised by the equal distribution of all work, with each writer contributing four pieces (either an introduction, epilogue or non-fictional commentary to accompany the sections, or short stories). *Tales I tell My Mother*, then, is an example of literary sisterhood in practice.

Showalter's *Daughters of Decadence: Women Writers of the Fin-de-Siècle* (1993) contests that 'women *were* a major presence in the new literary world of the 1880s and 1890s' (vii). Showalter argues that many of the writers in the anthology were previously neglected because of their preference for the short story over the novel (viii). Showalter's anthology attempts to rectify this situation by highlighting the existence of those stories that 'offer a feminist point of view on issues of sexuality, aesthetics, "decadence", and quest' (ibid.). Moreover, there is a second function to this anthology, as it not only brings together voices from the past but also speaks to the present. In reproducing feminist short stories from the *fin de siècle* in this anthology Showalter is consciously interacting with, what is for her, a contemporary feminist moment. Concluding the introduction she elucidates this:

> A century later, the utopian dreams of *fin-de-siècle* feminists have yet to be fully realised, but reading their stories we can take heart from their talent and their courage to look with hope to the new century, and to another beginning of a new world for women. (xix)

The affinities between the two periods is at the forefront of Showalter's project as she aims to show that, despite the passage of a whole century, similar problems remain for women and feminism's goals are still not fully achieved. In this anthology, Showalter unites the first and second waves to celebrate the literary manifestations of feminisms while contributing, through literature, to contemporary feminist conversations.

These anthologies are merely a glimpse of the plethora of publications that emerged from the 1970s onwards. Many other anthologies were published around the same time and were targeted specifically at drawing attention to lesbian relationships and women's erotic lives. These include Joan Nestle's *A Restricted Country: Essays and Short Stories* (1987), Sheba Collective's *Serious Pleasure: Lesbian Erotic Stories and Poetry* (1989) and the subsequent *More Serious*

Pleasure (1990) (all of which were published by Sheba Feminist Publishers), as well as *Erotica* (1998), edited by Margaret Reynolds with a foreword by the contemporary author Jeanette Winterson. The combination of fictional and non-fictional short writings across these collections highlights the importance of both modes of writing in championing feminist politics. The growth in the number of women's short story anthologies published coincides with the rise of second-wave feminist politics, suggesting it was deemed a relevant literary medium for the publication of women's narratives. The anthology also highlights the connection between women's feminist short story writing and the non-fictional feminist writing that burgeoned during the same period.

While Gail Chester has suggested that 'as the 1990s went on, the number of feminist anthologies being published waned' (2002: 200), this assertion overlooks the array of publications that were spurred on by the growth of third-wave feminism in Britain and America. Nearly twenty years after publishing *The Body Politic*, a landmark text for the Women's Liberation Movement, Michelene Wandor published *Once a Feminist: Stories of a Generation* (1990). Collecting together voices of the women's movement and preserving records of the past, this collection also speaks 'to the present about the experiences of the past' (7). In many ways, this anthology is a dialogue between second- and third-wave feminists. In 1999 Natasha Walter edited a collection of essays on contemporary feminism for Virago Press, entitled *On the Move: Feminism for a New Generation*. Both the title and Walter's introduction to this collection make it clear that this is a book defined by young and/or 'new' feminist voices, suggesting a break from second-wave feminism or the 'mother' generation. Further, Walter herself admits to disagreeing with some of the views forwarded in the anthology, stating that 'no one will agree with everything that everyone says in this book. But despite that there is the possibility of finding common ground and building on it' (4). *On the Move* typifies third-wave feminism's acceptance of diversity and openness towards disagreement while still remaining anchored in the belief in women's equality and the necessity of a feminist movement for facilitating social and political change.

The anthology is a dynamic medium that can be affiliated with a particular cultural moment, intent on capturing the voices of any one moment, or bringing together voices from across history to speak in some way to the present. Accordingly, it has the capacity as a form to challenge the simplistic, linear narrative that has come to dominate feminism's story by prioritising instead the overlap and disconnect between different feminisms across the decades. Although the anthology has gained currency at different points in time – most notably during the second wave – it also transcends affiliation to any one specific strand of feminist political thought, to unite women's voices, experiences and artistic expression and offer a valuable literary space for women's writing, especially short story writing. In the discussion of femininity, marriage, domesticity and sexuality, I will draw on short stories published in *The F Word* (2011), an anthology published by Granta in which feminism and fiction are truly united, and *Kin: New Fiction by Black & Asian Women* (2003), which aims to 'reflect the diverse nature of what constitutes being black and/or Asian in Britain today' (McCarthy 2003: 2). These are just two anthologies, of many that have been published in recent years. However, both of these collections explicitly foreground the importance of feminist politics, indeed, including this as part of their rationale, and therefore stand out as significant contributions in the context of this study.

Chapter overview: key moments

The perceived affinity and dialogue between the short story and feminist politics is demonstrated in the following five chapters, which illuminate some of the key themes to preoccupy contemporary feminisms. Chapter 1 focuses on the issue of femininity and how the female body is represented by women writers. This chapter attends to the ways in which sex and gender interact and how heteropatriarchal discourses have established sociocultural expectations of femininity. Subsequently, the textual analysis reveals how women writers use the short story to critique and challenge patriarchal assumptions. Space, and a woman's right to occupy space, provide the opening point of analysis through a reading of the narratives of Byatt and Tremain, before turning to the issue of women's behaviour and stereotypes. Focusing on the writings of Atkinson, Barker, Hall, Kay and Tremain, the second part of the chapter explores how their short stories depict and reflexively critique femininity in order to make visible, problematise and even subvert this cultural construct. Finally, the discussion illuminates the ways in which femininity is often understood in relation to a young and white female body. Subsequently, this closing section pays attention to narratives which foreground bodies 'other' to this normative model and asks how this challenges the concept of femininity and, in turn, what this might tell us about contemporary feminisms.

The politics of motherhood have been a reoccurring focal point of feminist debate. Chapter 2 commences by contextualising the notion of institutionalised motherhood and engaging with the writings of Shulamith Firestone, Adrienne Rich and Julia Kristeva. The literary analysis focuses on the control of women's bodies and societal expectations in the work of Roberts and how the critique of motherhood apparent in these narratives reflects a tendency of much second-wave feminist thought. The second section of this chapter considers the writings of Simpson and how she invokes the narrative brevity of the short story to heighten not only the sense of spatial constraint the female protagonists, who are mothers, experience, but also the temporal constraints felt by those without a child, who are aware of their ageing bodies. 'Maternal Loss' explores the ambivalence at the heart of motherhood and feminism while questioning how understandings of the maternal contain broader meanings and significance across cultures and in the context of migration narratives. The concluding commentary engages with the topic of feminist generations and reflects on the ways in which motherhood has been explored and reworked as a central feminist motif at different points since the 1980s.

The themes of marriage and domesticity have been important issues in feminist discussions and signal the enduring relevance of personal politics, which is why they are the focus of Chapter 3. Beginning with 'Historical Issues', which focuses on narratives of marriage and domesticity that invoke the past, the analysis raises questions about the momentary nature of the short story and its ability to engage with history, as well as the significance of intertextuality. The subsequent discussion moves on to consider how narratives challenge the notion of 'marital bliss', the repercussions of unmarried status for women, and, through the story 'Red Sari', how issues of cultural difference impact on the politics of marriage. The section entitled 'Domestic Duty' foregrounds the gendered politics of domesticity and how this is shaped by, while shaping, feminist politics, before the final section focus on ethnicity and ageing, and how the traditional domestic landscape is unsettled by the presence of these discourses.

In keeping with the desire to consider a spectrum of gendered and sexual identities, Chapter 4 explores the politics of masculinity, deliberating how a consideration of masculine identity corresponds with a feminist agenda and why this is important for mapping a progressive feminist politics. Since the 1980s masculinity, more specifically 'hegemonic masculinity', has been a focal point of gender and sexuality discourses. The short story writings of Mantel, Hislop and especially Tremain reflect, critique and trouble such understandings of masculinity through the issues of work, sexuality and the differences between male and female bodies. As with the historical strand of Chapter 3, in this chapter there is a focus on history and one particularly significant historical moment for men and masculinity: the 1980s. Through a reading of the literary representations of Margaret Thatcher, in the context of the work of Judith Halberstam, Chapter 4 highlights one of the ways in which queer theory and postmodern feminism have also informed recent feminist debates.

Reflecting the shift in critical fields, as with Chapter 4, the analysis in Chapter 5 foregrounds gendered identity and focuses particularly on the politics of sexuality. The section on transgressive female sexuality examines sexuality as a site of political resistance for women, and considers the impact of such discourses on a wide range of female bodies. The notion of choice is crucial to any discussion of sexuality, and through a reading of Kalbinder Kaur's story 'When English Girls Hold Hands', this chapter considers the implications of sexuality and women's choice in the context of race and ethnicity. Taking a range of short stories, I scrutinise the dialogue these narratives perpetuate between seemingly diverse feminisms. The final part of this chapter questions how the politics of queer theory interact with feminisms via the locus of sexuality in the writings of Kay and Ali Smith, before concluding the chapter with a discussion of Janice Galloway's 'We're Not in This Together'.

Finally, the Conclusion opens with a discussion of Helen Simpson's 'The Festival of the Immortals' and Barbara A. Graham's 'Next of Kin' and explores the ways in which the imagery and metaphors deployed in these short stories offer a means of rethinking the relationship between feminist discourses: what does the momentary nature of the short story reveal about feminisms? Following this, the Conclusion reflects on the themes and issues that have emerged throughout the chapters and draws together the various 'moments' of discussion by returning to the overarching questions first posed in this Introduction. As such it will offer insights into how and why the short story has been, and continues to be, a useful literary vehicle for engaging with feminist politics. However, the Conclusion will also reflect on the potential limitations of literature to propagate a productive politics which can influence and bring about social change – namely due to the importance of experiential, affective relationships between the reader and the text. Importantly, it will also consider how differing feminisms 'speak' to one another. In keeping with a tendency of many wonderful short stories, and extending the discussion of the anthology posed in the Introduction, the Conclusion will be open-ended in that it will offer some horizon scanning, and consider the position of British women's short story writing and feminism now, by reflecting on how new forms and trends in the literary marketplace are perhaps altering the way feminist stories are being told.

Notes

1. In the wider international context, 2013 saw the Canadian short story writer Alice Munro receive the Nobel Prize for Literature and Lydia Davis win the Man Booker International Prize.
2. In an article published in 1996, Hanson herself acknowledges the benefit of moving beyond the connection between women's socially marginalised position and the status of the short story to focus instead on the representation of women's experience in the genre: 'Whether or not women were (or are) in fact "outside" language and culture is, in a sense, beyond the point, which is that they have felt themselves to be excluded in this way' (142).
3. The 'Ruskin Weekend', as Wandor refers to it, was a weekend in February 1970 when the political conference 'Women's Weekend' was held at Ruskin College, Oxford. It marks a critical turn in women's consciousness raising and political formation and signals the beginnings of the unified Women's Liberation Movement.
4. Examples of this convergence of the personal and the political in writing are especially apparent in an American context and include Barbara Findlen's *Listen Up: Voices from the Next Feminist Generation* (1995); Rebecca Walker's *To Be Real: Telling the Truth and Changing the Face of Feminism* (1995); and Daisy Hernández and Bushra Rehman's *Colonize This! Young Women of Color on Today's Feminism* (2002).
5. Michelene Wandor is also the editor of *The Body Politic: Women's Liberation in Britain, 1969–1972* (1972), the first major non-fiction anthology to emerge out of the Women's Liberation Movement, as well as *On Gender and Writing* (1983) and *Once a Feminist: Stories of a Generation* (1990). *Once a Feminist* will be discussed later in this chapter.

Chapter 1

Femininity

Femininity is a complex terrain and one marked by a plethora of tensions and contradictions, especially in the context of contemporary feminisms. While the feminine and the feminist have often been positioned as incompatible discourses, in the twenty-first century a body of literature and debate has embraced femininity and suggested that for 'Girlie girls, "femininity" is not opposed to feminism, but is . . . central to a politics of agency, confidence, and resistance' (Munford 2007: 274). In addition is the competing critique which focuses on how post-feminist discourses of empowerment mask the politics of class, sexuality, race and ethnicity which marginalise those who do not adhere to the hegemonic model. In *Black Beauty*, Shirley Anne Tate (2009) refers to this hegemonic model as 'white beauty's iconicity', which she defines as 'implicitly heterosexual, age conscious, purportedly classless and [seeking] to obscure its racial markedness' (11). The subject of femininity, then, is one which prompts questions about race, ethnicity, class, sexuality and age. Femininity taps into the heart of feminist discourses as it speaks to the construction of the category of woman but also because it intersects with a plethora of broader socioeconomic and cultural issues. Crucially, it has been an enduring feature of feminist debate, riding across the various waves, which in itself highlights the complexity of both the issue and feminist discourse.

After a brief survey which considers the way in which femininity has been theorised in relation to a range of other media and genres, this chapter discusses the representation of femininity through three key themes. Firstly, I consider the relationship between space and the female body through a reading of A. S. Byatt's (2011) 'NO GRLS ALOD, INSEPT MOM' and Rose Tremain's (1983) 'The Colonel's Daughter'. The second section focuses on notions of appropriate female behaviour with regard to body image and violence, before the final section illuminates the ways in which femininity is often understood through association with a young and white female body. Subsequently, that closing section pays attention to narratives which foreground bodies 'other' to this normative model and asks how this challenges traditional understandings and conceptualisations of femininity and, in turn, what this might mean for the ongoing relationship between feminism and femininity.

Femininity and genre

In recent years the tension between femininity and feminism has emerged in scholarship on soap opera, women's magazines and the media more broadly. It seems appropriate to reflect on this body of work for what it reveals about the ongoing academic dialogue between femininity, feminism and genre. Interestingly, the formal structure of soap opera includes interweaving stories and a narrative disruption that refuses straightforward linear progression or a tidy resolution, and the genre is governed by temporal demands. All of these elements can be mapped on to the short story (brevity and open-ended narratives) and short story collection (interweaving stories). Likewise, soap opera critics have noted the genre's everyday subject matter, its emphasis being placed on marriage, birth, death, divorce, and familial quarrels and dynamics, and have even proposed (somewhat problematically) that it is a feminine discourse (Geraghty 1992: 41). Paving the way for discussions of women and soap opera, Tania Modleski (1994) suggests that soap opera provides narrative pleasure for women by validating women's experience and depicting scenes to which they can relate (93). Taking this further, Martha Nochimson (1992) proposes that because of the genre's perforated narrative it is a form 'opposed to strategies of domination' (39), and is in fact a *resistant* 'feminine discourse' (2). While Geraghty asserts the feminine credentials of soap opera, for Nochimson soap opera contains a feminist potential. The feminine and the feminist are fractious concepts in the context of this debate, and in suggesting a genre is gendered there is a danger of propagating reductive essentialisms.

As with soap opera scholarship, Ros Ballaster, Margaret Beetham, Elizabeth Frazer and Sandra Hebron, in *Women's Worlds: Ideology, Femininity and the Woman's Magazine* (1991), investigate the relationship between femininity and the genre of the woman's magazine. Drawing on the formal features of women's magazines (open-ended, heterogeneous, fragmented), they argue that women's magazines 'contain, within single issues and between different titles, many competing and contradictory notions of femininity' (22). However, they also note that it 'is important to resist claiming the cyclical or open-ended form is *essentially* a female quality, rather than a culturally learned distinction of gender' (30). This warning signals why the feminine and the feminist have often co-existed uneasily: the foregrounding of the feminine qualities of genres often results in the negation of any feminist potential they contain. Or, more importantly, the prioritising of the feminine reaffirms women's association with the private sphere and revives gendered binary assumptions. The space of women's magazines is particularly vital, as it is a textual space in which social norms, rules and codes of conduct shape understandings of femininity. Nadia Sanger (2009) discusses the significance of South African magazines in constructing racialized and sexualised femininities, arguing they are 'influential agents of socialisation, privileging and normalising particular types of discourses about gender, sexuality and race' (138). As such, magazines are a space in which the double bind of femininity is realised: 'women learn that they are valued for their (hetero)sexual bodies, but even as they devote energies to perfecting them, the ideal remains largely unattainable' (Wesely 2002: 1183).

The media is a significant cultural space in which gendered subjectivities are constructed and where, in recent years, feminism has been increasingly debated. Equally, academic feminism has paid much-needed attention to the cultural space of the media and produced insightful analysis of the trends and tendencies of representation. As Hilary Hinds and Jackie Stacey (2001) summarise:

> the history of the representation of feminism in the British press during the last 30 years might be characterised as being marked by a shift from the monstrous outsiders of the 1960s and 1970s to the incorporated Ms of the 1990s. (155)

Referring to the shift from depicting feminists as so-called bra-burners through to the more popular image of the 'Girlie girl' and 'girl power' culture in the new millennium, Hinds and Stacey offer a fair summation of the media's narration of feminism. However, they also attend to the limitations of such linear accounts of media imaging by acknowledging the prevalence of 'uneven and multiple significations' during this time (ibid.). Thus, the emphasis of their study falls on the complexity of feminism and femininity as cultural categories and scrutinises the mutating relationship between these two discourses since 1968 (ibid.). These established engagements with the politics of femininity and feminism, then, illuminate the multitude of ways in which these discourses are negotiated in popular culture. In extending this discussion to the short story genre, this chapter furthers such analysis while recognising that both feminism and femininity are textually mediated (Taylor 2003: 183).

Spatial boundaries

In 'NO GRLS ALOD, INSEPT MOM', A. S. Byatt scrutinises the way public space is shaped by gendered social assumptions, and how this often results in women's expulsion from that public space. While the title of the story is based on a 'notice attached to his bedroom door by my five-year-old grandson' (31), Byatt's narrative moves away from the private space of home to explore how universities have, historically, applied similar gendered rules to that of her five-year-old grandson. From the unequal balance of colleges at Durham University (seven men's and three women's colleges) to the single-sex unions of Oxford and Cambridge, the story sheds light on the inequalities at the heart of some of the UK's most celebrated educational institutions. Reflecting on teaching at University College London for eleven years in the 1970s and 1980s, the narrator (implicitly Byatt) identifies The Houseman Room as a particularly pleasant space. However, this is swiftly undercut with the realisation that 'until very recently . . . The Houseman Room had, of course, been reserved for men' (34). The relative currency of gender segregation in public space, and the hierarchical power implications, are more fully realised with the closing discussion of how the 'UCL Professors' Dining Club . . . did not invite women professors' (35). That certain spaces remain the preserve of a particular white, middle-class male elite is foregrounded in Byatt's story, which offers a scathing critique of supposedly 'politically forward-looking, rational, unprejudiced' institutions which perpetuate old-fashioned and outdated gendered ideas (34).

The story's title, 'NO GRLS ALOD, INSEPT MOM', invites the reader to draw parallels between the public spaces of the university, with the men's common room and 'Professors' Dining Club', and the five-year-old grandson's rules about his own private, bedroom space. Although a seemingly flippant remark in which a young child attempts to assert ownership over his private space, this sign reveals the ways in which these broader conceptualisations of gender segregation and space are internalised by individuals at a young age. Further, with the title page of the story marking the point of entry in to the narrative, the act of reading this story mimics the crossing of a threshold into a new space. This connection is intensified by the inclusion of a picture, in between the title page and story's opening, which depicts a traditional, almost archaic, wooden door. Thus, the space of the short story symbolises the privileged university rooms outlined in the narrative, and the brevity of the short story accentuates the reader's sense of being in an enclosed space. In this respect, the medium of the short story works with the grain of the narrative to illuminate the relevance of spatial boundaries and provoke the reader to reflect on their own positionality and history with public and private spaces.

In Tremain's story 'The Colonel's Daughter', space plays a significant role in the exploration of gender relations and, in particular, offers an insight into the interaction between femininity, masculinity, patriarchy and feminism. The story is structured entirely around the intersection of divergent spatiotemporal moments, in the sense that the story moves between different characters' perspectives over a period of time. As such, the story is very much a narrative jigsaw which is slowly pieced together. The main characters create this narrative tapestry, and these include the protagonist Charlotte, her parents (Colonel and Lady Browne), the Browne's butler Garrod, Charlotte's fiancé Jim Reese and, finally, the writer Franklin Doyle. All of these characters, with the exception of Franklin, are connected from the beginning of the story, whereas Franklin's narrative only interweaves with this familial group after he sees Charlotte in hospital.

The story opens when Colonel and Lady Browne are away on holiday and Charlotte visits her old family home in order to steal her parents' valuables. Charlotte's motivation for this theft is that she hopes to support her partner Jim, a struggling musician, financially. Importantly, it is the chiming of the clock that connects the narratives of Charlotte, Colonel and Lady Browne, and Garrod. As Charlotte walks through the hall in her parents' home 'the grandfather clock chimes ten' (1999: 4). The clock's physical enunciation of a specific time is the stimulus for the narrative to shift focus and become centred on the other characters. More specifically, it moves to the Swiss Alps, 'at this precise hour, in Wengen, [where] Colonel and Lady Amelia Browne are served coffee – excellent Viennese coffee – in the comfy lounge of the Hotel Alpenrose' (ibid.). Anchored by the chiming of the clock, a sound that represents a specific temporal moment, but because of its echo also rings beyond that moment, the narrative fluidly moves across spatial boundaries.

In the process of stealing from her parents' home Charlotte fatally injures the servant Garrod. Although the details of this event are somewhat ambiguous, the narrative implies that Charlotte hits Garrod over the head. Following the robbery, in which Charlotte takes 'loops of pearls, diamonds stiffly jointed into necklaces and bracelets and inset with emeralds' (10), she returns to the flat she shares with Jim, and, victorious, declares the act 'the most perfect thing I've done' (11). However, Jim 'can't look at Charlotte with her eyes like coal, so he turns away and leans his head against the wall. I want to break her, he thinks now' (ibid.). The source of Jim's anguish is that, in her vanity, Charlotte 'relegates me, miniaturises me' (ibid.). While Jim previously describes how 'he doesn't *feel* rage' (8; original emphasis), and how 'his anger is contained' (ibid.), here his anger is 'pushing and bursting till it hurtles from him and he sees it arc and fall in Charlotte's body hurtling over into the air' (11). While previously Jim 'thinks' about hurting Charlotte, here his actions cause Charlotte to hit her head on 'the grey metal of the typewriter', and she is subsequently taken to hospital (ibid.). Crucially, in her action Charlotte usurps Jim, in gendered terms, by taking on the traditionally masculine role of provider.

Before Jim lashes out at Charlotte in anger, when he is in their flat awaiting her arrival home from the robbery, Jim admits that 'her intelligence suffocates him' (8). Jim continues to make reference to an article Charlotte is writing entitled '*Eve and the Weapons of Eden*' (9; original emphasis). Following Jim's attack on Charlotte, the police arrive at the couple's flat. Looking through their belongings, Constable Richards finds Charlotte's article and discovers a secret feminist message hidden within the work. At this discovery Constable Richards 'bites on the Dentyne, sighs, sets the papers down, rubs his eyes. "Frightening muck!" he whispers to himself' (16). Formatted in the shape of a rectangle, the hidden message reads, 'our movement, like our sister movements of the eighteenth and nineteenth centuries, is hobbled not only by public apathy and public pig-ignorance but also by lack of money' (17). By clearly aligning Charlotte with the women's movement, her subsequent debilitation, because of Jim's aggression, is metaphoric of men's scepticism and resistance towards women's liberation. Significantly, by the time Charlotte is seen leaving the hospital in a police car her mother, Amelia, is in a state of disbelief. Amelia cannot believe her daughter is a criminal or that she would steal from her own parents. However, when Amelia asks her husband, 'how could you imagine Charlotte doing a thing like this? She's not a criminal!', Colonel Browne responds, 'in this society . . . she is' (33). According to her father, Charlotte's crime lies not in stealing her parents' valuable belongings but in her feminist allegiance.

It is Charlotte's social transgression that 'this society' denounces. In turn, her imprisonment functions symbolically in the narrative and reinforces the prominence of patriarchal power in the face of feminism and alternative performances of gender identity.

Despite Charlotte's actions being firmly driven by her desire to save Jim, when travelling in the police car she realises that she

> hasn't 'saved' Jim Reese. Pride and anger prevented this. She is punished for her arrogance. And he, in the flood of his male violence, has rendered her useless to the women she has worked with, worked for, when to them too she planned to offer more. (34)

Seemingly, in this patriarchal society, nobody escapes unscathed. Despite her wish to help men and women, Charlotte is imprisoned for theft and for the murder of Garrod, who dies the day after the robbery. Notably, Charlotte perceives that it is Jim's 'pride and anger' that prevent him from accepting her help, which itself was only supposed to offer Jim 'a birth of self-respect, a birth of energy and purpose' (33). In other words, Charlotte's power and status, partially because of her family's wealth, but also because she usurps the traditionally masculine qualities of action and authority, challenge Jim's own masculine identity.

In Byatt's and Tremain's short stories space plays an important role in understanding gender relations. Arguably, the brevity of narrative space in the short story heightens the awareness of spatial confinement, accentuating the narrative content further and demonstrating how form and content intertwine in short fiction. Space is shown to be influenced by gender discourses but, equally, spatiality challenges the traditional perceptions of gender binaries as well. Of course, in each story this is far from simplistic and neither author presents a 'correct' or 'rectified' representation of the situation through a straightforward reversal. Instead, both stories critique the positionality of women within social and private space, but, ultimately, also acknowledge the complexities of reworking such relations in a nonbinary fashion.

Stereotypes: behaving like a woman

Kate Atkinson is a well-known, popular contemporary author, whose bestselling books have been turned into television series, and who has successfully published fiction that straddles the boundaries of literary and crime fiction. While Atkinson has attracted critical attention, this remains relatively sparse. Monica Germanà (2010) discusses the 1995 novel *Behind the Scenes at the Museum* in relation to Scottish women's gothic and fantastic fiction, and Sinead McDermott (2006) explores the same novel's representation of the family. Fiona Tolan (2009) recognises the political approach of Atkinson's debut novel, calling it 'a mid-1990s feminist interaction with postmodernism deconstructions of historiography' (275). Clearly, then, Atkinson's writing lends itself to a broad range of critical approaches. More significantly, Helen Mundler (2009) critiques Atkinson's sole short story collection, *Not the End of the World* (2002), as marking a transition in the author's writing: 'the affiliation to postmodernism and to metafiction is worked out with much greater subtlety, making the commentary on narrative fiction the more complex and interesting' (195). Thus, Mundler scrutinises the creative contribution this collection makes to literature, alongside the apocalyptic aspect of some of the stories. Although the notions of feminism and femininity are not explicit in Atkinson's writing, or indeed in the scholarship that engages with it, her treatment of female characters in the short stories proffers some fruitful material for reflecting on these tropes.

In 'Transparent Fiction' (2002), Atkinson introduces the character of Meredith: a young woman who has 'gone through life borrowing other people's personalities rather than going to the trouble of developing her own' (48). An American currently living in the UK, Meredith is established as a woman who lives in the moment. Her relationship with Fletcher is viewed as a 'temporary liaison' (53) and she experiences an 'odd malaise' in England which she suspects is due to 'an overabundance of history' (ibid.). What is especially interesting about Meredith is the tension which resides at the heart of her character. She is depicted as pursuing a carefree existence, devoid of material attachments, yet her doctoral research is into Telomeres, which the narrative reveals to be about the longevity of life as: 'the longer our telomeres, the longer we live' (57). In this narrative space, the reader is confronted with conflicting and quite contradictory messages about Meredith which, subsequently, reflect the constructed nature of identity. Such representation of character is a common feature of short stories, which often portray 'human identity as a subject in process, so that characterisation tends toward only partial realisation' (March-Russell 2009: 134). However, in Atkinson's narrative, it is the specifically female body which is partially realised and this leads to feminist critique. In this regard, the characterisation of Meredith echoes with Carole Jones' (2015) notion of 'feminine disorientation',

a term she uses to signal the 'present confusion, uncertainty, and contradiction . . . central to the contemporary experience of female selfhood' (388). Attempting to avoid the problematic phrase 'crisis of
femininity', Jones positions this feminine disorientation alongside the
emergence of neoliberal post(-)feminist regimes which

> construct a series of double entanglements in offering female freedoms
> while simultaneously exerting constraint through reinvigorated patriar-
> chal pressure to conform to limited models of femininity, the contradic-
> tions of which exert a dangerous, irreconcilable tension on individual
> women. (398)

Through this lens, the conflicted nature of Meredith's character, then,
is a manifestation of the broader complexities that emerge from this
double entanglement of femininity.

Crucially, the performed nature of identity is directly connected to
notions of femininity: 'Meredith knew that most men would rather
have Air Stewardess Barbie in bed with them than a girl with a doctoral thesis' (50–1). There is a level of subtle critique around femininity and desire in Atkinson's narrative through the figure of Meredith.
The conflict between an authentic and performed self is brought to
the fore, but this time it is expressed through the imagery of the
female body and what makes a woman attractive and desirable to
a man. Seemingly, Meredith measures her own existence and worth
through a heteropatriarchal lens, and arguably it is this framework
from which she seeks to break free and this is the motivation behind
her carefree lifestyle. The story closes, 'Meredith Zane ran into the
future for ever' (67), and with a poetic twist Atkinson's narrative
closure is both forward-facing and conflicted as the future and eter-
nity merge. In the narrative space of the short story, in which brevity
dictates a more fleeting interaction with characters and situations,
the notion of feminine disorientation is foregrounded, as uncertainty
and contradictions remain the defining narrative features.

Comparatively, Nicola Barker's 1996 story 'G-String' (in Barker
2003) is a comical depiction of a woman's relationship with underwear, and in the process, the story offers a double-edged critique
of femininity, sexuality and the notion of a feminine ideal. The
protagonist, Gillian, is vividly described from the outset as: 'thirty-
four, a nervous size sixteen, had no cheekbones to speak of and hair
which she tried to perm. God knows she tried' (26). In a long-term
relationship with Mr Kip, who 'was an ardent admirer of the great
actress Katharine Hepburn' (ibid.), Gillian is acutely aware that
Katherine Hepburn is intelligent, slender and beautiful, and thus

'everything a girl should be' (ibid.). Katharine Hepburn is located as the ideal woman and her characteristics are normalised and, resultantly, become the standard by which femininity and womanhood are measured. While Gillian silently acknowledges that Katharine Hepburn 'was *old* now, too' she does not verbalise this thought because 'naturally she didn't want to appear a spoilsport' (ibid.). The detailed description of Gillian establishes the way in which a woman's identity comes to be mediated through the figure of the *other*. In this case, Katherine Hepburn is positioned as the archetype of female beauty and it is against her standards which Gillian is judged and, subsequently, judges her own self-worth. However, from the story's opening there is a clear disjoint between the superficial image and the reality of the situation.

The tension between the ideal and the reality is furthered with Gillian's experience of purchasing underwear, to accompany the 'expensive dress in white chiffon which didn't at all suit her' (27). For her 'big night out' to the local Rotary Club with Mr Kip, Gillian attempts to emulate his ideal woman but, as Jeanie swiftly tells her, the dress makes Gillian look 'like an egg-box' and she needs to wear more suitable underwear to prevent this 'lumpy-humpy' appearance (ibid.). Consequently, Gillian purchases a G-string, itself a symbol of 'a modern girl' and thereby assumed to be an object a woman should admire (28). However, an unpleasant evening together is compounded when the wiper breaks on Mr Kip's beloved Aston Martin and Gillian is forced to venture into the wet weather to locate the missing part, before resorting to removing her underwear, cutting the G-string with her Swiss Army knife, and creating a rope-like attachment to manipulate the car wipers manually (30). Upon seeing Gillian's underwear Mr Kip is shocked: 'Good gracious! . . . You could at least have worn some French knickers or cami-knickers or something proper. Those are preposterous' (ibid.). Seemingly, as a woman Gillian is continually conflicted by what is expected of her. When attempting to fulfil the ideal of femininity and to appear attractive to her partner she is then shamed for being inappropriately dressed. The standards that shape femininity are revealed in 'G-String' to be complex and contradictory, resulting in an ambivalent negotiation exposed to be troubling for women. Crucially, liberating her body from the G-string also empowers Gillian to unshackle herself from Mr Kip's manipulation and control. Finally, she stands up for herself (signalled by her no longer using his preferred affectation of 'Mr Kip'): 'I've really had it with you, Colin . . . with your silly, affected, old-fashioned car and clothes and *everything*' (ibid.). Having removed the uncomfortable underwear

Gillian 'was victorious' and, as the story ends, she is positioned as 'a truly modern female' (30).

The invocation of the 'G-string' in Barker's story is a pointed engagement with a garment of clothing that has been a site of intense debate, particularly in relation to feminism. Rosalind Gill's work on choice and agency (2007) offers one summation of this fixation that took hold from the mid-1990s to the mid-2000s, when

> low slung hipster jeans, exposing the familiar 'whaleback' (visible G-string) and a pierced belly button became almost mandatory-wear for many groups of young women. So widespread and uncontested was this fashion that advertisers coined the term 'the midriffs' to refer to this generation/ sensibility. The fashion might have attracted mild opprobrium in certain domains, and negative comments about 'muffin tops' (the bulge of flesh above the jeans) when worn by women deemed not slim enough to carry off the look. (71)

Thus, the G-string is embraced as a sign of female empowerment for a younger generation, but it is also a weapon used against women's bodies to denigrate those who do not conform to the idealised model of femininity (signalled by their 'muffin tops'). Situated in this context, then, Barker's story 'G-String' is a vivid response to a particular moment in time in which women's bodies are understood in relation to this garment. However, given the characterisation of Gillian, with the specific details about her figure, along with the tone of mockery and ironic humour that pervades the story, there is also an element of critique to this narrative which seeks to redress heteropatriarchal and misogynistic conceptualisations of women's bodies.

Jackie Kay's story 'Mini Me' (2012) takes the form of a diary, which is used by the narrator, Pat, to record the progress of her diet. The very first entry reveals the difficult battle Pat faces in trying to lose weight when she visits a sports shop: 'You're supposed to be supporting people tae get healthy and there you ur discriminating – no support for ower 36 DD!' (191). The realisation that she cannot purchase a sports bra that is large enough for her breasts promotes the response of shame and simultaneously anger. Following a few hours of shopping, the first hurdle appears when 'ma tummy rumbles' and, 'pure starving' she resorts to a '*caffe latte*, the skimmed milk is mair *fattening* if yir on a diet, so I believe – this is the conundrum – and an almond croissant' (192). The notion of a 'conundrum' encapsulates the relationship between Pat's desire to lose weight and the difficulty she experiences in dieting, which runs throughout 'Mini Me';

a fact only further emphasised by the repeated return to '*Day* One' of the diet throughout the narrative. With this reoccurring failure to diet, female consumption is a prominent feature of the narrative as Pat indulges her love of food, sharing this pleasure in the diary. If, as Andrea Adolph (2009) suggests, a consuming woman exemplifies the potential agency of the female body and can provide a basis for exploring many aspects of femininity (10), then the initial sense of failure and lack of agency suggested by Pat's narrative is complicated by this act of consumption. Yet again, the female body is located as a site of contradiction, and the motif of negotiation re-emerges to complicate any simplistic relationship between femininity and body image.

In critiquing Foucault's approach to the body, and the emphasis he places on the cultural inscription of the body, Adolph (2009) argues that such an approach 'leaves out the interiority of the body and the body's intellectuality' (6), and proposes a greater focus on the intellectual and material body instead. A key element of this work focuses on the implications of the reader's response to the text, and Adolph draws on 'transactional' response theory to consider the way in which fictional texts that deal with female consumption and body image are also 'dependent upon readers' embodiment' (26) Taking this further, she argues that embodiment is not simply a means of understanding the character, but also 'the narrative composite of a text' (ibid.). In the context of Kay's short story, such an approach to the body, text and the reader attains currency with regard to feminist politics. Kay's use of regional dialect is a prevalent feature of the narrative, and it distances the reader from the text by slowing down the reading process. Those unfamiliar with this particular Scottish dialect (Glaswegian) are forced to pay close to attention to the words in a bid to decode meaning. At the same time, this use of language also adds to the detailed characterisation of Pat, accentuating the intimacy of the diary format, which undoubtedly brings the intellectual as well as the physical body of the character into the text. However, the use of dialect also reinforces the significance of the reader, who is an active participant in the reading of the diary, and therefore the telling of this story. Accordingly, primacy is granted neither to the reader nor to the text but both are equally important; a relationship Adolph argues is synonymous with the interactivity between the mind and the body (ibid.). Thus, the format of the short story further complicates the representation of body politics as the 'represented body within the text recalls for a reader that reader's own body' (ibid.). The level of inherent complicity, therefore, complicates the feminist dynamic of the text, which undoubtedly alters depending on the experiences, embodiment, and therefore response, of the reader. 'Mini Me' is a story not just of Pat's bodily experiences but of those of the reader too.

The significance of an 'other' in 'Mini Me' is furthered by the fact that Pat's motivation to lose weight is directly linked to the comparisons she makes with the bodies of other women. For example, she imagines giving 'masell the figure o' Michelle Obama', and while that might require her being a little taller she still believes it to be 'do-able'; after all, 'getting fit makes ye taller tae' (193). The reader's insight into Pat's thoughts illuminates her desperation to lose weight, but it also cultivates a critique of the discourses and consumerist organisations which profit from bodily insecurities and the habits of so-called yo-yo dieters. Likewise, it is not just the slim figures of other women that shape Pat's desire to shed weight; she is acutely aware of how other people look at her as an overweight woman, with 'the snooty-nosed people that look doon at you, sneakily eyeing your midriff. A' the people that talk to you like yer stupit' (195). Interestingly, a story which initially sets out in an intimate fashion, through the diary medium, soon begins to reference the wider social pressures which shape Pat's mindset and determination to lose weight. Consequently, the story foregrounds the way in which individual 'choices' surrounding bodily appearance are often influenced or even enforced by sociocultural expectations.

In this respect, 'Mini Me' can be seen as a response to neoliberal agendas and feminist discourses which suggest individual choice and freedom are defining features of women's experiences of femininity. Counter to such notions, 'Mini Me' problematises such assertions by emphasising the complex terrain individuals negotiate in their embodiment of gendered identity. Such a depiction draws on contemporary conceptualisations of girls and young women which acknowledge that their bodies are subjected to a series of contradictions, as they are 'generally represented as having (or being) too little or too much; as too fat or too thin; too clever or too stupid, too free or too restricted' (Griffin 2004: 42). Such contradictions result in young women experiencing a permanent state of dissatisfaction with their bodies and a persistent desire to achieve something 'other'. Clearly, these often invisible sociocultural ideologies have an impact on the physical and mental wellbeing of women, and it is such consequences that are realised in 'Mini Me'.

The story's title emerges from a particular section of the story, when Pat is trying to convince herself that she can lose weight.

In fact, 'mini me' takes on an identity as a new person in her own right:

> I huvtae believe she's possible, this *mini me*, like I've got something invested in her materializing. And before she's even here, what you huvtae say is *this is it* this time, you're gonnae hang on tae her? You are no gonnae let her go. Right? (193–4)

This 'new' figure of 'mini me' reveals the impact that body image has on Pat's sense of self. This is reinforced when she confesses to herself that 'I'm a bit o' an alien when I'm skinny; I don't recognize masell' (194). Despite the protestations that Pat is trying to lose weight for herself there is a clear disjoint between her desire to be skinny (because this is what society and culture tell her is the acceptable bodily manifestation of a woman) and her own sense of identity and self-identification. Thus, the materiality and the intellectuality of the body are strongly interwoven through the figure of 'mini me'. The final diary entry on '*Day One Hundred and Forty-Three*' (209) depicts Pat's night out with her friend Jenny. However, far from celebrating her friend's weight loss, Jenny expresses concern and even 'looks appalled', which swiftly wipes the smile off Pat's 'thin face' (210). It is only in the company of Jenny, who 'doesnie look at me like the people at work do' (ibid.), that Pat reflects on how isolated and alone she has been while losing weight. In becoming the 'mini me' she longed for, Pat has experienced sacrifice, isolation and 'solitary confinement' (ibid.). Thus, in striving to emulate a certain image of female bodily beauty Pat has subjected herself to some intensely negative emotional experiences. The 'Mini Me' diary, then, provides a compelling insight into the relationship between cultural ideals of the youthful, slender female body and the consequences that perpetuating this image has for those who do not adhere. Crucially for feminism, the consuming female body resides at the juncture of subjectivity and embodiment and, therefore, can speak profoundly to contemporary understandings of femininity.

While 'Mini Me' explores the psychological and physical implications of femininity discourses on a woman's body, Sarah Hall's 'Butcher's Perfume' (2011) challenges the stereotype of physical weakness and, indeed, meekness often associated with feminine behaviour. Narrated by a young woman called Kathleen, 'Butcher's Perfume' is her story about the Slessor family. The oxymoronic nature of the story's title sets the tone of the narrative, which brings together seemingly oppositional qualities of masculinity and femininity only to challenge such binary conceptualisation. The story opens with a focus on Kathleen's friend Manda, Kathleen's entry route into knowing the Slessor family, and describes a graphic scene of female violence in which Manda recalls how she had 'beaten two girls at once' (3). The reason for Manda's violence has 'nothing to do with her size – it never does with girls' (ibid.); instead it is attributed by people in the local town to the fact that Manda 'came from gypsy stock' (4). As such, 'Butcher's Perfume' not only offers a critique of femininity, but challenges the stereotypes and general preconceptions of 'being a gypsy'. In doing so, 'Butcher's Perfume' is undercut with the politics of social class and racial difference as these discourses run throughout the story.

While sociocultural stereotypes suggest that violence is not a trait associated with femininity, and therefore consequentially with the female body, in 'Butcher's Perfume' it becomes the most natural attribute of Manda's identity. In fact, this appetite for violence even infiltrates her physical appearance as, when Manda has Donna Tweddle 'by the throat' (6):

> Her face wasn't pretty and smiling the way lads like girls' faces to be. Manda had her good features, those fire-dog eyes among them, and a heavy chest at fifteen, but that wasn't it. What she was doing suited her, and she was lit up, the way someone plain looks better when they sing, when suddenly it seems they have bright colours under a dull wing. (7)

In this instant, Manda is transformed by the violent act. While she does not adhere to the normalised assumptions of female beauty – typified by the description of being 'pretty' and 'smiling' here – Manda does light up, albeit in a more animalistic manner, through this act of aggression. This is reinforced when, later on, she releases Donna from her grip and the 'brightness left her too' (ibid.). Nonetheless, despite displaying characteristics that are stereotypically associated with masculinity, Manda does not escape the biology of her female sex and, after having sex with a family friend, she falls pregnant. Thus, through the power of description, Hall's short story complicates the notion of masculinity and femininity and the reader is drawn into an opaque portrayal of gender identity.

In keeping with the detailed depiction of female violence, Hall's narrative does not shy away from confronting the reader with the physicality of Manda's experience, even if it is mediated through Kathleen's eyes:

she took two pills for her abortion, and I held her shoulders while she
was sick. She said the nurse had told her not to look when she went to
the toilet, but she had looked down into the bucket by her feet. It wasn't
like period clots, just a ball of tubes. (12)

With this portrayal of abortion, the story articulates the challenging experiences of the female body. Furthermore, with the performance of traditionally masculine characteristics by the female body,
'Butcher's Perfume' reinforces the discrepancy between sex and gender, thereby challenging the cultural and social naturalisation of sex
and gender continuity. The end result is a short story in which some
of the most normalised attributes of femininity are unsettled.

The 'other' woman

The stories discussed so far in this chapter have all tended to centre
on young, white, Western female bodies, which in itself reveals how
notions of femininity are commonly mediated and understood in
contemporary discourses. In considering the 'other' woman, then,
this final section of the chapter explores how issues of race, ethnicity and ageing offer fruitful ways of revisiting femininity and offer
further insight into the ways in which this gender identity is socioculturally constructed and maintained. However, by interrogating
this construction of the 'other', such an approach also opens up
the possibility of understanding some of the nuances and inconsis-
tencies of femininities. Michèle Roberts' story 'Playing Sardines'
(2001) exemplifies such a point as the concepts of young and old
are brought into play. The 'sardines' of title refers to a childhood
game in which children hide in small spaces, often tightly packed
together like sardines in a tin, while another child seeks these
hiders out. This is a game of the imagination and it celebrates
the potential fear *and* joy to be found in darkness. Roberts uses
this notion of 'playing sardines' in a variety of ways, all of which
function to rewrite ideas about ageing, women and contemporary
feminisms. Following the association of sardines with people, the
phrase 'playing sardines' also suggests 'playing people', or 'playing with people'. If after puberty play, with all its connotations of
pleasure and self-fulfilment, is supposed to be renounced in favour
of caring for others, Roberts challenges this binary opposition by
suggesting that play is relevant later in life too and can transcend
its association with particular ages. In many ways, then, the title

implies that Roberts is herself playing games with her characters and readers.

'Playing Sardines' centres on a woman who marries an architectural historian from Venice, only to realise that she is in love not with him but with Italy. The story opens with the protagonist having bought a tin of sardines from the market, purely because 'the tin they came in was foreign and beautiful' (1). She keeps the tin and never eats the sardines, and the object becomes a thing of beauty in her life. This establishes one reason for the story's title. However, it is when the protagonist sits outside at a dinner party, smoking a cigarette, that the other meaning is revealed to the reader. She tells Federico, a servant of the house, about the game 'sardines'. Language divides the pair, as she does not speak Italian well, therefore her telling of the story serves a greater purpose in sharing with the reader the pleasure she took in the game:

> I wanted to convey how the house was plunged into darkness and so transformed into a mysterious new landscape, how the point of the game was hiding yourself, in an impossible place no one normally ever went to or would ever dream of finding you in, and then waiting for someone to discover you. Of course you hoped it would be the person you loved the most, the person in whose presence you loved the most. (17)

Imagination fuels this game and transforms an ordinary situation into a 'new landscape'. It is the relationship with others that truly defines the pleasure the protagonist takes in the game. The primary hope is that the one person you love would find you first, but 'if you were unlucky, all too soon one by one, the others would find you, and pile in, giggling and whispering, which was when the game became truly sardines' (ibid.). While the name of the game refers to the numbers of children squashed in a small space together, the real desirability of the game is the potential pleasure of being intimate with just one person. Thus, the story reveals that while play is associated with youth and childhood innocence, even then, it is a means of masking the pleasure of intimacy that comes about from being close to other human beings. In short, even at this early age play becomes associated with sex and, vice versa, the story challenges the idea of old age equating to a lack of playfulness.

Comparatively, Tremain's story 'The Darkness of Wallis Simpson' (1999), from her fourth collection of short stories of the same name (2006), scrutinises the politics of memory in the context of the ageing female body and the implications of forgetting for individual identity. Issues of ownership and knowledge are paramount in this story, which uses the imagery of darkness and light to symbolise the individual's ability to know and remember. Beyond fiction, the life of Wallis Simpson has become a public story, a fact exemplified by the multitude of biographies of her and the 2011 film *W.E.* Indeed, it is partially to these non-fictional and supposedly authoritative recollections of Wallis that Tremain's short story responds. As such, 'The Darkness of Wallis Simpson' is about *reclaiming* the figure of Wallis as much as the story's focus is upon the act of remembering. Tremain's narrative attempts to retrieve Wallis from the public gaze through an individual, personal story. Accordingly, tensions surface in this story between the inner self of Wallis and the outer self, as constructed by society. By revealing this identity conflict, 'The Darkness of Wallis Simpson' challenges the ways in which totalising historical narratives overlook the individual and produce only a particular type of knowledge.

The motif of darkness is established with the 'shadowy' setting of the room Wallis inhabits in old age (3); a stark contrast to her previous life in the public spotlight. However, this motif of darkness and light is more complicated than a pure binary opposition because darkness suggests, and indeed includes, moments of light and vice versa. Like the narrative moment, and the short story that is at once immediate yet suggestive of things beyond, these motifs work together to create tension and blur boundaries. Opening in 'the shadowy room' in Paris, with her companion who insists on keeping her alive 'until you remember' (ibid.), Wallis only exists in this spatial darkness. Although Wallis' 'sentences turn to goo' (4), the reader is still privy to her inner thoughts. This narrative perspective enhances the conflict between the external perception of Wallis (society's view) and Wallis' internal self-knowledge and identity, which Tremain privileges here. After all, far from her being 'GaGa' (3; original emphasis), as the companion and world suppose, Wallis' memory does still function and produces coherent images and thoughts which drive the story's narrative.

Moreover, the internal stream of consciousness perpetuates the darkness and light motif. Wallis describes how

> the room is so damn dark – with just these thin movements in it, these shadows she can't make out – it's mortifying, like she's watching some old flickering TV picture, or even not watching, but trapped *inside* an old TV, a ghost made out of light, longing to join the world beyond the screen, the world of the TV watchers, pink as candy, warm and

rounded, with their haunches nudging up close to each other on their chintzy divan. How comely these brightly coloured people seem! As if nothing cold would ever touch them. (4)

Literally, the 'thin movements' are Wallis' companion and maid moving around in the darkness of her room. However, given the significance placed upon the 'darkness', and the resonance of memory as a void or lack, this scene functions metaphorically. Accordingly, 'these shadows she can't make out' become the memories which Wallis desperately tries to grasp and reclaim as her own. Developing this reading, the 'old flickering TV picture' extends the metaphor as her memory and history become a television image affected by a bad signal. Within this passage Wallis goes from watching the television, unable to see it fully, to being 'trapped *inside* an old TV'. This movement from subject to object (viewer to the viewed) reflects Wallis' current position in her bed, watched by the companion who attempts to 'retune' Wallis. Importantly, this also reminds the reader how history has constructed Wallis as a one-dimensional figure, 'a ghost made out of light', whose life has played out on the television screen.

At the story's conclusion, instead of naming Edward, an act the companion positions as the ultimate act of remembrance, Wallis refers only to 'the pale little man' (44). Thus, the story's ending proffers knowledge beyond the moment as 'when the *Maître* comes pestering her next time, this is what she'll tell her: "I've remembered him," she'll say. "He was too pale to have a name. I always called him darling"' (46). The story's conclusion remains in the future: it '*will* be put to rest' (ibid.; emphasis added), thus destabilising the assertive conclusion of a historical past that 'knows' Wallis. Conversely, the story propagates instability and offers a forward-facing liminality. Giving Wallis a voice is not a straightforward act of reclamation. When Wallis finally lifts herself up and taps on the window pane the crowd of reporters below the apartment moves forward, calling her name, as if 'seeing a ghost' (43). Wallis is simultaneously alive and dead to the journalists, an almost translucent figure. Hearing their voices calling her name triggers a memory in Wallis: 'oh, she can remember this: people calling her name. People reaching out their hands to her, trying to touch her' (43–4). Making reference to the manner in which the media pursued Wallis during her relationship with Edward VIII, this scene connects her past life with the present.

However, the version of the story that Wallis remembers provides an alternative narrative to the one that Maître Blum demands, or to the story told by other people about Wallis. Here, Wallis remembers how the man that loved her was gentle to her and 'never got mad at her. Never called her an American bitch' (44). Instead, Edward 'got mad at the world' and the way it treated Wallis by depicting her as the 'mannish', 'coarse' and 'too American' woman who caused a king to abdicate (Tremain 2010a: n. p.). The description here reveals how the public dislike for Wallis during this time was transposed onto her body and marked in gendered terms. In 'The Darkness of Wallis Simpson', Tremain negotiates between the darkness and light, the past and the present, and draws on the brevity of the short story to sketch an imagined, miniature portrait of Wallis that challenges social preconceptions while revealing the way in which gender categories are not simply affirmative identity labels but can be used negatively to deride individuals. Equally, the story seeks to insert the ageing female body into a mainstream narrative. After all, while the story of the young Wallis has been repeatedly told, in Tremain's narrative the elderly Wallis re-emerges from the shadows.

Issues of memory loss also reside at the heart of Aminatta Forna's short story 'Haywards Heath' (2010), which was shortlisted for the BBC National Short Story Award. In tracing his lost love and travelling to visit her at a nursing home, the ageing, black, male protagonist, Attila, is confronted with a woman who no longer recognises him. Instead, Rosie smiles at Attila and exclaims, 'what a coincidence! He's coming to see me any time soon. I'm waiting for him. Maybe you two will meet' (14). While Rosie remembers Attila, she only remembers the younger version of him and therefore cannot identify the man in front of her, in the present, as her former love. With the movement between the present and the past of Attila's memory, the reader is confronted with portraits of Rosie, both young and old. Attila 'examined her offered profile for a few moments. How much beauty there was still' (13), and the beauty associated with the young female body is shown to reside still in this older woman. Later, when taking a turn around the garden, Rosie stretches out her arms, provoking Attila to think of 'a memory of a photograph of her in the exact same pose. Where was it now?' (15). The double distance in this image, as Attila can only remember the photograph he does not physically possess, replicates the emotional distance between the couple. At the same time, the physicality of Rosie's body creates a synergy between these two moments as the younger version re-emerges in the figure of the older woman. Accordingly, such imagery brings into question the notion that beauty and youth (two concepts frequently associated with femininity) are solely applicable to the young female body. Seen through the male eyes of Attila, who expresses as much affection for this ageing Rosie as he did for the younger woman, this depiction also challenges the assumption that for women to be worthy of competing within the heterosexual market they must look youthful (Sanger 2009: 140).

The unsettled relationship between youth and age is also mirrored through Rosie's childlike behaviour. After stealing a sweet from a box on an old woman's lap in the garden, 'Rosie gave an impish giggle, the sweet bulged in her check' (16), before she pleads with Attila to come and visit her again. Hoping that Rosie will eventually remember him, Attila returns two months later with a box of sweets to give to Rosie. However, he is confronted with an unexpected image: 'Rosie, cradled by the arms of the young, African worker' (17). Thus, Rosie's childlike behaviour is only one element of her regression into the past, as the words: 'Shall we do another turn, Attila? Another turn. What do you say?', which are directed at the young careworker whom Rosie has mistaken for Attila, illuminates her loss of memory and sense of time and place. With a bittersweet poignancy the story closes with Attila sitting down and watching as Rosie dances with this young man. This closing scene is fuelled with sadness, yet beauty, and the unspoken but implicit reality of the story is that Rosie is a woman suffering from Alzheimer's disease. 'Haywards Heath' is not only a story which challenges the long-established association of femininity with youthful female bodies; it also proffers an alternative and often untold story of the realities and experiences of the ageing mind and body, subject to illness. Forna exploits the brevity of the short story to provide a snapshot of life in the immediate moment. The ambiguity around any sense of closure leaves the reader on the cusp, replicating the emotions of Attila, and thus furthering the sense of longing.

In comparison, 'That Polite Way That English People Have', from Andrea Levy's collection *Six Stories & an Essay* (2014), is the story of a young Jamaican woman named Blossom who is setting out on a journey to England to train as a nurse. Having worked from a young age, Blossom has saved for years to pay for a passage to England and to travel 'in style' (62). The story's title, 'that polite way that English people have' (59), is a phrase repeated at various points throughout the story by the protagonist and narrative voice, Blossom. Indeed, Blossom is strongly influenced by English society and attempts to emulate the behaviour and characteristics of English high society. After all, she has spent ten years as a nanny for 'one of the foremost English families in Jamaica' (ibid.), and for Blossom, this means she is more informed than most Jamaicans on what it means to be

English. In this respect, Blossom's passage to England, during which time she changes her name to Hortense, is depicted as a transitional experience in which she attempts to shed her previous identity as a Jamaican woman and, instead, to replicate the characteristics of a high-class English lady. Significantly, the well-documented argument that 'whiteness functions as the unmarked, uncritiqued norm' (Sanger 2009: 140) is revisited in Levy's story as Blossom's desire to assimilate with English culture draws attention to the normalisation of whiteness.

The difficulty of Blossom's transition to Hortense re-emerges throughout the journey; firstly when the 'rough and uncouth' man (63) who carries her trunk on to the ship, and sees the luxury passage Blossom has purchased to travel to England, reminds her that, 'you're a nigger' (64). Here, skin colour is not only a material embodiment which defines racial identity, but is used metaphorically to regulate the behaviour and aspirations of the individual. The subtext of this statement aims to remind Blossom of her ethnic *roots*, regardless of her aspirational *routes*. Moreover, as Hortense, she engages in dinner with fellow passenger Philip Keyes (71). When he escorts her back to her cabin and asks if she would like 'a night cap', Hortense misunderstands the meaning of this phrase (taking it literally), and responds 'that I did not usually wear anything on my head when I slept' (ibid.). While the intention behind this question was actually an implicit proposition to extend their evening further and comes with sexual undertones, Hortense is oblivious to such implications, highlighting a gap in cultural knowledge and drawing the reader's attention to her performance of Englishness, as opposed to a native English identity. In *Black Feminist Thought* (2000), Patricia Hill Collins argues that the theme of journey is linked to the affirmation of self for black women (131). Further, proposing that self-definition is an important aspect of black feminist thought, she contends that: 'Black women's lives are a series of negotiations that aim to reconcile the contradictions separating our own internally defined images of self as African-American women with our objectification as the Other' (99). Understood in this way, Blossom's journey in 'That Polite Way That English People Have' provides one example of such a complex negotiation, and the transition to Hortense signals an attempt at self-definition.

Despite such cultural limitations, Blossom (as Hortense) does perform a particular version of English femininity through her choice of clothing. For dinner on the ship she wears her best dress, and she 'brightened up this green dress with a strip of yellow satin ribbon across the low neckline and over the puffed sleeves. And I finished the whole look off with a small piece of ribbon as a bow in my hair' (68). The choice of materials, shape of the neckline and accessories all contribute to the stereotypical image of femininity. The conscious attempt to project a certain image of femininity (as shaped by under-standings of Englishness) is reinforced through the encounter with fellow traveller Petal. Blossom describes Petal as looking 'so dressed up with her ribbons and lace, trying to look high class. But I could tell she was rough' (69). For Blossom, the false pretence of civility (Englishness) is illuminated further by the fact that Petal 'wiped' with her napkin rather than 'dabbing it at the corners of her mouth like English people do' (ibid.). Crucially, through Blossom's perception of Petal it becomes clear that Blossom's attempts to project a particular persona (as Hortense) is in fact an attempt to shed her Jamaican identity and to assimilate into English culture. Upon first seeing Petal, Blossom describes 'a Jamaican woman as black as night' (ibid.). The blackness of Petal's skin is equated with her identity as being 'even more' Jamaican than Blossom. Thus, in the context of race, ethnic-ity and culture, the performance of femininity and of feminine roles is not simply a result of patriarchal constructions of gender iden-tity, but also reveals the hegemonic dominance of a particular white, Western feminine identity. Hortense attempts to perform an aesthetic of feminine beauty and, in the process, hopes to appease the gaze of the Western eye. By bringing such a construction of beauty and femininity to the forefront of the story, Levy's story attests to the significance of femininity for racial politics and feminism, reminding the reader that 'color consciousness and the pursuit of whiteness is the backdrop for contemporary definitions of beauty and femininity' (Hunter 2005: 29).

A central motif in the story is the coat Blossom purchases from her employer, Mrs Roberts, based on the advice that 'since the war the cost of coats in England had become very high and that this coat I was purchasing from her was the best quality money could buy' (59–60). Blossom trusts her employer and buys the coat with the confidence that it 'would be the finest coat in England' (59). The coat becomes a symbol of hope and represents Blossom's faith that England will provide her with a better life. While the coat is a neces-sity of life in the cooler climate of England, as the story progresses, it becomes assimilated with England in Blossom's mind and her affec-tion for this fashion object reflects her belief in England as a country. Given Blossom's investment in the coat, it is especially significant that the story ends with Petal telling Blossom that 'this is an ugly coat' and that her 'employer has sold you a very old-fashioned coat' (75). While Blossom positions herself as culturally and socially superior to Petal throughout the story, in the end it is Petal who issues the final judgement. Thus, while Blossom's story begins with her claiming to have 'seen how life can be' (62), especially in comparison to her unrefined, uneducated, country mother, by the story's end these assertions of privilege and cultural capital are undermined. Nonetheless, Blossom's possession of the coat reveals the importance of social and economic capital in the pursuit of femininity, which, consequentially, reminds the reader that 'beauty is still a form of social capital which continues to be racialized and contested' (Tate 2009: 10). Significantly, Blossom's ability to purchase the coat and a comfortable passage to England recognises that class and economic capital are important mobilising factors in her attainment of this 'new' identity.

In summarising extant scholarship detailing the relationship between feminism and femininity, Riley and Scharff (2012) highlight that 'the construction of feminism and femininity as mutually exclusive is an old one . . . that continues to be reproduced in contemporary media . . ., academic feminism . . ., young women's talk . . ., and popular culture' (208). While this does provide a fair summation of how the relationship between feminism and femininity has been conceived, the prioritisation of a binary understanding of these two concepts is problematic. Understandings of femininity as either anti-feminist (as associated with second-wave feminism) or pro-feminist (as symbolised by the 'girlie girl' and post-feminism) only perpetuate simplistic narratives about what, in reality, is a complex issue. The stories discussed throughout this chapter have all contributed creatively and critically to representations of femininity and have sought to scrutinise the manifestation of femininity discourses across temporal and cultural moments. However, these narratives by no means provide a clear 'answer' to the question of how femininity and feminism should be defined. While all of these stories do attest to the fact that femininity is traditionally understood in relation to the young, white, middle-class, Western female body, many of these stories take this further and seek to unsettle the assumed interdependence of this relationship. Certainly, this body of women's short story writing provides diverse stories to the broader narratives of femininity, and its engagement with feminisms.

Chapter 2

Motherhood

The politics of motherhood is perhaps one of the most prominent points of debate upon which feminist theory and practice have evolved since the 1960s. Indeed, the centrality of motherhood to feminism is recognised by the wealth of theoretical and academic writing on the subject. Importantly, Elaine Tuttle Hansen (1997) summarises how 'the story of feminists thinking about motherhood since the early 1960s is told as a drama in three acts: repudiation, recuperation, and . . . an emerging critique of recuperation that coexists with ongoing efforts to deploy recuperative strategies' (5). While the first of these acts is given over to feminist thinkers such as Betty Friedan, Kate Millett, Shulamith Firestone and Simone de Beauvoir, who in one way or another illuminate the interconnection between women's oppression and their assumed affiliation to motherhood, the second act in this story is an attempt to 'reclaim and reinterpret motherhood and revalue difference' (ibid.). Seemingly, then, just like the story of feminism, the issue of motherhood becomes framed as a site of progress based on difference. However, as Lauri Umansky (1996) acknowledges, 'feminist discourses of motherhood have also evolved along trajectories more complex than that of the negative to the positive' (160). This chapter aims to explore further the complexities at the heart of feminism's engagement with motherhood and to move away from this drama in three acts. By reading a range of short stories by Michèle Roberts, Helen Simpson, Kate Atkinson and Andrea Levy, this chapter highlights the multitude of ways in which writers have negotiated the often complicated terrain of motherhood, and sought to offer a diverse spectrum of experiences and understandings of the subject, by exploiting the formal qualities of the short story and short story collection.

Significantly, much of the theoretical debate on motherhood emerges from an American context; the focus on British short stories, therefore, offers a means of countering the predominance of American feminist thinking on the subject by focusing on the insights provided by British literature. If, as Ann Ferguson (1997) proposes, 'the experience of mothering [alone] can tell us little about the conception of motherhood prevalent in a society at a certain time' (39), then it is hoped that the focus on literature will provide a means of understanding the ontological realities of motherhood while enabling a critique of the sociocultural discourses underpinning maternal constructs. While American scholars shaped the motherhood debate from the 1960s through to the millennium, there has been a notable shift in the medium of debate with the rise of the internet and online spaces such as Mumsnet. The popularity of Mumsnet is noteworthy because through this online space 'it is possible to see how personal experiences are being publicly articulated in ways that tap into and seek to shape the public-political agenda' (Gambles 2010: 36). Mumsnet illuminates the very reason that motherhood has always been a significant site of debate for feminism: it blurs the traditional boundaries of private/public and personal/political.

In reading short stories, this chapter continues to pay attention to the intersection between the public and private spheres by considering what the personalised narratives contribute to public understandings of motherhood. In other words, how do literary depictions of motherhood creatively contribute to contemporary feminist understandings? Simultaneously, to what extent are the individual narratives shaped by and reflexive of feminist theory? This chapter commences by discussing Roberts' short stories and the ways in which they perpetuate the theoretical premise of institutionalised motherhood, before moving on to more recent short stories by Simpson. With this focus on Simpson's short stories I also reflect on what the short story collection offers as a textual space for depicting experiences of motherhood. The final part of this chapter centres on issues of maternal loss and offers an opportunity to consider how ethnicity and race inform understandings of motherhood, as well as the way in which the concept of the maternal resonates on a metaphoric level with issues of gender, race and identity.

Institutionalised motherhood: Michèle Roberts

In 'On Imagination' (1998), Roberts contends that the mother figure is simultaneously sentimentalised, despised and blamed in society and culture (21). As a result, women struggle to locate an 'image of sensual loving delight between mother and daughter' (ibid.). For Roberts, this results in a battle in which 'we search for the image, try to make one, to make one up' (ibid.). Extant criticism on Roberts' fiction stresses the relevance of feminisms to her narratives, with a significant focus on French feminism and theories of the maternal. Most notably, Sarah Falcus (2007) outlines how, like Luce Irigaray, Roberts' work explores 'the contradictory and problematic representations of the mother, attempting to break the silence of the mother without reinscribing her in the position of object and threatening women with further marginalisation' (17). Similarly, Hanson analyses the mother figure in Roberts' novels *A Piece of the Night*, *Wild Girl* and *Flesh and Blood*, published in 1978, 1984 and 1994 respectively, alongside the short story 'During Mother's Absence' (1993), arguing that 'feminism provided the terms through which identity could be tested, questioned, and challenged, but was itself questioning and fluid – hence the diversity of the fiction it inspired' (230).

The mother figure is a central concern in Roberts' first collection of short stories, *During Mother's Absence* (1994a). The need to conjure the mother, reaffirm a maternal existence and reclaim motherhood dominates many of her short stories. At the same time, each story portrays alternative images of the mother, thus allowing a spectrum of images to constitute the category of 'mother'. 'Anger' is the opening story of the collection; it is told by an omniscient narrator but throughout the first half of the story it repeatedly takes the perspective of the mother, Bertrande, as the point of narrative focalisation, and it is with this section of the story that I begin. Broadly speaking, 'Anger' is a story of two parts and centres on Bertrande before moving on to focus on her daughter, Melusine. 'Anger' challenges the idea of the contented mother because Bertrande's emotions are dominated by anger and resentment towards her child. In fact, Bertrande's anger, described as 'the fire inside her' (9), and the difficulty she has bonding with the baby result in her dropping the baby in the fire. This event is depicted in a natural and unsurprising manner: 'the fire was near Bertrande. Bertrande was near the fire', and so, 'Bertrande dropped the baby in the fire. She said it was not an accident' (ibid.). The simple, consequential relationship between Bertrande standing near the fire and dropping the baby in jolts the reader as the flow, and therefore supposed logic of the action, is at odds with the specifics of the act.

Immediately, this story resonates with Adrienne Rich's *Of Woman Born: Motherhood as Experience and Institution* (1992). In the chapter entitled 'Anger and Tenderness', Rich recalls how,

I was haunted by the stereotype of the mother whose love is 'unconditional'; and by the visual and literary images of motherhood as a
single-minded identity. If I knew parts of myself existed that would
never cohere to those images, weren't those parts then abnormal,
monstrous. (23)

Importantly, Rich identifies the stereotype of motherhood and the culturally perpetuated notion that it is a 'single-minded identity'. As she
reveals, those who neither experience motherhood in this way, nor perform the role adequately, are deemed monstrous. In 'Anger' Bertrande
is established as an outsider in relation to the rest of the community.
She lives with her husband Guillaume above the village, 'in their small
house tucked into the side of a steep hill' (1). Bertrande's geographical
position symbolises her status as an outsider and her social ostracism
manifests itself upon her female body. Even prior to throwing Melusine
into the fire, Bertrande is marked as a non-normative woman because
her 'hands were the largest of any woman's in the village' and they were
'puckered with scars' (3).

The narrative voice embeds the opinions of Bertrande's neighbours within the story to mirror the social critique that she experiences. Early on, these women 'other' Bertrande, a fact symbolised
by their perception of her large hands, her singing of strange songs
and her cursing of her husband in a 'guttural voice', which are all
viewed as being antithetical to womanliness (4). The villager wom-
en's voices embody the mindset outlined above by Rich (the coherent
image of the unconditionally loving mother) and reflect the internalisation of patriarchal values by women. In 'The Straight Mind'
(1992), Monique Wittig argues that the discourse of heterosexuality
has become normalised to the point of invisibility in society and,
hence, it is impossible to speak in a language outside it. As such,
the default position of society can be referred to as heteronormative. Echoing Wittig's 'straight mind', here the village community
exemplifies a 'maternal mind'. Roberts' depiction of the neighbours
suggests that the discourse of motherhood has undergone a similar
procedure to that undergone by heterosexuality. Here, love and happiness for the child and a general embracing of motherhood have
functions akin to those of heterosexuality. Importantly, the reader's
insight into the internal and external perceptions of Bertrande, and
the ways in which they conflict, allows the reader to critique societal
discourses that seek to shape, inform and even control women's bodies. Thus, this formalistic feature, of moving between differing narrative perspectives, is critical to the facilitation of feminist critique.

The cause of Bertrande's social exclusion stems from two issues: firstly her behaviour in the woods, where she collects flowers not 'to dry them for tisanes. Oh no; she pressed them, stuck them on squares of sugar paper, and hung them on the wall' (3). Such creativity is decadent and therefore deemed wasteful, thus inducing scorn. Secondly, her status as childless is unnatural, according to the community, as 'you never saw Bertrande's hands . . . caressing a child. Married for ten years, she appeared incapable of conceiving an heir' (4). Crucially, being childless suggests a lack of fulfilment of the category 'woman'. Thus, when Bertrande does fall pregnant the other women of the village 'could welcome her as one of themselves' (ibid.). This reflects Rich's feeling that "I only knew that to have a child was to assume adult womanhood to the full, to prove myself to be "like other women"' (25).

This initial acceptance of the pregnant Bertrande by the community is soon revoked when they perceive her behaviour to be 'too proud and angry to pass unnoticed' (5). Bertrande is seen collecting 'roots that were well known to bring on young women's monthly flows' (ibid.). Although this is wrongly perceived to be a naive mistake on Bertrande's part, as opposed to an active desire to abort the baby, nonetheless the priest remonstrates with Guillaume that he 'should not let his wife roam so far from home into the woods to collect roots' that could harm her and the child (ibid.). Here, the maternal body is under male control and it is her husband's responsibility to ensure that Bertrande conforms to the standards of 'womanly' and 'motherly' behaviour.

The male control and responsibility for women depicted here recall Shulamith Firestone's *The Dialectic of Sex* (1973), in which she argues that it is sex privatization and women's status as reproducers that cause their original and continuous oppression, and men's subsequent power (74). Invoking *The Dialectic of Sex*, 'Anger' elaborates the premise that culture creates 'an unnatural psychological dichotomy' of the good/bad woman, and that this 'personality split is projected outwards on to the class "women": those who resemble the mother are "good", . . . those unlike the mother . . . are sexual, and therefore "bad"' (Firestone 1973: 62). Through the figure of Bertrande, Roberts reflects the way in which patriarchy controls women's bodies, especially through motherhood. Consequently, 'Anger' critiques the way in which society defines and controls, or to use Rich's word *institutionalises*, motherhood.

Following the birth of their daughter Melusine, Bertrande's behaviour still refuses to conform to societal expectations. Instead, she looks 'contemptuously' at her husband and does not allow the women to 'touch the baby with holy water' (8). As a result, the women proclaim that, with 'such a mother, what prospect was there for the child?' (ibid.). This comment foreshadows the story's later focus on Melusine's non-normative body and behaviour, and highlights the emphasis Roberts places upon the shared experiences of the mother and the daughter in this story. However, before this, with the collection of wild roots and by dropping Melusine in the fire, Bertrande challenges the stereotype of the contented mother. Crucially, 'the priest tried to sort out the right words. Bertrande. The baby fell in the fire by accident' (9). Again, the priest attempts to control Bertrande, and here he quite literally rearticulates her actions so that they adhere to social expectations. Regardless of the priest's attempts to revoice Bertrande, she still becomes known as 'a monster' (10). Thus, the anger of the title is not just Bertrande's literal rage, as the opening of the story suggests, but a wider anger at the social expectations that define motherhood and women's bodies more broadly.

The second story in Roberts' collection is entitled 'Charity', and it furthers the critique of women's motherly behaviour. The story is broken into five subsections, each of which centres on different elements of maternal experience, and which can be summarised by the story's closing sentence: 'The Lady of Perpetual Succour Mrs Charity Auntie my young erotic mother' (62). Emphasised by the lack of punctuation, this closing remark merges all of the mother figures together, reflecting how they are all as important as the next in providing physical or spiritual maternal guidance to the story's protagonist, Marie. The name of the narrator is only revealed via Karen, a girl in Marie's class at the local Catholic school. Responding to a passage from the Bible, Karen comments:

> It's about Charity . . . it says in the book that Charity means loving everybody but loving men is wrong Sister isn't it unless you're married and even then you can only love one well Sister is it true what everyone says that Marie's auntie went with men for money she was a whore everyone knows that it's true isn't it. (57–8)

Concerned with the oppressive religious discourses within which the girls are educated and the social class divisions that are emphasised by the charitable scholarships awarded to Marie and her friend Mary, this middle section of the story also illuminates the conflict between charity and sexuality. According to Karen, Marie's aunt is placed in direct conflict with notions of religious charity as, by selling her body,

Marie's aunt is a whore and implicitly un-Christian. While religion is a dominant element of the story and the nuns at the school provide physical, but more importantly spiritual, 'mothering' to Marie through the preaching of scripture, it is the traditional, physical maternal figures upon whom I will focus here; Marie's birth mother and her aunt, the woman who raises her.

The maternal body frames the story's narrative and remains a pertinent feature throughout, as section one opens with the image of breastfeeding, a bodily function that re-emerges in section five with the figure of Mrs Charity. Likewise, the middle parts of the story meditate on the physicality of Marie's aunt's body and focus on her sexuality and sexual attractiveness. The story's opening is relatively short (two pages), and recounts Marie's dream of her 'young erotic mother' (31). As with the closing section, this part of the story is told in the fictive present when Marie has reached adulthood, as opposed to the childhood perspective of the middle, narrated through the medium of memory. In this dream Marie and her mother 'watch each other undress' after being soaked in the rain and then Marie's mother 'turns back the blue quilt on the bed, and I [Marie] slide in next to her' (32). While lying in bed against her mother's warm flesh, Marie describes how

> I lay my hands on her hips and pull her close, kiss her soft mouth, her shoulders, stroke her hair, the wet silky place between her legs. The storm drums on the roof. She kisses and caresses me. Her smell grows stronger, like a garden after the rain. She offers me her breast, round touching kissing sucking biting, then my swollen cunt boils over and I come. (ibid.)

The act of breastfeeding becomes sexualised as the dream reveals Marie's desire for her lost mother. It is the 'milky fullness' of the breast, as Edith Frampton calls it in her discussion of Roberts' breastfeeding narratives (2006), which symbolises the corporeal presence of the mother. Following Hélène Cixous' (2001) belief that 'women write in white ink' (2045), this dream passage reunites the bodies of mother and daughter while suggesting a language between them, in the form of the milk. Cumulatively, Roberts tries to find a place for women, and specifically female bonds, but not in the realm of spoken language, rather in the unspoken dream and between female bodies.

Marie's mother is an absent presence throughout the story. By comparison, Marie's aunt is an extremely physical bodily presence.

Marie recalls how 'Auntie was not what you would call a good-looking woman most of the time, except in the afternoons when she got tidied up for her visitors', and she, 'didn't look anything like the other children's mothers' (34). From the outset Marie's aunt is distinguished as not fulfilling the traditional and socially accepted role of mother; based on bodily manifestations she does not perform motherhood adequately. Instead she always 'wore bright red lipstick and could talk with a cigarette in her mouth' (35), marking out her strong physical presence throughout Marie's childhood. It is through Marie's description of her aunt that she is 'normalised', as Marie does not see anything unusual in her aunt's behaviour. After all, Marie is cared for, well fed and given suitable freedom and autonomy to be who she wishes. It is only when 'forced to become aware through other children's gibes and rhymes, that she [Auntie] was odd and therefore bad' that Marie's perception shifts (38). Thus, through this child narrator's perspective 'Charity' challenges the definition of motherhood and reveals, through the childhood innocence of the narrator, the ways in which motherhood is socially conditioned.

While Marie's narrative alludes to afternoon visitors and how being 'good meant not getting home from school until four o'clock every day in the week' (25), the implication that Marie's aunt is a prostitute is left to the reader to decode. It is not until the fourth section of the story that Marie discovers the truth about her 'Auntie', which results in her being slapped and left with a bruise (59). Arriving home early and rushing into the house, Marie finds her aunt lying with a man 'like in a photograph' (58). However, as she 'looked at her bare white bosom', she sees how the man 'curled in her arms and sucked at one of her breasts like a baby' (59). Echoing the opening dream scene, the breast is this time eroticised and the man becomes infantilised in Marie's eyes. From this point on, Marie 'realised that something was broken' and in witnessing this scene her relationship with her aunt is irreconcilably damaged (ibid.). Thus, the maternal body in 'Charity' is the site of both female kinship and sisterly destruction, as the sexual act that Marie associates with the maternal bond is shattered.

With *During Mother's Absence*, Roberts embraces the polyphonic nature of the short story collection and uses it to critique the institutionalised version of motherhood while proffering alternative images (both negative and positive) of being a mother. In the process, Roberts fiction puts forward a notably second-wave approach by emphasising mother–daughter relations and women's bodies in general. Indeed, this literary representation questions the formation of the category 'woman' more broadly and thereby reflects one of the bedrocks of second-wave feminist politics. With these various portrayals of motherhood the notion of an absent presence emerges in relation to the mother–daughter relationship. The narratives illuminate how, even if physically absent, the mother–daughter bond lives on beyond the material confines of existence because of female embodiment and women's shared experiences. Likewise, the titles of both stories – 'Anger' and 'Charity' – symbolise the differing reactions to the politics of motherhood, and what it means to be a woman. On the one hand there is anger, a desire to transgress the patriarchal institution and reject social expectation. On the other hand exists charity and the belief that women's identities, bodies and connections should be celebrated and embraced by women and for women. As such, these two stories exemplify the diverse affective nature of feminism as it moves between the politics of anger and charity.

Temporal and spatial constraints: Helen Simpson

Motherhood emerges as a prevailing theme in the writings of Simpson. As a writer who has published solely in the short story genre, Simpson's work offers insights into the ways in which this textual space can be exploited to illuminate truly the narrative's thematic preoccupations. Ailsa Cox has discussed Simpson's short stories on numerous occasions, acknowledging the breadth of her writing, from highlighting the way in which Simpson uses the form to foreground theatricality (2008) through to discussing her critique of the literary marketplace (2013a) and the use of circularity in the short story collection (2013b) . Likewise, writing in the *London Review of Books*, Tessa Hadley (2006) states:

> Simpson writes stories about all sorts of things, but the ones about family life and motherhood set the tone for each collection. And her choice of form (she only writes short stories) may well be influenced by this material no sooner grasped than gone, these shape-changing offspring. (26)

Like many other commentators Hadley highlights the strong focus on motherhood and domesticity in Simpson's stories. The foregrounding of time in the short story offers Simpson an innovative way of engaging with these feminine *and* feminist concerns. If, as Hanson suggests, 'the novel is the most obviously mimetic of literary forms, especially *vis à-vis* the concept of time, [and] the short form may be seen as its necessary foil, questioning by its very nature and structure novelistic assumptions about extensive time and material reality' (1985: 172), then Simpson exploits the short story's ability to critique these mimetic assumptions and, in the brevity of the short story, reveals the implications of a lack of time for women's experiences of daily life.

The narratives' temporal restrictions are reflected in the individual stories' content: making the most of time, lack of time, pregnancy and labour, adolescence and periods of change and transition. Furthermore, the centrality of time to women's lives is positioned as especially significant in relation to motherhood. As Melissa Benn (1998) argues, 'women with children talk about time all the time: feeds, sleep, how many days they are at work, what they manage or don't manage to do at home. Time torments them: time is a treasure' (64). Like the short story genre, for mothers the issue of time is defined by tension, and here it is both tormenter and treasure. Individual stories' dependency on time to drive or control the narrative, reflecting women's lived experience, thus marks the merging of the genre's formal features and narrative content. Significantly, in her analysis Benn asserts the importance of Simpson as a writer: 'Let us at least acknowledge how unusual it is for a writer like Helen Simpson, quick-witted epiphanous drawer of short stories, a quintessential modern writer, to break the silence in a *Best of Young British Novelists* collection' by engaging with issues of motherhood (20). Benn's passing reference to Simpson's work highlights the scarcity of fictional representations of women's lived experience and the daily rituals of motherhood. This is a point that Simpson acknowledges in 'With Child' (2006b), when she refers to motherhood as 'uncharted back then in the 1990s' (n. p.). Thus, part of the 'edginess' of Simpson's subject matter comes from the fact it is an under-discussed (and suggestively undervalued) topic in fiction.

In 'Hey Yeah Right Get a Life' (2001b), the reader is first introduced to Dorrie, who is positioned as an archetypal stay-at-home mum. She has had three children in the space of four years: 'she had broken herself into little pieces like a biscuit and was now scattered all over the place' (153). However, despite this feeling of fragmentation, she 'felt a sick thud of relief that it was not two years ago when she had been racing against the clock to get to work pretending to them that all this had not just happened' (159). Thus, while Dorrie's daily life throughout the story is presented as stressful and both emotionally and physically draining, it becomes a blessing in comparison to her previous attempts to juggle childcare and work. Nonetheless, her failure to manage both work and motherhood, and 'to keep both worlds up in the air', mean that she 'knew she had failed' (ibid.). Implicitly, Dorrie measures her success as a woman against contemporary notions of women 'having it all' (an issue I have already discussed in the context of the 'Mummy Wars' and post(-)feminist politics elsewhere) (Young 2015). Crucially, in this short narrative space, there is an intensity to Dorrie's emotional response to motherhood. The reader is exposed to the time pressures and subsequent negative response Dorrie experiences and this raises questions about the illusion of motherhood as an ideal against the everyday reality of the experience.

The claustrophobia experienced by Dorrie is reworked in 'Café Society' (2001b), as Simpson uses the versatility of the short story genre to produce a much shorter narrative. The narrative brevity compresses the issue of time, space and the ability of these mothers to converse. The opening, when 'two shattered women and a bright-eyed child have just sat down at the window table in the café' (233), immediately situates the story, yet it also suggests a universalism that this could be any two women with children. The story is constituted by passages in standard font and those that are italicised, with the latter representing the women's thoughts. The fact that these italicised passages dominate the majority of the story illuminates the struggle these women have in speaking and, consequently, expressing themselves and connecting emotionally. When the story closes and Frances and Sally 'have exchanged little more than two hundred words inside this hour', the question is asked, 'how much friendship can you base on that?' (242). 'Café Society' fictionalises what Hollows (2000) calls women's 'common experience of oppression' (5), and highlights how this shared experience does not always translate into women's solidarity. It can, in fact, also prevent women from coming together. Simpson's use of the brevity of the short story form to depict a specifically female experience demonstrates how the short story often establishes 'the primacy of "an experience" directly and emotionally created and encountered' (May 1994: 133).

Simpson's narratives also engage with the notion of time through the issue of maternal loss, or time running out. 'Early One Morning' (2006a) follows a mother, Zoe, and her daily car journey, taking her son to school. Living in London means the two-and-three-quarter-mile route takes Zoe and her son George forty-five minutes. Time becomes the anchoring motif of the story, and it shapes the narrative and Zoe's life. Moreover, marking its difference from the stories in *Hey Yeah Right Get a Life*, here this seeming drain on Zoe's time is embraced as her opportunity to spend quality time with George. After all, the counter-current that runs throughout the story is Zoe's awareness that time with her son is running out as he grows up; a point illuminated when he gets out of the car without kissing her goodbye, leaving Zoe upset until he sneaks back to kiss her without his friends seeing. Compared to the experience of the mothers that have no time in the previous collection, here time is viewed in a new light as the narratives focus on the phase when children are growing up and adults become aware of the fragility of time.

This notion of time running out extends to Zoe's own life, as she tells George and his school friends Harry and Freda, who share the journey, that 'time goes by slowly at school. Slowly. Slowly. Then, after you're thirty, it goes faster and faster' (266). The balance of this utterance reinforces the point Zoe makes, as the punctuation around 'slowly' breaks up the sentence structure, as opposed to the flow of 'faster and faster'. Life is presented here as a finely balanced experience. Crucially, when asked why this happens Zoe responds, 'I don't know . . . Maybe it's because after that you somehow know that there'll be a moment for you when there isn't any more' (ibid.). Here, death begins to loom large in the story, as being aware of one's own existence also comprises an awareness of one's mortality. Being a mother, and children growing up, serve as a reminder of one's own ageing body as well. Significantly, the end always being in sight in a short story foreshadows the emphasis on temporality in Simpson's narratives.

Similarly, 'To Her Unready Boyfriend', from the collection *Dear George* (2001a), rewrites Andrew Marvell's poem 'To His Coy Mistress' (published 1681). However, in another playful adaptation that returns to the Restoration period, Simpson's story results in a woman trying to encourage her partner to have a child. She argues that 'it's all right for you, you're like the popes in the Renaissance, you can go on fathering children till you're eighty-three' (115), whereas for women time is limited. Simpson plays with Marvell's original text to invoke contemporary narratives which remind women that their ageing bodies are time-limited with regard to having children. Moreover, unlike in Simpson's other stories, here motherhood is embraced and a child is described as altering 'the balance between us' for the better (116). The narrator assures her partner that 'a child would turn the direction of our eyes away from the withering and fattening of our over-familiar selves towards the pleasure of a fresh new presence growing' (ibid.). Described as a unifying presence, a child is heralded as the saving of this relationship as opposed to causing its demise. In invoking Marvell's poem, Simpson situates gendered notions of time in dialogue with each other. While Marvell's poem opens with the lines, 'Had we but world enough and time, / This coyness, lady, were no crime', in 'To Her Unready Boyfriend' the idea of a woman's biological clock is invoked. Instead of the man's impatience being the driving force, Simpson's narrative is consumed with the woman's fear that she will run out of time to have children. Time is *engendered* and the male and female perspectives are placed in conversation through this textual allusion.

'Constitutional' (2006a) follows its unnamed protagonist and narrator as she walks around the Heath outside the school at which she teaches in the lunch hour (again, specific temporal barriers frame the narrative). Having recently discovered that she is pregnant, and commencing this walk straight from returning from her friend Stella's funeral, the relationship of life and death is at the forefront of the protagonist's mind. The story is contained within a one-hour time frame – a fact the narrator makes clear from the beginning – and as she completes her circular walk all the anticipation grows towards the conclusion. Furthermore, the focus on time, she confesses, 'is getting to be a bit of an obsession but then I suppose that's only natural in my condition' (323). The effect of the narrative and literal circle, combined with this focus on time, is to bridge life and death and to associate the story with the circle of life.

Alongside the physical clock the story also draws on notions of a woman's biological clock, as the narrator shares her surprise at finding out she was pregnant after her GP encouraged her to stop taking the pill and 'give my system a rest, she suggested, time to get back in touch with my natural cycle again now that I was so much less fertile because of the years' (329). Building on the passing comments in stories like 'Early One Morning', where Zoe acknowledges it is increasingly common for women to have children in their thirties (269), and 'Burns and Bankers' (2001b), where Nicola is proud of giving birth to twins at forty (220), here the narrator's pregnancy defies the popular assumption about women being too old to have children. Furthermore, the story also invokes the work of feminist theorist Julia Kristeva (1981), who positions cyclicality as being related to notions of female subjectivity (16), as Simpson appears to advocate a sense of a specifically feminine type of time with the protagonist becoming 'emboldened by contact with my own inner calendar' (329). Thus, from the time pressures faced by women in their daily lives through to issues of a specific type of women's time, Simpson's narratives offer an expansive feminist engagement with notions of time.

Narrating maternal loss

The experience of maternal loss has already been touched upon in the discussion of Simpson's story 'Early One Morning', which portrays the anxious tension felt by a mother as her son gets older and becomes more independent, and this shift in relationships is the driving force behind Kate Atkinson's story 'Wedding Favours' (2002). Opening with the poignant line, 'This was it then. The moment Pam had never really anticipated had come to pass. Her son had gone' (243), the reader is confronted, directly, with the wrenching emotions of Pam and her profound sense of loss. While it is swiftly clarified that her youngest son, Simon, had not gone 'far and not for ever . . . but gone nonetheless' (ibid.) it slowly emerges that he has left home and gone away to university. As he is the final one of her children to 'fly the nest', Pam's sense of loss is palpable. As she reflects, when her husband Alistair left her it was 'somehow inevitable' and when her daughter Rebecca went to university 'she'd still had Simon' (ibid.). However, now, with Simon's departure, combined with the fact that she has recently been made redundant, all that is left for Pam to do is to make wedding favours with her friend Maggie as a means of supplementing her pension income. While for upbeat Maggie this new-found state of being child-free and without a full-time job means they are as 'free as birds' (252), conversely, Pam is left wondering 'how could a sugared almond signify anything, let alone happiness?' (254). In the same situation these two women offer extremely differing responses, thus highlighting the nuance required when discussing women's experiences of motherhood. Importantly, this narrative exchange reveals that motherhood, and what contributes to feelings of loss, are always personal and individual. Accordingly, there cannot be a single definition of what it means to be a mother, which emphasises the importance of feminist discourse also not resorting to simply offering a single reading of the subject.

Throughout the story there is a strong sense of haunting, with the insertion of absent voices and the focus on home spaces. From the beginning of the story Simon's voice is present in the narrative, with side comments and echoes that respond to or extend his mother's thoughts: '(*I'll be back at half-term, for God's sake*)' (243). The use of parenthesis and italics denotes this shift in voice and it visibly breaks the flow of Pam's thoughts. This device also unsettles the linearity of the story as it creates a narrative movement between the past and the present while offering insight into this maternal relationship. The juxtaposition of these two voices serves to heighten the differing responses to the same situation here: his mother's profound sense of loss is a source of frustration for Simon. While his mother still views him as a child, Simon is setting out on a more independent life in which he views himself as having grown up; it is this newly embraced identity which Pam struggles to accept. The passing of time is central to this story, as Pam's loss is not just occurring in this narrative moment, but is furthered by the stark realisation that while 'your children were like a knot of fear that you carried around inside you all the time' (249), they may not always be a physical presence in your daily life. Instead, all that remain are the voices of the past haunting the memories of the present; a description which resonates with the story of feminisms and the ways in which the critics and activists of the past always infiltrate the present and even future developments.

Alongside the use of voice, space is also significant in 'Wedding Favours'. When she returns home from taking Simon to university for the first time, Pam 'wished he could just stay in his room for ever and then she'd always have someone to look after and would never be on her own' (246). Interestingly, it is 'the bad mother part, she supposed' (ibid.) which thinks in this way. A seemingly passing thought is actually a very telling remark and it chimes with the discussion earlier in this chapter of institutionalised motherhood. Part of Pam's response to this loss is shaped by her understandings of what it means, as defined by society, to be a mother. Crucially, in the case of Pam, this appears to be not just *a*, but *the*, defining element of her identity as a woman. With this realisation Pam mourns: 'what happened when you'd plotted the whole course of your life by your children and then they weren't there any more?' (261). Pam's rhetorical question haunts the reader and introduces an element of accountability into the narrative as the reader is asked to respond to Pam's emotions.

Notably, time and space collide at the story's end when Pam reflects on how: 'you were always waiting for them to walk back in – not as themselves, not as they were now, no – what you expected (what you dreamt of) was that they were going to walk through the door and be three years old' (263). There is a flexibility, and even fluidity, to the understandings of time and motherhood in this story. Here, Pam laments the feeling of emptiness and constant anticipation caused by the wait for her child's return, but there is also the acknowledgement that it is impossible ever to relive or recapture the past. For Pam, a mother can only ever dream of a child returning home, and the image here acts as a metaphor for the child's return to the maternal body. However, the future, too, is unreachable and is merely an expectation and dream based on the past. Temporality, therefore, is unsettled, a point reinforced by the open-ended and forward-facing 'closure' of the narrative. Significantly, this narrative of a mother's loss and desire to return to the past chimes with the narrative of contemporary feminisms. The imagery of the mother is often employed in relation to second-wave feminism, when it is being conceived as a historical movement contained within the 1960s–1980s. Thus, reading 'Wedding Favours' provides a literary looking glass through which we might understand the complex temporal relationships of differing feminisms. It is never a simplistic return or departure to a past moment; instead the past always infiltrates, informs and shapes the present even while looking towards a future: it does not have to be an either/or binary relation.

Similarly, Roberts utilises the notion of maternal loss in the story 'Your Shoes' (1994a), which is narrated entirely from the perspective of a mother. Her daughter has recently run away and the story becomes a one-way conversation in which the mother addresses the missing daughter. It establishes a leitmotif in the shoe, as this image weaves throughout *During Mother's Absence* and Roberts' later short story collections. As the bereft mother stands in her daughter's bedroom she reflects how someone 'half-mad, with grief that is, might pick up a shoe from the rug and hold it like a baby. Someone like me might do that. As if the shoe might still be warm or give a clue to where you've gone' (73). Suffering from the loss of her daughter, the mother clings to objects that are imbued with her memory. The shoe becomes a surrogate for the daughter as the mother tries to imagine being 'in her daughter's shoes', in both the metaphorical and literal senses of the phrase. She describes them as 'rebellious shoes' because, looking at their position in the room, they point towards the window and door as though they 'wanted to get out, to get away just like you did' (74). The narrator rectifies this and the shoes are 'stowed in the wardrobe. Just in case', locked away 'to grieve in the darkness' (ibid.). The shoes grieving in darkness symbolise the mother's emotions and her desire to stow her daughter away in their family house. Finally, later in the story, the shoes become a symbol of hope when the mother tells the doctor, 'she'll be back soon, I'm sure of it, why, she hasn't even taken her new shoes!' (77). In this single image resides a spectrum of meanings, as the conflicting emotions of the mother are externalised and symbolised by the daughter's shoes.

It is the internal first-person narrative perspective that facilitates this story's representation of motherhood, and it reveals a range of emotions and thoughts about the narrator and, associatively, the role of being a mother. As the story draws to a close the mother begins to believe that 'it's my fault you've left home to sleep rough God knows where' (80). This assumption mutates into an imagined accusation: 'Go on, blame your mother, everyone else does, I'm a failure as mother. I didn't give you enough of whatever it was' (ibid.). External forces cause the mother to feel as though she has failed and that society judges her. In turn this is projected onto her daughter:

> Next thing you'll be saying it's because I didn't breastfeed you, or because I didn't pick you up every time you cried. At night you cried so much, in the end I used to shut the door on you and go back downstairs. I was exhausted. Your father slept through most of it, he said it wasn't his job. (ibid.)

Reinforcing the ways in which the role of mother is externally defined and certain expectations are placed on how one performs motherly duties, it is the body that becomes the site of judgement. This passage also critiques the unequal division in parenting as it is deemed the mother's role, not the father's, to be up at night and provide the primary care for the baby; an issue Firestone aims to rectify. This shift in the care dynamic is the first demand Firestone makes for an alternative system of reproduction (1973: 193). In this passage, the pressure overpowers the mother and she 'shuts the door' on her daughter. Crucially, Roberts does not criticise the mother but instead the tone is sympathetic to the narrator and mother. What the narrative does criticise is the social conventions that *create* the pressure upon women and mothers.

As with 'Wedding Favours', 'Your Shoes' ends with a return to the maternal body as the narrator imagines her daughter is in the room: 'I hold you to my breast and rock you like my mother never rocked me' (82). Reasserting the breast as the locale of female connection, the narrative stresses the importance of women's bonds. Importantly, there is an oxymoron apparent in the notion of 'bonds' because they are positive in emotional terms but crippling in physical terms. By foregrounding the imagery of bonds in these narratives, Roberts explores the tensions inherent in this concept and uses this imagery to reflect on the uncomfortable tensions that can exist in familial relationships. Importantly, in relation to feminism these bonds are both real and imaginary.

Motherhood is a prominent theme in Andrea Levy's collection *Six Stories & an Essay* (2014), and it is one of the ways in which this collection engages with the issue of cultural difference. In the essay which opens the collection, 'Back to My Own Country', Levy reflects on her parents' experiences moving from Jamaica, where they were living a comfortable middle-class life, to England, 'the fabled Mother Country that they had learned so much about at school in Jamaica' but which failed to live up to their expectations. In England, her parents 'were poor and working class' (6), yet 'they must accept what this country was willing to give. They were, after all, immigrants' (7). The fissures between dreams and reality, the 'them' and 'us' of native and immigrant status, and between Jamaica and England establish the tone of opposition and cultural difference which pervades Levy's collection. Nonetheless, it is the belief that 'my heritage is Britain's story too' and that it is time to 'put the Caribbean back where it belongs – in the main narrative of British history' (19) which drives Levy's stories and the collection as a whole. Importantly, it is the understanding of England as 'mother' which defined her parents' experiences with the country, yet, by the end of this essay, the tone is one of defiance, provoked by the hierarchical relationship such an understanding cultivates. Prior to even reading the stories within the collection, then, the reader is made aware that the political impetus driving them is deeply embroiled with generational and familial tensions.

In 'The Empty Pram' the narrator has recently arrived from Jamaica, it is 1948, and she is 'eager to start my new life in this Mother Country' (97).[1] Again, we see the repetition of the mother figure's association with England, and the overarching narrative teases out the issue of cultural differences and assimilation. When an English boy arrives at her door, with his 'two skinny white arms awkwardly clasped . . . to his chest' holding a baby, the narrator is forced to wrestle the 'poor baby from him' (97). At this point the boy begins 'wailing' and runs away before the narrator can discover the whereabouts of the baby's mother. As she goes outside she sees a pram and once again is reminded of the differing approaches to motherhood across cultures: 'mothers in this country often left their babies outside so they might breathe some fresh air; they seemed to have no fear of it being abducted' (99). A cultural norm in one country appears strange and even dangerous behaviour in another. When she discovers that this pram is not empty, there is a 'peaceful sleeping infant' inside, the narrator is left 'confused' (ibid.) before hearing a scream and, 'following the sound of commotion', walking around the street corner to see 'a group of three English women looking aghast into another pram' (ibid.).

It is at this point in the narrative, as she returns the baby to the mother, that the narrator most severely experiences the feeling of being a social outsider and 'foreigner'. As she tries to ask if the baby belongs to one of them the women look back 'with an expression so full of terror . . . Six eyes popped wide in their sockets and three mouths fell open at the sight of my black face' (100). This horrified response is heightened by their actions of leaning 'to grab the baby' and subsequently 'all three shielding the baby between them' (ibid.). Pertinently, because the reader is viewing this exchange from the narrator's point of view, and is fully aware of the kindness behind her actions, the description of these three English women confronts the reader with the vivid realities of life as an immigrant in England at this time. As the narrator tries to explain, to give voice to her actions, she is merely confronted with 'faces slowly creased into frowns' as the English women cannot understand her (ibid.). Mistaking her actions for an attempt to steal the baby, the women call for the police. It is only when the young boy who initially took the baby witnesses this and finally explains the situation, that 'another of the women started clapping her hands with relief that I was not the devil' (102). However, even here, the narrator is not fully 'redeemed' in the eyes of the English women, with one of them thanking her while at the same time scolding that 'you should have told us what happened' (ibid.). Of course, the irony of this is acute for the reader, who is fully aware that the narrator did attempt to explain, but that these English women failed to understand. Consequentially, the story brings into question issues of responsibility and authority and challenges the assumed position of privilege the English women assume.

The tension at the heart of this story, which plays out through the trope of maternal loss, is one of cultural difference and misunderstanding. Indeed, this is the image on which the story closes: 'Then all three women began patting me like a dog . . . as they discussed together whether I would like a nice cup of tea' (ibid.). It is an issue which re-emerges in the proceeding story in the collection, 'February'. Another story which was inspired by Levy's mother (106), 'February' tells of how her mother, when asked to 'describe winter in your own words' for her evening class, was given a 'C minus for all her effort' because her description 'is not what February is like at all!' (108). While her mother has 'described the winters in Jamaica – her child-hood Februaries' (107) this is not something that the English teacher recognises and, in this instance, this is literally marked on the page of her story. The English perspective is given dominance in 'February' as the position of teacher is empowered either to validate or to deny the accuracy of this story. Consequently, the Jamaican version of winter is deemed incorrect. While the narrator in 'The Empty Pram' is left voiceless, feeling like a 'dog', with other women speaking *about* rather than *with* her, in 'February', although a Jamaican voice is present, it is swiftly denied any authority. In this respect, both of these short stories also offer a commentary on the difficulties of feminism engaging with and even being representative of different cultures and ethnicities. These narratives raise questions about agency and voice by asking who is really speaking and, importantly, is anybody really listening?

Levy's literary depiction of Jamaican women's experiences in England reverberates with Gayatri Chakravorty Spivak's claim that 'the subaltern cannot speak' (1988: 302) and, as she proposes, that if Western women really want to help they first 'must learn to stop feeling privileged *as a woman*' (2006: 187). In 'February', especially, the white Western woman is located at a site of privilege and author-ity and the consequence of this is the silencing of the non-Western voice. Levy's short stories creatively articulate a fundamental prem-ise of postcolonial feminism, as outlined by Robert Young (2003):

> Feminism in a postcolonial frame begins with the situation of the ordi-nary woman in a particular place, . . . It will highlight the degree to which women are still working against a colonial legacy that was itself powerfully patriarchal – institutional, economic, political, and ideological. (116)

Through these narratives, set in recent history and in a specific time and place, Levy illuminates the cultural tensions between women and in turn offers a critique as to why Western feminism cannot speak on behalf of the non-Western woman in the present either: it does not fully understand the immigrant voice in these narratives, so how can it ever be representative of these women? The closing of 'The Empty Pram' with the English women deciding whether or not the narrator, and cultural 'other' in this scene, would like the ultimate symbol of civilised English society – the cup of tea – is emblematic of the ways in which cultural assimilation is often

viewed as being about the 'other' culture conforming to the dominant culture. However, in telling the story from the point of view of
the Jamaican immigrant, Levy challenges the reader to consider the
'other' perspective for herself and to begin to understand that there
is also a different story to be told, a story which does not carry
'with it the authorizing signature of Western humanist discourse'
(Chandra Talpade Mohanty 1984: 335).

Motherhood and feminist commentary

The figure of the mother becomes particularly significant when thinking about the relationship between differing feminisms, and it has
frequently been utilised in narratives which seek to 'define' the similarities and differences between second- and third-wave feminisms.
In such instances, third-wave feminism is viewed as a response to the
fractious tension that developed in the 1990s between second-wave
and post(-)feminisms, as it resolves to embrace multiple feminisms,
including the overlaps and dissonances. Despite the often generational (and therefore implicitly divisive) claims about the third wave,
because of its name it is positioned as explicitly building *upon* the
work of second-wave feminists, not breaking away from them. In
these prevalent narratives of contemporary feminism, it therefore,
symbolically, evokes the generational metaphor of the mother and
daughter. This metaphor plays out in Simpson's short story 'Lentils
and Lilies'[2] through the issue of matrophobia as the story's narrator,
Jade, rejects the life choices of her mother in an attempt to find her
own life path. In this respect the story is a narrative of generational
conflict.

From the opening Jade is clear that 'she would never be like her
mother, making rotas and lists and endless arrangements, lost forever
in a forest of twitching detail with her tense talk of juggling and her
self-importance' (145). However, at the same time, Jade is repulsed
by stay-at-home mothers: 'Imagine staying in all day, stewing in your
own juices. Weren't they bored out of their skulls? It was beyond
her comprehension' (147). Jade, then, is not simply a teenage girl
rebelling against her mother and the generation before her, but can
be read as a symbol of third-wave feminism's attempts to negotiate
the turbulent binary options pre-established by patriarchal society
for women. When Jade meets an unnamed mother in the street and
is hijacked into helping her because her daughter has stuck a lentil up

her nose, Jade positions herself as a modern feminist and implies that this woman is behind the times. Jade remarks, 'you'd think it was the fifties, men roaming the world while the women stayed indoors. The personal was the political, hadn't she heard?' (150).

The problem with Jade as a character is that she fails to acknowledge fully the socioeconomic framework which her own mother, this 'flabby womany-ness' of the stranger (149), and women more broadly have to negotiate in their everyday lives. While Jade attests that:

> If she ever found herself in this sort of situation, a man, babies, etcetera; when the time came; IF. Well, he would be responsible for half the childcare and half the housework. At least. She believed in justice, unlike this useless great lump (151)

she assumes, without any attempt to understand the context, that this woman has freely chosen to live her life in this way. The narrative reveals Jade's inability to consider the broader social construction of motherhood and the economic factors that might have led to these women staying at home to raise their children. Instead, Jade believes that she has adequate free choice and agency to change this situation as an individual. Subsequently, the reader is asked to critique all three narrative positions: Jade's, her mother's and this other woman's, in order to understand the complexity of navigating the private and the public spheres for women.

In conclusion, the diversity of experiences and multitude of emotions displayed in these short stories illuminate the complexity of motherhood and highlight why it has been, and remains, such a pertinent element of feminist debate. Rather than understanding feminism's engagement with motherhood as a linear trajectory, what these narratives reveal is the overlap, synergies, differences and reoccurrences that emerge across different moments in time and which signal the ongoing importance of motherhood to contemporary feminisms. Furthermore, the symbolic attachments to motherhood, at the heart of feminist discourse's deployment of the 'feminist foremother' motif, serves to remind us of the implications for feminism itself which are bound up in any analysis of motherhood. While it has been suggested that 'it is impossible for feminist theory to avoid the issue of mothering and it is impossible for feminist theory to resolve it' (DiQuinzio 1999: xx), what these short story narratives reveal is that, in part, this paradox is not important. What is important, however, is that stories continue to be told about motherhood and feminisms, irrespective of whether these stories embrace, challenge, rethink or merely reflect on the embodiment, practices and realities motherhood produces for women.

Notes

1. This story was commissioned by a woman's magazine but never published because the editor 'declared that this story was not suitable for her readers . . . It was too controversial' (95–6).
2. 'Lentils and Lilies' was published in Natasha Walter's anthology *On the Move* (1999a), a text that prioritises the feminism of 'young women'.

Chapter 3

Marriage and Domesticity

> The synthesis of 'house' and 'wife' in a single term establishes the connections between womanhood, marriage, and the dwelling place of family groups. The role of housewife is a family role: it is a feminine role. Yet it is also a work role. (Oakley 1990: 77)

In *Housewife* (1990), Ann Oakley highlights the important contradiction inherent in the concept of the 'housewife' and captures the entwined nature of marriage, the family and domestic responsibilities for women. In recognising the role of housewife as one of 'work', Oakley also points to why marriage and domesticity have been a central issue for feminism: they are a pivotal locus upon which the public/private debate plays out. The often-told story of feminism, marriage and domesticity follows a similar pattern to that of motherhood in that it wavers between rejection and/or reclamation and often invokes the tropes of progress and/or regression. Reflecting on domesticity and feminism, Joanne Hollows (2000) notes how 'feminists came to see the family as a key source of their oppression and, therefore, political' (4). This intersection of the personal, individual experience and the wider political agenda is particularly pertinent in the context of marriage and domesticity. In *The Feminine Mystique* (2010), Friedan labels 'the problem that has no name': the social and cultural discourses that promote women's self-sacrifice, as women are conditioned to care first for their husband, children and home (5). By 2013, Anna Coote and Jacob Mohun Himmelweit assert the ongoing relevance of Friedan's work by highlighting how, 'fifty years on, there's a different, but closely related problem. It is not so much enforced joblessness and domesticity that afflict women today, as the combined pressures of paid work and caring' (90). Seemingly, then, regardless of any grand narratives which imply a trajectory of progress and difference across so-called waves of feminism, in actuality there is a far more complex temporal overlap across cultural moments in which reside differing responses to the issues of domesticity and marriage, in a feminist context. It is not a story of either progress or failure, but instead should be understood as a complex, shifting and always situational discourse which is both personal and political.

The temporal intersection between the past and present in relation to the politics of domesticity and marriage is perfectly articulated in Lionel Shriver's introduction to the fiftieth anniversary Penguin edition of *The Feminine Mystique*, in which Shriver points to the relevance of Friedan's polemic to women today in the context of 'New Traditionalism'. Shriver writes, 'any woman seriously considering the new "freedom" to choose housewifery and motherhood as a substitute for a demanding career should watch every episode of *Mad Men* back to back, and then read this book' (2010: xi). New Traditionalism is explicitly bound up with notions of a feminist backlash, and it implicates discourses of domesticity and women's liberation. Accordingly, the home becomes women's sanctuary and the 'new traditionalist discourse centralises and idealises women's apparently fully knowledgeable choice to abstain from paid work in favour of hearth and family' (Genz and Brabon 2009: 52). The domestic sphere is located as a site of female autonomy and independence, but, crucially, as part of this redefinition of domesticity, the 'backlash not only warns women that they cannot "have it all" and must choose between home and career, but also makes the choice for them by promoting wedded life and domesticity as a full and fulfilled existence' (ibid.: 55). Thus, as the label indicates, 'New Traditionalism' is a paradox in which coercion and social conditioning construct the domestic sphere as an autonomous space and a 'free choice' for women, while in actuality impeding its fulfilment as such.

Given the complexity of personal politics in relation to marriage, the family and domesticity, in exploring women's short story writing this chapter, once again, foregrounds the momentary nature of the genre as a means of extricating the ambivalent position of these discourses and attempting to give due recognition to the lived experiences of women. However, in prioritising the moment and the story of the individual, this raises questions about the ability of a broader feminist political movement ever to 'speak' coherently and bring about social change. The first section of this chapter focuses on historical narratives and therefore problematises the story of marriage and domesticity as being one of progress and change. By drawing on the short stories of Kate Mosse and Helen Simpson it is possible to see the synergies across the decades, and even centuries, with the contemporary being placed in dialogue with the past. The relationship between marriage and domesticity provides a focal point for the second section of this chapter by considering stories which narrate the realities of everyday life as experienced by many married women; then the final section considers Ali Smith's contribution to *Refugee Tales*, alongside two of Zadie Smith's short stories, to explore how the domestic landscape is complicated further by the politics of immigration and ethnicity. While feminist theory has predominantly discussed the issues of marriage and domesticity in the context of a notably white, middle-class Western context, the writings of black, Asian and ethnic minority women writers can provide insight into what these issues mean when the politics of race and culture intersect with gender.

The past and the present

The relationship between the past and the present is not solely a feature of Kate Mosse's short stories, but pervades the pages of her novels too. As Katherine Cooper argues, Mosse's 2007 novel *Sepulchre* is a form of 'female gothic' which explores themes of female agency and liberation through discourses of 'powerlessness and imprisonment' (Cooper 2012: 153). Similar tropes resonate in Mosse's 'The Mistletoe Bride' (2013) as well, as Mosse utilises the short story form to offer an almost portrait-like exploration of femininity and female agency. 'The Mistletoe Bride' tells the story of a young woman on her wedding day who, following a traditional game of hide-and-seek, remains hidden, and subsequently trapped, inside a large chest for centuries to follow. Thanks to the frontispiece to the story, which states 'Bramshill House, Hampshire, October 1935', a precise specific time and place are established, before the revelation that there are multiple layers to the temporal shifts in the story: the initial past of 1935 is displaced as the 'mistletoe bride' begins to tell her story and the reader is 'carried back to that first December so very long ago' (4). Due to this temporal movement, a sense of haunting shapes the narrative space as the reader is transported from the contemporary moment of engagement with the text, to the narrative present of 1935, all the way back to the past and the wedding day itself. By invoking these various historical moments, the narrative establishes synergies across history which makes the subsequent critique of marriage – as symbolised by the wedding ceremony – especially pertinent.

The trope of femininity infiltrates the depiction of the wedding day as her new husband, Lovell, calls the narrator his 'fairy bride' and describes her as being 'lighter than air' (6). In a setting which is filled with the 'scent of lilies' (5), there is an abrupt disjoint when the narrator confesses that: 'I must learn to call him husband' and 'I must learn to wear my new responsibilities more lightly' (ibid.). The repetition of 'I must learn' in these expressions illuminates that the performance required of a new wife is not a natural one and that she must educate herself as to how to behave in order to conform to certain societal expectations. Crucially, this pressure to perform femininity is, ultimately, the reason for her death. The decision to conceal herself in the chest during the game of hide-and-seek is driven by two desires: 'I think of how pleasant it would be to lie down and rest. Then I imagine Lovell's face as he opens the chest and sees me looking up at him, framed in lace and tulle, and my mind is made up' (9). It is the thought of looking like a still portrait, a woman framed by delicate materials, and therefore creating an image of beauty for her husband which affirms the decision to hide in the chest. Her own comfort at resting for a while is secondary in this thought process; ultimately it is Lovell's imagined response which shapes her decision.

The tensions which arise due to the differing historical moments are replicated in the actions and thoughts of the protagonist. Even when thinking about where to hide, the mistletoe bride is conflicted: 'I need to be well hidden, the game loses its charm else, but not so well concealed that Lovell loses patience in the search' (8). The sense of compromise at the heart of this statement symbolises the larger sense of compromise that the narrator experiences in becoming a wife. After the door to the room in which she is hiding is blown shut, and the chest is accidentally locked, the narrator simply closes her eyes and passively waits for Lovell to find her. However, when she falls asleep and the search continues, 'if they saw the chest, they saw it was locked fast from the outside and did not think I could be there' (10–11). With a bitter irony her fate is sealed: 'I died as I had lived. Quietly, gently, leaving little trace' (11). The description of her death reminds the reader of the earlier description of the lightness of the bride and the trope of femininity once again re-emerges, but this time in association with death. Suggestively, then, Mosse's story offers a cutting portrayal of the consequences of marriage and the ensuing forced performance of femininity in the role of wife. The depiction challenges the traditional understandings of the female body in the 'natural' roles of bride and wife, critiquing such normalised assumptions with this act of retelling.

Importantly, Mosse includes an 'Author's Note' at the end of each story in the collection which provides further detail about the inspiration and context for each narrative. Having first discovered the story of 'The Mistletoe Bride' in a book on folklore and myth, Mosse traces the various versions of the story, as retold by men in fiction and song. This paratextual detail is revealing in that it both emphasises the origins of short fiction in oral storytelling, myth and folklore and illuminates a history of this story as carved out by men. Mosse's version of 'The Mistletoe Bride', therefore, can be understood as a response to these previous versions and a means of reasserting a female voice in this particular literary history.

From the same collection, 'Sainte-Thérèse' opens with a poignant reflection on the significance of the moment: 'In the blinking of an eye can the world shift . . . Between one catch of breath and the next, the rest of forever defined by that single, solitary moment' (111). For the story's protagonist Hermione, the encounter with a statue of Sainte Thérèse in a church in the French town of Montolieu changes her life. While the story is set in the contemporary era (France in the summer of 2003), it draws on a figure from history and a statue which was physically carved in the past. The story focuses on a couple, Hermione and Leon, who have been married for ten years. From the story's outset it is clear that their relationship is troubled: 'As usual, Leon seemed to think it was her fault the morning hadn't gone well. For at least half an hour he had been picking away at her, criticising her' (112). Hermione now accepts that Leon takes 'pleasure in putting her down', and while she despises herself for tolerating his behaviour she is resigned to the face that 'their patterns were set' (ibid.). However, on this day Hermione's perspective alters and she realises she does not have to conform to the usual routine and run to Leon seeking forgiveness; after all, 'she had done nothing wrong' (114).

In breaking these well-established relationship patterns, Hermione walks over to the local church. Going into the side chapel Hermione describes the scene as 'like a room in a giant doll's house', and she feels the urge to 'smash' to pieces the glass which protects pieces of material and feathers: 'Protecting them from whom? From what?' she questions, it 'all repulsed her' (117). As she stands in this space, she 'realised she was twisting her wedding ring on her finger' and the feelings of repulsion and claustrophobia, at being trapped inside a space akin to a doll's house, become associated with her own marriage through the symbolic act of playing with her wedding ring. Later, as she runs from the church, only to collide accidentally with the statue of Sainte Thérèse, Hermione suddenly feels a sense of calm, and she reaches out to brush away a cobweb from the statue: 'in that moment, no more than a pinprick of time, she was touched by a presence' (119). Although Hermione does not believe in saints or spirits, she 'knew that her world had shifted' (ibid.). As she leaves the church she is no longer wearing her wedding ring, which lies at the foot of the statue. It is unclear whether this was an intentional act by Hermione, but nonetheless her subsequent actions are certainly deliberate: she takes a taxi to the airport and boards a flight home without Leon. In a single moment, then, a life is altered.

After years of 'bullying and belittling' Hermione reasserts her identity outside the marital relationship, and the final paragraph considers how, 'years later, friends would still talk about how Hermione came back from that French holiday a different woman', 'you could see it in her eyes' (120). Poignantly, this narrative closure signals to the future, the 'years later', and also echoes the middle of the story and the description of the statue's eyes, which Hermione momentarily believes to be 'living eyes' (119). As such, temporality is once again troubled in this story which refutes the notion of simplistic linearity. With a statue, a figure from the past, shown to alter the present and even future of a woman's life there is an awareness that the past, present and future are never isolated concepts. Equally, with the middle of the story and 'a pinprick of time' sending the reader back to the opening sentences of the story, 'Sainte-Thérèse' is a narrative of the moment, but one which is acutely aware of the relationship across and beyond moments as well. From this story it is possible to see the potential power of the moment for effecting change, but more significantly, 'Sainte-Thérèse' illuminates the importance of female communication across the generations. Read metaphorically, Mosse's story provides a compelling analogy for feminist relations too. Such an approach echoes Lucie Armitt's analysis of Mosse's Languedoc trilogy, in which Armitt (2014) suggests the novels, metaphorically, signal the importance of 'maintaining an active dialogue between the voices of different generations of feminism' (154).

Comparatively, Simpson's short story 'Good Friday, 1663', from *Four Bare Legs in a Bed* (1991), is littered with quotations from a sermon as it, just like Mosse's stories, refers the reader to a very specific point in history. These references provide a structure for the narrative but also create a dialogue between religious preaching, importantly, the institution that defines marriage, and the unnamed narrator of the story. The story is an oblique reference to John Donne's poem 'Good Friday, 1613. Riding Westward'.[1] It is set on Good Friday; the poet is travelling west but his thoughts turn to the Holy Land in the East. The poem is a meditation on the poet's own sins and his desire 'to receive / Corrections' (lines 37–8) and to be purified. Throughout, the poem poses a series of philosophical questions as the poet reflects on his inner soul. Using this original poem as a starting point, Simpson's story is set fifty years later on the cusp of the Restoration period. 'Good Friday, 1663' critiques the institution of marriage and sees a wife bemoan her marital situation. Importantly, in setting the story fifty years later than Donne's poem, Simpson establishes a dialogue between these two moments that also recognises the shifts in under-standings of gender in this period. As Katherine M. Quinsey (1996) summarises,

> it is now commonplace that the seventeenth century spans the shift from an earlier concept of gender as a variation in an essentially unified human nature to a hardening of gender categories, which theorized female as distinct in essence from male in all levels of existence. (1)

In 'Good Friday, 1663' Simpson challenges the introspective thoughts of the distinctly male poetic voice, concerned with sin, religion and redemption in Donne's poem, to offer instead a female voice preoc-cupied with the burdens of marriage and children.

The narrator of 'Good Friday, 1663' sits in the church listening to Parson Snakepeace preach 'only sermons from the old dead Divines' (19) and she remarks in disbelief that her husband 'claimed *me* for his wife!' (20). While the parson recites the crucifixion of Jesus Christ, the protagonist transposes an historical, canonised event onto her own life. Echoing 'Four Bare Legs in a Bed', by the story's end the protagonist sees how her 'husband sits beside me like a ball and chain. A pack of squalling infants will do the rest, forging my binds link by link' (29–30). The narrator describes herself in an image akin to that of Jesus Christ at the crucifixion; restricted by binds 'link by link' (30). In 'Good Friday, 1663', as there is across all of the stories discussed here, there is a tendency to pinpoint a very specific histori-cal moment. Mosse and Simpson use specific moments in history to highlight synergies across the ages. As such, affinities in women's lives from the early modern period to the present day are implicit in these stories and they force the reader to question any assumptions they may have about linearity, progress and a difference between the past and the present. As these stories revel in telling us, it is never quite as simple and straightforward as that.

Marital bliss or duty?

The collection *Four Bare Legs in a Bed* instigates Simpson's fictional engagement with a distinctly white, middle-class society and the politics of heterosexual relationships. Seemingly traditional in nar-rative scope, in fact, as Nicholas Lezard points out, 'Simpson is the writer who most famously went where male writers were either too frightened or bored to tread: examining the "ever after" that follows the supposed happy ending' (2012: n. p.). This is epitomised by 'Four Bare Legs in a Bed', which tells the story of a married couple from the perspective of the wife. Throughout the story both husband and wife remain nameless, a device that instigates character ambiguity and results in the scenes holding greater resonance for the reader as she attempts to fill in the gaps. Moreover, it evokes a sense of commonality as these unnamed individuals, this recently married couple, could be any and every couple. The narrative emphasis falls on the woman's experiences pre- and post-marriage and the impact that they have had on her own sense of identity. Early on in the story she recalls how she felt the night before her wedding:

> I looked back down half-a-dozen years and saw my secret self at thirteen or fourteen. I had never felt incomplete alone, nor had I ever trembled for security. Now I had a premonition that my privacy and self-possession, which harmed nobody and were my only important treasures, would be things of the past the day after tomorrow. My saying yes to a wedding appeared in this illuminated instant as self-betrayal. (4–5)

Here, there is a sense of two women in existence with the 'secret self' signifying the former, younger, part of this woman which she feels she has lost in marriage. It is in the 'illuminated instant', a temporal moment of clarity, that the protagonist becomes aware of herself and acknowledges the potential threat that becoming a part of somebody else means to her. Indeed, it is her 'privacy' and 'self-possession', markers of her individuality and sense of self-belonging, that are threatened by marriage.

The wife's premonition, recollected in this passage, comes to fruition in the remainder of the story as her husband slowly infiltrates all areas of her existence, including her dreamscape. In an attempt to unshackle herself from his control she reveals how:

> Sometimes I slide my ring off before we go to a party, but he makes me put it on again. That left-handed ring finger is the weakest of the ten, always the first to let you down during a vigorous scherzando; there are sets of arpeggios based exclusively round strengthening its feebleness. It is also the more sensitive, the one women use when following such instructions as, Pat [*sic*] this feather-weight creme lightly into the fragile skin tissue which surrounds the eye area. (6)

Seeking to liberate her body and mind from the consequences of her marriage, the removal of the wedding ring becomes a powerfully symbolic act that the husband quickly prohibits. Moreover, the impact of marriage, for which the wedding ring is a metonymy, is that the husband infiltrates the wife's body, signalled by the left-handed ring finger being 'feeble'. In a fluid connection the narrator reminds the reader of the popular beauty guidance women receive about using this finger to apply eye cream: the female body is 'fragile' and only a delicate touch will suffice. Like marriage, the woman's beauty regime is constructed around her assumed 'weaker' status, and culture becomes concerned with, and empowered by, protecting the female body.

For the protagonist and narrator, sex is also altered following marriage, as 'conjugal life correctly conjugated reads: libido libidas libidamus libidatis libiDON'T' (5). This play with Latinate words reveals the steady transition from sexual pleasure to simply sexual 'DON'T'. It is 'goodbye to the pure uncomplicated glee which can spring up between strangers, leading them out of their clothes and towards each other in a spirit of, among other things, sunny friendship' (ibid.). The story suggests that the problem for this woman stems not from the heterosexual relationship per se but the institutionalised product of marriage. No longer friends, later in the story she describes her husband as 'upend[ing] me, he takes no notice of anything above the waist' and she becomes like an animal as she feels 'he cages me' (13).

Throughout the story there are numerous other instances of the husband's psychological control, from his interrogative reaction to her returning home late after a night out with a friend through to his overt disgust when she wolf-whistles at him stepping out of the shower, which results in his condescending observation that her behaviour is 'not exactly very feminine, is it' (11). In a similar vein, and with a remark that foreshadows the politics of Simpson's later short stories, he spitefully threatens that '*you* need a baby. *That* would sort you out' (8). Here, motherhood provides the ultimate means of controlling his wife and keeping her inside the home. With this montage of exchanges, and the blend of past and present tense, memory and experience, the wife's life is construed, through her first person narrative, in a manner that evokes the reader's sympathy for her.

Issues of enclosure and control are reflected in the structure of 'Four Bare Legs in a Bed', which opens and closes with discussions of the wife's dreams, and this ensures a cyclical element to the narrative. In the beginning the dream is celebrated. She addresses the reader, asking her not to 'let on to the Old Man', continuing that 'I think I can safely say I have slept with all the men and boys of my acquaintance' (3). It is through dream-fantasy that the narrator's sexuality comes to be most fervently expressed. However, by the story's conclusion, when the dream re-emerges it is to lament how the husband, for a second time, has invaded her space by featuring in her dreams. Because of this invasion the protagonist bemoans how 'I will never more be private' as, 'like a censorious turnip, my husband is staring in' (18). Deploying the story's ability to avoid tidy resolution and instead open up a new beginning (or in this instance return to an earlier beginning), 'Four Bare Legs in a Bed' depicts feelings of claustrophobia and utilises the short story's brevity to do so.

In Simpson's 'Give Me Daughters Any Day', during a period of convalescence Ruth's grandmother, Vesta, comes to stay with Ruth and her husband Denzil. Like the couple in 'Four Bare Legs in a Bed', Ruth and Denzil are recently married and tensions fester as they negotiate their individuality in the context of marriage. Moreover, Ruth finds herself in the conflicting position of being caught between her husband and grandmother as inter-familial differences emerge. Vesta criticises Denzil for not being a 'real man' because he teaches English, which is not a 'proper subject' (31). Denzil's arrival home at five o'clock is interpreted by Vesta to mean that his job does not qualify as work. As her grandmother disparages her husband, Ruth defends Denzil and subsequently their life choice. Ruth asserts that 'women don't like only doing housework and having babies these days . . . We want to be independent and fulfilled too' (ibid.). Distressed by such feminist sentiment, Vesta tells Ruth that she talks 'a lot of rubbish' (ibid.), and this exchange highlights the generational conflict that surrounds issues of work and family life choices.

Complicating this initial friction is the fact that, despite Ruth's defence of Denzil to Vesta, the reader is also privy to Ruth's exchanges with Denzil, in which marital tensions surface: 'Why did I get married' asks Ruth, to which Denzil retorts 'Not that again' (32). As Denzil's remark highlights, there is reoccurring resentment between the couple, stemming from their marriage. Indeed, Ruth comes to replicate her grandmother's opinion when, following a bitter exchange, Ruth tells Denzil he is selfish because he 'comes in at five o'clock, miles earlier than other men, and you sit around with your bits of paper while I'm up and down stairs with her bloody lemon barley water and rice pudding and pots of tea' (40). Thus, just like child-rearing in the author's later stories, here it is caring for others as part of a marital relationship that instigates issues of gendered work inequality, according to Simpson.

Simpson's story 'Heavy Weather' follows a couple, Frances and Jonathan, after the birth of their second child, Matthew. Frances is

suffering a form of post-traumatic stress and has reoccurring night-
mares, 'where men with knives and scissors advanced on the felled
trunk which was her body' (120). Since the birth, three months ago,
Frances reflects on how 'she had not had more than half an hour
alone in the twenty-four since his birth in February. He was big and
hungry and needed her constantly on tap' (119). Because of this
demand on her time, mental and physical exhaustion take hold of
Frances. At a key moment of becoming, in 'Heavy Weather' it is the
loss of selfhood that is most apparent. The story spans the family holiday in Dorset. This temporal break only heightens Frances' despair
because, after the holiday, 'Jonathan would be back at the office with
his broad quiet desk and filter coffee while she, she would have to
submit to a fate worse than death', with the constant demands of the
children (135). When they visit Thomas Hardy's cottage on holiday
the couple are reminded of their shared pleasure in reading Hardy's
work. Matthew purchases a copy of *Jude the Obscure* for them to
read to each other in bed, 'when we've got a spare moment' (126).
This concept of a 'spare moment' strikes a chord with Frances and
she cannot hide her surprise at such a thing existing. The couple's
divergent understanding of the ease with which a 'spare moment' can
be found highlights their differing life experiences since the birth of
their children. This is particularly significant because it is through dis-
cretionary time that an individual's freedom and agency are realised,
and this 'free time' signals an ability to pursue personal goals. Later,
while Matthew finds time to stop for five minutes on his way home
from work to read the novel, Frances is left dealing with the fact she
is not 'allowed to belong to *my* self any more' (137; original emphasis). The fact that Matthew can carve out a 'spare moment' to stop
and read typifies the gendered inequality of the domestic roles within
their relationship.

In 'Heavy Weather' Frances tells Matthew how she 'was thinking, what a cheesy business Eng. Lit. is, all those old men peddling
us lies about life and love. They never get as far as this bit, do they'
(126). The 'this bit' which is being referenced here is the daily life
of marriage and children. While Frances notes that the 'great men'
of literature frequently depict the happy-ever-after ending, they fail
to explore the domestic rituals that govern everyday life thereafter;
an issue Simpson's narratives aim to rectify. Importantly, with the
reference to *Jude the Obscure*, 'Heavy Weather' invokes an unhappy
marriage (the characters Sue and Phillotson are introduced to one
another by Jude and they marry only for Sue to become dissatisfied
with Phillotson and subsequently leave him) and a narrative of social

ostracism (following Jude and Sue's cohabitation out of wedlock). Thus, Simpson draws on an established representation of marriage while simultaneously offering her own depiction of contemporary married life. Through this intertextual reference, she develops the initial critique of the 'ever after' by placing it in dialogue with other narratives, and portrays motherhood to be a significant element of that 'ever after' and sense of domestic duty as experienced by many women. Thus, the politics of motherhood, marriage, domesticity – all issues most readily associated with the personal sphere – are located as enduring sites of contestation and are problematic for women to navigate. As such, 'Heavy Weather' implies that, like the dark clouds which are difficult for the sun to break through, these issues are 'foggy' subjects for contemporary feminisms and that, arguably, there is not a simplistic answer which will suit everybody, but a need for every woman to negotiate these terrains for herself in the endeavour of bringing about change.

Victoria Hislop's 'The Zacharoplasteion' (2012) tells the story of a young woman, Angeliki, who works with her mother, Sofia, in the family 'zacharoplasteion' (a shop which sells sweets and desserts). The first encounter with Angeliki is through her mother's eyes, as Sofia sees her: 'floating down the aisle, all white, radiant, smiling her angelic smile' (57). However, Angeliki is walking not down a church aisle to be married, but down the aisle of bread trolleys. From the outset Sofia's disappointment at her daughter's unmarried status is clear, and the narrative includes asides such as 'left on the shelf, like last year's biscuits' (ibid.) and 'all her school friends were long since married' (58). Regardless of Sofia's success and creativity in baking sweets and desserts, she is judged by her mother for her 'single state', over which the older woman obsesses (61). Importantly, the narrative privileges the reader to know Angeliki's unexpressed thoughts on the matter, and it is revealed that this is a conscious decision on the part of Angeliki, who 'would wait for ever rather than compromise' (ibid.). While Sofia wants nothing more than for her daughter to conform, and be 'like other girls' (59), Angeliki refuses to sacrifice her sense of selfhood and principles simply to appease those around her. Thus, Angeliki challenges the social and cultural expectations which surround young women and critiques the 'rules' and guidance that suggest a woman's happiness depends upon being married and conforming to traditional domestic roles.

While the conflict over marriage cultivates a sense of longevity in the narrative, by referencing events which affect an entire lifetime, significantly the story pivots on one single moment. Midway through the narrative there is a temporal shift as the reader is told that the previous year, something had happened 'that her mother would never understand. It was a moment when everything changed' (62). From the ensuing narrative the reader learns that Angeliki met a man, when he visited the shop, 'studying appreciatively the variety of sweetness on display' (ibid.). While the regular customers 'seemed to exist in a state of misery', this stranger makes Angeliki smile, laugh and feel complete (65). The 'delighted interest' he takes in the shop is a refreshing experience for her and it is this sudden awareness, of what it feels like for somebody to pay attention and not simply to take for granted such delicacies as 'normal' and expected, which is responsible for her emotional awakening. While it is a fleeting moment, nonetheless, 'nobody before or since had stirred her in the way he had done', and while there is speculation that Angeliki's heart must previously have been broken, hence her rejection of male advances, the story concludes: 'But Angeliki knew that her heart had been woken, not broken' (66). The moment alters her understanding and enables her to realise that the 'natural' transition from daughter to wife, to fulfil a predefined role dutifully, is not the only option for her. As such, the story closes with an optimistic glance to the future and to the hope of alternative opportunities to those assumed destinies.

'The Zacharoplasteion' provides interesting, metaphorical readings of relationships and speaks to feminist politics in a particular way. Angeliki's encounter with the 'stranger' signals the importance of engaging with those outside the established and normalised cultural context. In this respect the story acts as a metaphor for how feminism needs to learn from those outside the dominant standpoint in order to understand and address diversity fully. While Angeliki has long been subjected to her mother's desires (which reflect those of the culture in which the women reside), it is by recognising the 'other' that clarity about her own identity and wishes is provided. The story also offers a critique of generational relationships, specifically that of the mother and daughter. Throughout the story there is a continual tension surrounding the issue of marriage, between her mother's desires for Angeliki to marry and Angeliki's own wishes not to feel compromised or pressured into following a 'natural' life trajectory. This mother–daughter dynamic nurtures a binary understanding of marriage and domesticity and, subsequently, reflects one of the most problematic elements of feminism's story. As Astrid Henry suggests in *Not My Mother's Sister: Generational Conflict and Third-Wave Feminism* (2004) 'when we remain stuck in feminism's imagined family, we lose sight of the myriad relations feminists have with one another as well as the possibility of cross-generational identification and similarities' (182). The wave metaphor has often led to differing waves being pitted against one another, as the daughters rebel against their mothers, and reject their mother's feminism. However, through the narrative perspective of Angeliki such a simplistic relationship is reconsidered. By articulating the individual motivation behind the decision to contradict her mother's wishes, 'The Zacharoplasteion' challenges the act of feminist rejection and thereby the story of feminism as being marked by progress and difference.

In contrast, Amanthi Harris's 'Red Sari', published in the anthology *Kin* (2003), depicts a clash of cultures when the bride-to-be rejects the traditional red sari her mother wishes her to wear in favour of an ivory dress she sees in a wedding magazine. With the meeting of British and Indian culture, 'Red Sari' acts as a metaphor for cultural assimilation, hybridity and the negotiation of identity politics in the context of migration more broadly. The comparisons between India and Britain pervade the story with references to visiting 'a part of town like a town in India, but with Debenhams and Argos, and Tesco and an Iceland' (105), and her mother's scornful comments that 'back home they would not argue, no?', when she speaks with another mother (109). A sense of conflict marks the relationship between mother and daughter, as the story reveals the daughter's unexpressed thoughts in response to her mother's words. Such conflict is compounded by her marriage being to someone who, as her mother remarks, 'won't know about our customs after all' (107), implying this is a multicultural wedding to a non-Indian man. Thus, the reader is placed in a privileged position and witnesses the turmoil faced by the second-generation immigrant daughter as she attempts to negotiate the expectations of her Indian heritage alongside her own identification with and assimilation to British culture.

The story closes with the revelation that the daughter was 'married in the dress from the magazine' and she walked around in 'cool ivory silk', wearing 'thin threads of silver' in her ears (110–11). The refusal to wear the red sari and large gold earrings, which would have required the painful procedure of making larger holes in her earlobes, marks the assertion of her transition into British culture, as she wishes to embrace the traditions of that culture into which she is marrying. However, the ending of 'Red Sari' is complicated because it is not a simple narrative of rejection of the family tradition and Indian heritage. Finding the red sari years later, the daughter feels the 'plum red and gold folds' and decides she 'could design a dress . . . a sari-dress, have it made. It would certainly be different, and perfect and mine' (111). In stark contrast to the opening image of the bride in the magazine, whom she desires to become in the ivory wedding gown, in this closing passage there is a recognition of her individuality and identity. A critical part of that identity is hybridity – symbolised by the 'sari-dress' – as she accepts that this is what makes her 'different' and 'perfect'. In 'Red Sari' the ending provides a sense of resolution and is fundamental to the politics put forward in the story.

Implicitly, then, 'Red Sari' suggests that narratives of migration are about a process, a journey, which does not stop at the moment of arrival. For first-, second- and third-generation migrants there is an ongoing negotiation between the domestic space that has been left behind and the new home being created. Family bonds and new relationships are all important aspects of this transition, and key moments shape that identity thereafter. Critically, marriage is an important element of this process. As an institution, which in different cultures is marked by a plethora of traditions and customs, in the context of generational migrant narratives a marriage is a significant moment which signifies a substantial identity renewal. Thus, while marriage has been a significant site of contestation in Western feminist debates, 'Red Sari' demonstrates that it is important not only in the context of gender discourses, but for understanding how women negotiate the politics of racial identity and cultural conflict too.

Altered domestic landscapes

The personal sphere, whether domesticity, relationships or home spaces, has preoccupied Western feminist debates over recent decades. However, while discussions have often centred on the ways gender relations are shaped by and shaping of these arenas, what happens when the politics of race and ethnicity are brought into the question too? In discussing British feminist thought, Floya Anthias and Nira Yuval-Davis (1983) problematise the concept of 'sisterhood' and the implicit notion of commonality which resides within this discourse. Instead, they argue that '*every* feminist struggle has a specific *ethnic* (as well as class) context' (62). Zadie Smith's short stories provide one such insight into how a specific gender and ethnic 'struggle' exists within the domestic landscape. In considering the short stories of Smith, it is worthwhile noting the broader critical discussions that surround her writing. Her novels *On Beauty*, *White Teeth* and *NW*, published in 2005, 1999 and 2012 respectively, have been subject to much interpretation, with a predominant focus being on issues of race, ethnicity, multiculturalism and postcolonial discourses. More recently, Lourdes Lopez-Ropero (2016) reads *NW* in relation to postcoloniality and postfeminist subjecthood, and thereby focuses on the intersection of ethnicity and gender. Accordingly, Lopez-Ropero suggests that by bringing women 'center stage' in *NW* this text marks a turning point in Smith's fiction (123). Following this appraisal, Smith's short stories 'The Embassy of Cambodia' (2013) and 'Two Men Arrive in a Village' (2016), which were published around the same time as and after *NW* respectively, both deal with the intersection of race and gender.

'Two Men Arrive in a Village', published in the *New Yorker*, scrutinises how the home space (in this instance represented by the village) is transformed in the context of non-Western cultures, thereby offering an alternative depiction of the personal sphere for women to that which dominates much feminist theory. Throughout the story the unnamed narrator draws the reader's attention to the act of storytelling and self-reflexively critiques the act of narration. After all, the story 'has the perfection of a parable' and, whilst unique, it is simultaneously 'representative', therefore illuminating a tension at the heart of the narrative: this is a story about a particular village and its inhabitants, but it could also be the story of many other villages and their inhabitants. An ambivalence and tension are also apparent in the descriptions of the teenage girls who 'are out in front of their huts or houses, wearing their jeans or their saris or their veils or their Lycra miniskirts, cleaning or preparing food or grinding meat or texting on their phones. Depending.' Such detail serves two functions. Firstly, it perpetuates the sense of this being a specific place while seemingly anywhere, with the nameless 'girls' being a broad descriptor. However, it also challenges the stereotype of the culturally 'other' woman as 'all the same' through Western eyes, wearing the same indistinguishable veil and 'confined' to the same activity. Instead, this story points to the individuality of these young women through a single word, 'Depending', which remains vague so as to challenge the reader to ask: depending on what? Confronted by the directness of the narrative, the reader is encouraged to critique her own subjective position and naturalised assumptions. The dynamic of this story ensures that the feminist politics is directly focused on the intersection of gender *and* ethnicity.

Despite the troubling scenes to which the reader is subjected, there is a poetic resonance to Smith's narrative in which the violent realities of everyday life are undercut through the conscious act of storytelling. When the young boy, whom his mother tries to conceal behind her skirt, steps out in a 'brave but reckless' attempt to challenge the two men, 'the tall dim one raised his gleaming machete and, with the same fluid yet effortless gesture with which you might take the head off a flower, separated the boy from his life' (n. p.). The sense of hope which the young boy symbolises is swiftly stemmed, and it remains for the women to act as protectors of the village and of the young girls:

> But the women! How proud we are, in retrospect, of our women, who stood in formation, arms linked the one to the next, in a ring around our girls, as the tall, dim man became agitated and spat on the floor . . . the pointless courage of our women at that moment, though it could not keep the men from arriving in the village and doing their worst – it never has and never will. (n. p.)

While all of the able-bodied men are out of the village, leaving the inhabitants seemingly unprotected, it is the women who stand together in an act of defiance to protect the younger generation of women from being raped. Although it is a futile gesture, as the two men soon break the circle, the image of this circle of protection is poignant in that it positions women as protectors of the home space against external forces. The narrative voice exudes a self-reflexivity, as the awareness of this being a retrospective retelling is brought to the fore. Significantly, this image is also one of different generations of women coming together, with the older generation protecting the younger women; accordingly it attests to the necessity of women uniting and of inter-generational dialogue.

Ambiguity prevails in the story's conclusion with the orality of telling stories, reporting events, being the final act:

> The next day the story of what happened is retold, in partial, broken versions that change depending very much on who is asking: a soldier, a husband, a woman with a clipboard, a morbidly curious visitor from the next village, or the chief's wife. (n. p.)

The phrase 'partial, broken versions' highlights how each individual interprets their experience of this event and creates their own narrative from it. However, this extract also emphasises the importance of the reader, or listener. Depending who the story is being told to, the details shift slightly in order to make the story more acceptable, palatable or relevant to that audience. 'Two Men Arrive in a Village', then, directly challenges the reader to reflect on her own act of reading this story and of piecing together the snippets of information which have been provided. When the chief's wife returns and visits the girls to ask for their accounts of the story, there is one who 'told her story in full'. Nonetheless, as the girl is about to reveal the real name this man provided her with the narrative stops, and the 'was –' is left open, with the reader in a state of suspense. The fact that the 'chief's wife stood up suddenly, left the room, and walked out in the yard' implies that the revelation of this man's name holds some meaning for her, but this is never disclosed to the reader. Thus, Smith's story draws on the brevity of the short story to interrogate how, in one moment, the lives of women can be irreversibly altered and the home space can be a site of danger and violence. The movement between the precise and the general, the sense that this is happening to specific people in a certain location while it could seemingly be any village, conjures a tension at the heart of the narrative, which is unsettling and challenging to the reader's understanding of women's experiences in the domestic space and provides additional meaning to the word 'home'.

The politics of race, gender and class are brought to the fore in Smith's short story 'The Embassy of Cambodia' (2013). Its publication in hardback as a single short story, by Hamish Hamilton, is certainly significant in what it reveals about short story publishing in the UK. However, curbing that initial sense of celebration that a publisher is championing the short story is the awareness that Smith is an author with strong marketability and a great deal of cultural capital in the literary marketplace. Publication issues aside, 'The Embassy of Cambodia' explores the politics of the domestic space for a migrant woman working in London. The fact that Fatou, the West African servant of the Derawal family, resides on the same street as the Royal Embassy of Cambodia establishes a bitter irony which reoccurs throughout the story, just like the 'Pock, smash. Pock, smash' (2) sounds that are repeatedly heard from the badminton court within the Embassy's 'high walls'. That Fatou walks past this building, and can only hear the sounds of the shuttlecock and witness the occasional glimpse as it soars through the air, symbolises the barrier between the poorest and wealthiest in this society. Equally, while the grandeur of the building is noted in the opening pages, chapter '0–3' undercuts this as the narrator, who remains an unnamed citizen 'from Willesden', describes how: 'Our minds tend towards the prosaic [not poetic]. I doubt there is a man or woman among us, for example who – upon passing the Embassy of Cambodia for the first time – did not immediately think: "genocide"' (6). The individual perspective, and experience based on racial, ethnic and social class factors, shape the response to this building and reveal the importance of acknowledging how the same space can hold different meanings depending on individual identities.

The chapters move between those focused on Fatou and ones which tell the story of this area of London and its inhabitants more generally. The focus in these sections is attuned to the politics of class and race, especially as Willesden is populated by 'almost all New People, though some of us, like Fatou, were, until quite recently, Old People, working the land in our various countries of origin' (40). This migrant voice speaks with authority about the community because 'I have been chosen to speak for them, though they did not choose me and must wonder what gives me the right' (ibid.). In undermining the very authority which has just been asserted, the narrative voice critiques the idea of speaking on behalf of migrants and highlights a problem: this community are often spoken about, have their stories retold, without actually being given any opportunity to speak for themselves. Similarly, 'a discarded *Metro* found on the floor of the Derawal kitchen' provides Fatou with the opportunity to 'read with interest about a Sudanese "slave" living in a rich man's house in London' (15). Here, the enslaved voice still does not 'speak' directly, as the journalist and newspaper mediate the story. Reading this story provokes Fatou to question whether she herself is a slave; however, 'this story, brief as it was, confirmed in her own mind that she was not' (ibid.). This is despite the fact that 'she had not seen her passport with her own eyes since she arrived at the Derawals', and she had been told from the start that her wages were to be retained . . . to pay for the food and water and heat . . . as well as to cover the rent for the room she slept in' (16). While Fatou does not recognise this situation as slavery, the reader is uncomfortably aware that Fatou's predicament is one of modern slavery and that her dependency on the family, and the psychological manipulation to which she is subjected, are ethically and morally wrong.

After saving the life of one of the Derawals' children, Asma, when she is choking on a marble, Fatou is aware that since then 'neither of the adult Derawals had been able to look her in the eye' (52). When she is fired, and Mrs Derawal struggles to explain the exact reason, it becomes clear that the parents feel guilt and shame that their domestic servant is the one who has saved their child's life. The only reason that Mrs Derawal gives for Fatou being fired is 'we have no need for a nanny' (64), even though 'Fatou had never cared for the children, not even slightly' (6). Fatou leaves the Derawals' house that same day, after the sad realisation that she does not even have a suitcase in which to place her few belongings. Fatou's narrative emphasises the precarious situation that many migrant women find themselves in, as dependents of wealthy families. The swiftness with which she finds herself homeless (although her friend Andrew offers her a place to stay and to help to secure her a job) recognises that the home space is not a site of safety and security. Indeed, for the migrant domestic servant, the home space and domestic sphere are a site of insecurity and enslavement in which equality is not an option.

In 2015 Comma Press published *Refugee Tales*, a collection of stories about real-life refugees and their experiences. The stories are told to and subsequently written by a range of writers. Amongst them, Ali Smith is the author of 'The Detainee's Tale', which was first published in the *Guardian* (June 2015). The story is set in a room in a London university; the reader is clearly placed in the position of listener and Smith self-consciously reflects on her own act of bearing witness to and trying to understand the story she herself is being told. What is captured on the page is a story which tells the horrific tale of this person's experiences of being held in numerous detention centres, while at the same time it is about Smith's own response to what she hears. Storytelling is used as a means of challenging the assumptions that are made about refugees and those detained due to their immigration status, and offers a perspective rarely heard in media coverage and government narratives about refugees in Britain. Importantly, after some contextual detail Smith swiftly moves to recount the detainee's tale: 'Here's what you tell me. It's all in the present tense, I realise afterwards, because it is all still happening' (755). Immediacy comes to the fore through the self-conscious act of storytelling in 'The Detainee's Tale', and the orality of the short story's origins is invoked in order to intensify the politics of the narrative.

As an orphan at the age of three and given to a man in the local village, the detainee describes, at the age of six, being sent to work on a farm. Suffering beatings and years of enslavement at the age of twenty-one, 'you run away' (767). The story charts the journey from this initial 'home' to eventually arriving in Luton, where the existence follows a distinct pattern: 'Room, van, warehouse. Warehouse, van, room' (800); thus the escape from one form of imprisonment only results in another. After the detainee writes to the Home Office for help, the consequence is arrest and imprisonment. The detention centre, as Smith discovers when she visits, is yet another form of prison, and she learns that there is no such 'thing as therapeutic help for people in detention', even if clearly 'you're traumatised' and suffering the 'terrible mental consequence' (912). Smith's deployment of 'you' intermittently throughout this section of the story acknowledges that in reading this story the reader is having the narrative mediated by another voice. There is a conscious desire here not to assume to speak authoritatively for this individual, but to recognise that this is an act of retelling, of giving voice to somebody who otherwise would remain voiceless. 'The Detainee's Tale' is an attempt to understand the realities of being a refugee and finding yourself living in the United Kingdom, but without the security of a home space. In fact, what is stressed in this story is the absolute insecurity of their situation:

> First it's prison, then detention. That takes two years. Then they release you for six months. Then they arrest you again. Back to detention, another six months. Then they release you. Any moment now they can arrest you again. They say: *We have accepted you are a victim of human trafficking.* But to go back to Ghana? You have nobody there to go to. Indefinite *leave to remain.* That means they'll arrest you again. They can, any time. (811)

This passage epitomises the sense of instability the Ghanaian orphan experiences in the UK. The irony is not lost in this tale that it is the *Home* Office that causes a great deal of this uncertainty and leaves the detainee in a constant state of flux and homelessness. In this context, the concepts of home, domesticity and the private sphere are devoid of any meaning as the realities of being a refugee, subjected to the indefinite detention policy, in contemporary Britain make such discourses irrelevant.

All of the tales in the collection unveil the ontological realities of being a refugee, while maintaining the anonymity of the person behind the tale. The story is accredited to the writer, but with full recognition that this is not *their* story. The act of telling and retelling is described by David Herd in the 'Afterword' to the collection, in which he suggests this creates 'the metaphorical sense of space . . . the cultural space' which these narratives require, as well as being a therapeutic process for many of the refugees. In this piece, he also recognises the significance of the publication: 'the geopolitical shift effected by the so-called "migrant crisis" makes the *Refugee Tales* project . . . all the more consequential' (Herd and Pincus 2016: loc. 1897), and the wider political implications of this anthology are abundant. The anthology is perhaps a particularly relevant medium for this project because it allows a range of stories to be told which are all anchored in the central theme: being a refugee and the realities of the government policy of indefinite detention. The political intent, the act of consciousness raising which drives the project, comes to the fore in this collection, as it is a means of portraying the diversity of experience as well as the commonality in the mistreatment and unethical situation of many refugees.

Conclusion

In Jane Rogers' 'Hitting Trees with Sticks' (2012), the home space is transformed into a site of lost memories as the elderly female narrator experiences extreme disorientation and memory loss (which it is implied is due to the onset of dementia), just like her own mother who has now passed. While her daughter, Natalie, is seen to be constantly trying to help her mother, such attempts are sadly futile as she continues to misplace everyday objects and eventually locks herself out of her home. The opening, with the narrator passing 'a young girl hitting a tree' (loc. 19), triggers a series of childhood memories for the narrator before she decides that hitting a tree with wood is 'against nature, it adds insult to injury. But maybe I am missing something' (loc. 26). This line hangs in the air, but soon takes on an ironic resonance at the story's end when the narrator, in her garden and angered by all the trouble the old almond tree has caused over the years, picks up the garden broom and marches over to start hitting the tree because 'it is time that old tree know it was beaten' (loc. 150). After following the narrator's spiralling thoughts and emotions, as she misplaces objects around the home, the reader is sent into a narrative loop as trying to follow the story's events becomes a difficult task. As such, the trope of the cyclical reverberates in both narrative content and structure of the story. The concept of 'missing something' lingers throughout the story, which shines a light on the often silent story of bodily ageing, which in turn transforms the home space and everyday domestic objects into alien entities that cause stress and confusion. Although the narrator can recall events from the past, in the present she remains confused and plagued by forgetfulness as her supposed home becomes almost foreign to her.

In his essay 'Imaginary Homelands' (1992), Salman Rushdie writes that 'the past is home, albeit a lost home in a lost city in the mists of lost time' (9). Rushdie suggests that the home is a place which the individual can never reach. It becomes an imagined space that one is always trying to capture. Thinking of home as real and imagined emphasises the ambiguous and porous characteristics that make it a location of multiple possibilities. While the imagined space of home is especially relevant in the context of migration narratives, for many British women the home is a very real space and one in which important gendered and cultural tensions exist. Equally, as 'Hitting Trees with Sticks' illuminates, the home space can also be transformed simply by the individual and, while once a site of familial happiness, for the ageing female body suffering from memory loss, it becomes a space of hostility and despair. In the last few decades, the politics of marriage and domesticity have come to define the home space in feminist discourses, and the reoccurrence of these issues throughout contemporary feminist debate illuminates their contentious, ambivalent and discursive nature. The politics of the personal and the domestic can tell important stories about women's lives and of feminism too.

Note

1. I am grateful to Helen Simpson for directing me to Donne's poem as the point of origin for this short story (private email exchange, July 2014).

Chapter 4

Masculinity

Masculinity studies is not necessarily the reactionary defensive rage of the men's rights groups, the mythic cross-cultural nostalgia of mythopoetry, nor even the theologically informed nostalgia yearning for separate spheres . . . . Rather, masculinity studies can be informed by a feminist project to interrogate different masculinities, whether real (as in corporeal) or imagined (as in representations and texts). (Kimmel 2002: ix)

The relationship between masculinity and feminism is undeniably one fuelled by anxiety and tension. The quotation above establishes the backdrop against which the decision was made to include a chapter dedicated to the theme of masculinity in this book. While the first part of the quotation from Kimmel's 'Foreword' to *Masculinity Studies and Feminist Theory* (2002) emphasises many of the fraught issues which have embroiled masculinity studies and feminism and often set them in opposition, the focus on how we can interrogate masculinity through the imagined sphere of representation is the primary purpose of this chapter. Importantly, as understandings of masculinity and femininity are based on the mutual opposition of sex and gender categories, it is necessary to analyse both elements of these identity discourses, which have contributed profoundly to contemporary gender relations and the enduring prevalence of patriarchy in shaping society and culture. In many of the short stories by contemporary women writers, the representation of men is crucial to the depiction of femininity as much as masculinity. As such, it is important to scrutinise the literary representation of masculinity for what it reveals about the politics of gender, sex and feminism today.

Following a brief overview which contextualises the theoretical perspectives surrounding masculinity, the next section of this chapter considers the work of Rose Tremain, paying close attention to how her short stories engage with history and, in the process, seek to unravel the construction of masculinity. With the shadows of the 1980s on the pages, many of Tremain's stories create a dialogue across temporalities which are further complicated by the reader's engagement with the text in the present. Indeed, throughout this chapter I continually return to how Tremain's short stories map some of the concerns of 1980s Britain and, through this, highlight the short story's ability to capture 'the moment'. In the following part of this chapter, 'The phallic makes the man?', through a reading of Tremain's and Victoria Hislop's narratives, sexuality is located as a key site for understanding the ways in which masculinity is constructed and positioned in society, as well as defined for the individual body.

The final section of this chapter pays close attention to recent literary representations of Margaret Thatcher, notably in the contentious short story by Hilary Mantel, and examines what this fascination with the so-called Iron Lady reveals about understandings of 'female masculinity'. The Thatcher era is often associated with the recession of the early 1980s, a high rate of unemployment, the decrease in manufacturing output, the Falklands War of 1982, the miners' strike of 1984–5, and Thatcher's personal branding as the 'Iron Lady'. In the context of these political, economic and social issues, contemporary understandings of masculinity underwent a significant reappraisal. Accordingly, the increased academic interest in masculinity arises in tandem with this cultural moment. Drawing on Judith Halberstam's work, this final section makes the case for understanding masculinity as an important theme in gender and sexuality debates and highlights how this can lead to a productive dialogue in and with feminist politics.

Theorising masculinity

The 1980s witnessed significant developments in the field of masculinity studies. In this period the term 'hegemonic masculinity' was first coined by R. W. Connell et al. (1982). Although the term first appeared in the 1980s, it is to Connell's *Masculinities* (1995; republished in 2005) that subsequent scholars tend to return for the most detailed account of hegemonic masculinity and the pluralised understanding of masculinities. Defining the term in this later book, Connell states: "'Hegemonic Masculinity' is not a fixed character type, always and everywhere the same. It is, rather, the masculinity that occupies the hegemonic position in a given pattern of gender relations, a position always contestable' (76). While white, middle-class, heterosexual Western man is usually taken as the embodiment of hegemonic masculinity, Connell signals the contestable nature of this position by emphasising its relationship with wider gender patterns. Crucially, while the 'number of men rigorously practising the hegemonic pattern in its entirety may be quite small', it still allows 'the majority of men [to] gain from its hegemony, since they benefit from the patriarchal dividend' (79). In other words, there is a secondary social existence to hegemonic masculinity in which those who are complicit with this form of masculinity, or who are striving to achieve the hegemonic model, perpetuate the prevalence of the discourse.

Hegemonic masculinity denotes the domination of one type of masculinity over another. As a discourse, hegemonic masculinity claims *and* sustains itself as the legitimate, authoritative and 'normal' form of that gender identity. Within the broader parameters of gender, by establishing itself as the gender norm, masculinity renders itself natural and subsequently becomes socially invisible. It is also through this normalised status that masculinity upholds patriarchy and subordinates all those outside the hegemonic position, on the basis of sex, gender, sexuality, race and class. With the politics of masculinity conceptualised in this manner, masculinity becomes located alongside the work of gender studies scholars and, in particular, it resonates with Judith Butler's theorisation of gender identity. After all, masculinity is performed upon and by the body, or as Butler argues, 'rather as an incessant and repeated action of some sort' (2010: 152). Acknowledging the socially constructed nature of masculinity, and rendering it visible, unsettle the supposed legitimacy of hegemonic masculinity. In this light, the hegemonic model may well be placed in 'gender trouble', but this does not constitute a masculinity 'crisis'. Instead, it affirms contemporary theorisations in which gender is deemed 'to be performative – that is, constituting the identity it is purported to be' (ibid.: 34).

Nonetheless, this 'troubling' of masculinity led to some arguing there is a 'crisis of masculinity' in late twentieth-century Britain. As Stephen Whitehead (2002) notes, 'as descriptors, neither men nor masculinity are fixed: they always have been and always will be somewhat transitory generalizations of identity' (58). Subsequently, Whitehead argues, the 'notion of a "crisis" can be seen . . . as a desire to change culture in order to maintain a "natural" gender order' (61). This phrase, 'crisis of masculinity', denotes the point at which masculinity studies and feminism most directly converge.

At the forefront of this 'crisis' debate is the work of Anthony Clare, who, in his book *On Men: Masculinity in Crisis* (2000), asserts that 'at the beginning of the twenty-first century it is difficult to avoid the conclusion that men are in trouble' (3). According to Clare, men's 'purpose, their value, their justification' are all under public debate and scrutiny (ibid.), and there is no shortage of suggested causes. Clare points out that at the

> top of the list is the growing assertiveness of women. As a consequence of the feminist revolution, so this argument goes, women are no longer prepared to be the property of men. In this feminist revolution, male power is being overthrown. Men, like colonists seeing this empire crumble, don't like what's happening. (3–4)

Clare's summation of the gender crisis is pointedly anti-feminist and somewhat misogynistic in that it posits women, and more specifically the feminist movement, as not just a, but *the*, root cause of men's identity problems. However, as Judith Kegan Gardiner (2002) argues, 'this talk of crisis, with its deliberate exaggerations and fomenting of anxieties, echoes the rhetoric of advertising' and suggests a greater antagonism between feminism and masculinity than truly exists (7).

Attempting to realign the relationship between feminism and masculinity, Tim Edwards, in *Cultures of Masculinity* (2006), proposes two types of 'crisis'. The first of these is the crisis from without, which is concerned with 'the perception that men have lost, or are losing, power or privilege relative to their prior status in . . . institutions', including the family, education and work' (8). Second, Edwards suggests, is the crisis from within, which

> is far less easily documented as it centres precisely on a perceived shift in men's *experiences* of their position *as* men, their maleness, and what it means. Most importantly, this often refers to a sense of powerlessness, meaninglessness or uncertainty. (ibid.)

While these two types of crisis are connected with and inform one another, the crisis from without tends to produce an image of masculinity in crisis en masse, something Edwards firmly rebuts. Instead, the crisis from within acknowledges that masculinity is, to return to Connell's work, 'a position always contestable' (2005: 76). In this light, individual crisis occurs because masculinity is 'a configuration of practice *within* a system of gender relations' (ibid.: 85). This notion of a crisis from within is especially relevant to this chapter because the short stories discussed, with their emphasis on the experiences of men, often reflect 'a sense of powerlessness, meaninglessness or uncertainty' (Edwards 2006: 8) through their internalised, masculine narrative perspectives. Consequently, the focus on masculinity at the heart of women's short story writing tends to rebut the 'woman blaming' tendencies demonstrated by a few critics, and instead illuminates why engaging with masculinity is important for understanding contemporary gender relations.

Rose Tremain: invoking history and critiquing masculinity

While Tremain's stories have been briefly discussed earlier in this book, given the in-depth attention paid to her writing in this chapter it is worth reflecting on her position within the literary canon and contemporary criticism. As a writer, Tremain has received limited critical acclaim and has herself noted in an article for the *Guardian* that 'I've had numerous opportunities to perfect the art of not winning', before going on to list a substantial body of literary prizes for which she has been shortlisted but which she has never won (2012: n. p.). Equally, academic criticism is sparse, with extant work focusing on the novels and, most often, the politics of masculinity. Indeed, in *Masculinities without Men? Female Masculinity in Twentieth-Century Fictions* (2003), Jean Bobby Noble analyses the representation of female masculinity in Tremain's 1992 *Sacred Country*. Similarly, Emma Parker (2007) argues that Tremain's novel 'subverts the myth that manhood is an inviolable state, or sacred country, inhabited by a privileged group of subjects: real men' (303), while Sarah Sceats (2005) reflects on Tremain's 'peculiar brand of feminism' (166), suggesting it is

> comprehensive in its focus; women's lives, in her novels, are lived in heterosocial contexts. Understanding women, their problems, their traumas, desires and aspirations, of necessity involves understanding men and the cultures in which they operate . . . Existential confirmation and belonging are, it seems, no more important for women than for men, but they are shown to be both problematic and difficult to achieve in what are essentially patriarchal societies. (166)

Following this summation, by locating the focus on masculinity within a broader feminist agenda, Tremain's fiction realises the importance of critiquing gender as a discursive category.

'Evangelista's Fan', the story from which Tremain's third collection takes its name (1995), depicts the consequences of a leader's rulings for an individual's personal life. Although this story is set in the historical past, affinities can be drawn between the protagonist's (Salvatore's) experience in early eighteenth-century Italy and late 1980s Britain. The uneasy relationship between public leadership and private situations mimics the tensions between working-class men and Thatcher's policies, as epitomised by the miners' strike. Moreover, by placing contemporary debates about masculinity in dialogue with individual historical experiences of identity and selfhood, the reader is reminded that 'masculinities come into existence at particular times and places, and are always subject to change. Masculinities are, in a word, historical' (Connell 2005: 185). The story opens in Italy in the aftermath of the French Revolution and with the king of Italy's decree that the years 1789–1815 are to be eradicated from the country's history. Tremain utilises this large, historical event as the narrative backdrop for the story, which details the effects of the king's decree upon the protagonist, Salvatore. Born in 1789, according to this decree Salvatore does not exist. Erased from the public sphere, he can live 'only in private' (5). Consequently, Salvatore leaves his family and their watch-making business and moves to England. However, once there, he loses the ability to make watches. Although it 'took him two months to understand the cause of his fear', he realises that his inability to make them 'grew out of his personal predicament after the King of Piedmont's decree' (9). The decree results in Salvatore's expulsion from his country, from his craft and from his own sense of self. In attempting to regain control of his life and work Salvatore becomes a 'REPAIRER OF TIME' (9; original capitalisation). Despite financially prospering as a repairer of time, because a stopped clock 'is a thing no Englishman can endure', Salvatore feels as though his new life 'was like a coat he wore' (10). Subsequently, he desires to be a man who can '*forsee*' [*sic*] time and therefore future events (16; original emphasis), because this ability to 'forsee' would imbue Salvatore with a sense of authority and control. Therefore, it would have allowed him to pre-empt the king of Italy's destructive decree.

Resolved upon this change in his employment, Salvatore decides that his future lies in making the barometer, 'one of the few scientific devices man has perfected that tell what is *going* to happen, not what is or what has been' (19). In pursuing this occupation he goes to work for Mr Sydney and Mr Simpkins at a shop which bears over the door the name 'FANTINO, E.'; the name appears on the instruments too (20). In taking this new job Salvatore agrees to disappear without a trace and to inform his current customers that he has returned to Piedmont. While Salvatore masters his new craft, Mr Sydney demands that 'you must become absolutely invisible until you are forgotten' (22). For the second time in his life, then, Salvatore becomes non-existent because of the rulings of others. The emphasis upon his employment is significant because, as Edwards asserts, 'work not only matters *to* men, but it is also part *of* them as a key dimension of their identity and masculinity' (2006: 8; original emphasis). Thus, Salvatore's problems at work contribute to a broader disruption of his masculine identity. Although, in the twentieth century, work became an increasingly important feature of women's lives, it is the traditional, persistent association of men with being breadwinners that maintains the significance of work in defining masculinity.

In *Wigan Pier Revisited: Poverty and Politics in the 80s* (1984), Beatrix Campbell engages with working-class men and women in an attempt to understand the contemporary situation of those living in different parts of Britain. Campbell's work is a feminist response to George Orwell's 1937 *The Road to Wigan Pier*, which she criticises because Orwell based 'his journey on the simple task of discovering the essence of working-class work and monitoring the degenerate landscape of mass housing' (1984: 116). Discussing the ramifications of unemployment for men, compared to its effect on women, Campbell states, 'the difference lies in the fact that unemployment for men means their exclusion not only from work but from the environment that makes them men, which is also their route to masculine class consciousness and class strength' (189). Further, she acknowledges the 'emotional cost, too. When unemployment means idleness it also means depression, self-hatred and pessimism' for men (209). Although Campbell is referring to a very different historical period, if we accept the synergies of 'Evangelista's Fan' with the contemporary moment of publication, Tremain's story, written in the aftermath of a period of high unemployment, contains traces of the fact that 'far from finding new opportunities, working-class men in the 1980s can no longer even be confident of securing the kind of jobs readily available to them throughout the postwar era' (Monaghan 2001: 5). As such, 'Evangelista's Fan' is a story of two moments in history in which the political landscape comes to define the experiences of the individual in poignant ways. Accordingly, the story challenges the conceptualisation of masculinity as suddenly in crisis in the contemporary era (as held by Anthony Clare). Instead, it illuminates that, throughout history, individuals have continually experienced an unsettling of identification with the hegemonic masculinity of the day.

Finally, with his second resurrection Salvatore becomes Evangelista Fantino; an Italian man invented by Sydney and Simpkins to give validity to their barometer because Italians are the experts in the trade. In adopting this new identity Salvatore 'talked to himself as if he were no longer Salvatore Cavalli, but some disinterested third party' (23), highlighting the rupture between his physical body and his sense of self and identity. When he becomes Fantino, E., his name 'is engraved on every instrument. The name, therefore, carries with it some years of prior existence that could go some way to redressing the balance of years lost as Cavalli, S.' (ibid.). It is via the physical instrument of the barometer that Salvatore, now Fantino, manages to assert his identity. Similarly, it is through external objects that he now has a claim to a past life. Crucially, his ever-shifting experiences in the present always return to his life in the past and thereby emphasise the ways in which individuals' lives are formed of an array of moments: the connection between the past and the present is not just a case of marking difference, but one of illuminating similarities too.

While 'Evangelista's Fan' focuses on a young man, in his mid-twenties, it is in 'Will and Lou's Boy', from *The Garden of the Villa Mollini and Other Stories* (1988), that the '*moment of engagement with hegemonic masculinity, the moment in which the boy takes up the project of hegemonic masculinity as his own*' (Connell 2005: 122; original emphasis), is most noticeable. 'Will and Lou's Boy' is told through the memory of its protagonist Dougie, who recalls 'the early summer of 1948, the year I got to be eighteen' (3). The story is a retrospective reflection on this formative time in Dougie's life, as he turns from a boy to a 'man'. The story is a dialogue across two moments in time which are only a few decades apart. As his mother tucks him into bed, 'Lou lullabyed' that 'you'll feel better when you're eighteen. You'll feel more like a man' (6). This comment by Lou suggests two things: firstly, that Dougie is currently not a man, he is something other; secondly, that there is a clear definition and image of what a man is and should be. Ironically, Lou's action here, of tucking Dougie into bed, undermines her assertion that he is becoming a man, because her action infantilises him. Furthermore, in suggesting that being a 'man' is defined by Dougie's age, the narrative signals the arbitrary nature of masculinity. After all, the assumption that one becomes a man at a certain age implies that other defining characteristics are less significant. On the night of Dougie's birthday meal, when he is 'full of beer', his parents, Will and Lou, remark that this 'is a new start, Dougie. This is your chance to start again' (9). The reason for Dougie needing this chance to start again remains unclear to the reader. However, what neither of his parents realises is that Dougie is actually happy with his current situation. By giving the reader an insight into Dougie's thoughts, the external opinions of his parents, who arguably stand in for society more broadly, are brought into conflict with Dougie's feelings. Ironically, it is revealed that it is only the fear that he is disappointing Will and Lou that worries Dougie; he is not concerned about becoming a man or having a fresh start.

The conflict between internal and external identity, and the constructed nature of the discourse, is also symbolised by the lottery ticket, number '879', which Dougie collects for the family's entry into the housing lottery. The housing lottery is a local government initiative in which current council tenants are entered into a lottery draw with the hope of being allocated a new house. The housing lottery triggers 'a malaria' in Lou as her desire to move out of their 'prefab' home is unbearable (6). However, following a conversation with his Aunt If ('If' being short for Iphigenia), Dougie's response to the ticket number, '879', also proves to be revealing:

> Aunt If said this was auspicious because 879 was a close-together group of numbers. I was the thin 7 in the middle, with Lou and Will leaning over me. Even now – and they're both long dead, actually – I still sometimes think of Lou as 8 and Will as 9. (7)

For Dougie, the closeness of the numbers replicates his family. However, as with Lou's action of tucking Dougie into bed, the 'man' Dougie is infantilised here. The way in which he attaches meaning to these numbers is almost childlike; a point reinforced by the way in which Dougie merges his parents' names, 'Lou and Will. Will and Lou. *Willou*' (4; original emphasis). Notably, the fact that 'even now', as an adult, Dougie thinks about his parents as these numbers indicates he still has a childlike perspective on life. When the winners of the new houses include '849', '859' and '869', his father retorts, 'shame we had the 7' (10). Unaware of the significance Dougie has attached to the number, Will's comment provokes Dougie to think, 'without me, they would have got lucky' (ibid.). Dougie blames his existence for Will and Lou's misfortune. As with Dougie turning eighteen, numbers are once again imbued with significance beyond their original function and reflect the ways in which meaning is often externally prescribed by others.

As well as providing a means of scrutinising the construction of internal and external identity, the inclusion of the housing lottery also reflects the social and political landscape of postwar Britain. In comparison with Orwell's depiction of Britain in the 1930s, Campbell argues that:

> Today the terrain is a quagmire. There is no archetypical proletarian, no homogenous working class, no symbolic essence of labour revealing the condition of the class, no essential culture expressing its interests and ambitions. On my journey it quickly became clear that there are many stories to tell and no generalisation will serve. (1984: 116)

The picture that Campbell paints is of a Britain in flux, in which traditional class identities are undergoing complex changes. According to her this is reflected in the housing situation. More specifically, she cites how, in the early 1950s, the housing minister, Harold Macmillan, 'stole Labour's thunder and promised 300,000 new homes a year. But they had to be cheap. So they *were* cheap, and nasty, and we now have a housing crisis which will endure beyond this century' (33). 'Will and Lou's Boy', with Lou's emphatic desperation to move into new accommodation and out of their prefab home, reflects the turbulent landscape and housing problems in Britain in this period. While Campbell notes how these new houses, the type Lou craves, result in another housing crisis in the 1980s, during the postwar moment they symbolise the hope and aspirations for a better life. Lou's dissatisfaction with the family's living situation, and implicitly their financial circumstances, illuminates a motivation behind her aspiration for Dougie to better himself, to become a man. For Lou, Dougie's fresh start is not just about his age; it is about breaking free from the constraints of social class that have impeded her own life.

Finally, 'Will and Lou's Boy' closes with Dougie's last day working as a park attendant (before he starts a new job at the hospital). As the narrative recognises the present moment from which the story is being told, Dougie reveals that he has worked at the park 'all my life' (11). He recalls:

> I told Willou this was my new start, and they were proud of me. But my last day at the park was one of the saddest things I can remember. They'd harvested the barley. I sat in the sunshine, staring at all the litter left among the stubble and thinking about my country. (ibid.)

Yet again, the childlike Dougie emerges as he refers to his parents as 'Willou'. Further, with the recognition of the past and present in this scene, he acknowledges his current act of remembrance: his reflection about 'my country' is suggestively a meditation on the sad state of the British landscape both then (in 1948) and in the narrative present. In *Wigan Pier Revisited*, Campbell refers to a 'landscape in transition' (31), and 'Will and Lou's Boy' maps the transition across the decades. Dougie's loss at leaving his beloved park is replicated in the pitiful state of his view; it is not just the urban housing estates that provoke sadness and despair. With the removal of the barley, a source of food and therefore sustenance, all that remains is 'litter', emphasising the demise and disintegration of the landscape.

From Tremain's fourth collection, *The Darkness of Wallis Simpson and Other Stories* (1999), 'Loves Me, Loves Me Not' tells the story of Frank Baines. Frank has recently arrived in London from the USA and finds the city 'too vivid and noisy, too purposeful, knowing and bright' (149). This brightness is associated with modern London and 'Mrs Thatcher in all her shades of electric blue, and her yellow hair' (ibid.), an unsettling scene in comparison to the war-torn London Frank holds in his memory. This earlier version of London was:

> Dark and slow and quiet. Dark railway carriages, on slow trains, where silence was preferred. Dark pubs. Dark little homes with, under the stairs, some deeper, incredible darkness in which a dog or a cat – or sometimes a child – lay sleeping. (ibid.)

This description reveals the security Frank discovers in the darkness of London, and it is the characteristic of the city which has remained in his memory over the years. Although the darkness refers to black-outs caused by the Blitz, for Frank darkness is associated with the London he loved, and, crucially, with Marie Smythe, the woman he loves. Moving from the gaudy brightness of contemporary Britain, the narrative relies on memory as Frank attempts to reclaim times gone by, and more particularly, the self he lost when Marie did not follow him to America as she promised. While Frank physically remains in this bright, new Britain throughout the story, it is via his memory that the narrative moves outside the present to recount events across the decades.

Fog imagery is prevalent throughout this story, but especially as Frank describes the moment when he waited for the ship to dock in New York, expecting Marie to step off it 'as a kind of film' (155). Frank tells his workmate Sol how he was standing 'in New York City and I'm at the waterfront early. And there's some fog or mist in the air and it's cold and I can see my breath' (ibid.). Located on the cusp with his position on the 'waterfront' (a position which serves as a metaphor for his life more broadly, as he is forever anticipating the arrival of his 'true love'), the 'fog and mist' distort Frank's vision. When Sol questions 'why fog and mist', Frank can only reply, 'dunno. But there they are. Then I pan out over the water. It's like the world ends there, in the mist, you know?' (ibid.). This image of the world ending highlights the importance of Marie to Frank. Her failure to arrive in New York marks the end of life for him, as he has envisaged it, and now he can see no further. For Frank, his life and selfhood are only complete if Marie is a part of it. Although in this scene the fog acts as a metaphor for Frank's failed hopes for the future, in the context of his act of storytelling the 'fogginess' of the scene emphasises the difficulty and unreliability of narrating via memory. In invoking the past, Tremain's narrative reminds the reader that, just like the future, it is plagued with uncertainty.

Suggestively, following Marie's failed arrival Frank's life remains in darkness, that is, until the point at which the narrative commences in the present moment of 1985 and the brightness of London. Having travelled to London, Frank has arranged to meet Marie at his hotel reception. However, after ignoring the ringing hotel room phone, as the receptionist calls to inform him Marie is at the hotel, Frank ends his lifelong attachment to the woman that broke his heart. Subsequently his connection to England is also terminated as he decides to let 'it go its unfathomable way' and focus on his life in America (163). 'Loves Me, Loves Me Not' highlights the interconnection between sexuality and identity in relation to hegemonic masculinity. The story emphasises the ways in which a single moment can shape, and in this instance haunt, a person's life as Marie has remained in Frank's thoughts to the fictional present day. Equally, it is in the brief moment when the hotel phone rings and Frank chooses to ignore it, thereby taking his revenge on Marie for jilting him, that he is finally able to move on. In this respect, Tremain's narratives suggest it is only through invoking, or in Frank's case engaging with, history that we can understand masculinity and gender relations more broadly.

The phallic makes the man?

Discussing the short story, Paul March-Russell (2009) argues that 'many short storywriters . . . view the form as a means of capturing the passing moment' (23). In the context of Tremain's work, March-Russell's observation is interesting because Tremain's short stories take further the association between the short story and the 'passing moment'. After all, Tremain's short stories focus on the immediate, passing moment and illuminate the potential inherent in the most fleeting of moments. However, her stories also celebrate the moment that has past, and by drawing on history, her short stories explore the synergies between the past and present. Furthermore, it is the use of two temporalities in the space of a single story that frequently perpetuates narrative development in Tremain's short stories. Likewise, it is in the discrepancy between a character's internal (personal) thoughts and external (social) perceptions that another dimension of narrative tension emerges. Thus, in the critique of identity, Tremain exploits the 'vertical' possibilities of short fiction and the potential of chronological disruptions. Such narrative movement is especially notable in 'The Crossing of Herald Montjoy', from *Evangelista's Fan*. This story follows the protagonist, Montjoy, a herald at the battle of Agincourt. The narrative focuses on Montjoy as he rides across the battlefield delivering messages between the two opposing (and fighting) camps. As he tells his nephew, Roland, his role as herald means he 'oversees the conduct of armies, but doesn't really belong to them. He's not a man-at-arms, but a man apart' (67). From the outset Montjoy is established as a man inhabiting an intermediate space, and the subsequent narrative also blurs the boundaries between the personal and private spheres, love and war. Importantly, while 'war is usually conceived of as a rite of passage, an opportunity for men to find themselves, to prove their masculinity and their capacity to tame their bodies and physical fears' (Rutherford 1988: 27), with the gentle and caring figure of Montjoy the connection between war and masculinity is complicated.

The story opens on '*a piece of ground near Agincourt. October 1415*', and the reader is told that Montjoy 'does not have far to ride' (67; original italics). Instantly, with this opening the reader is immersed in a specific historical moment. Moreover, it is the action of riding between the French and English camps that connects Montjoy's public role as herald with his private narrative of unrequited love. As the story shifts to 'a *piece of ground near the Manor of La Vallée. April 1412*', a repetition occurs because 'he did not have far to ride' (68; original italics). While, at Agincourt, it is the words of war Montjoy exchanges; in La Vallée, he delivers messages of courtship and declares his love for Cecile, the woman he wishes to marry. The description of these two scenes bears striking similarities; the only difference is that one depicts scenes of war and the other courtship. As a result, the reader is coerced into drawing comparisons between these two themes, which are stereotypically conceptualised in binary opposition to one another. Here, the momentary structure of the story, with the depiction of two discrete yet comparable events, problematises the binary understandings of love and war. On the one hand, these scenes remain separated, which seems to uphold the binary assumptions. Yet, at the same time, the similarities in description seem to undermine this relationship. Thus, in utilising the moment as a narrative device, Tremain imbues the story with a sense of tension.

The story culminates with the revelation that Montjoy's proposal of marriage is rejected by Cecile because she is already engaged to Monsieur de Granvilliers, with whom she is 'going to have a wonderful life!' (78). Returning to his parents' house, Montjoy proclaims, 'I don't want to speak about it. It or her. I don't want to talk about any of it. Ever' (80). With this rejection by Cecile, Montjoy is unable to speak. In losing her, he fails to achieve a heterosexual union. More particularly, the word 'Ever' in this passage suggests something beyond t the surface rejection and dismissal. Carrying, as it does, uppercase lettering, 'Ever' complicates the momentary nature of the story, and by being given its own sentence the word suggests a continuation beyond the initial moment. In this respect, the word 'Ever' reflects the tension between the momentary structure of the story and the historical setting. Implicitly, Montjoy's inability to achieve heterosexual courtship, in this one moment, has the potential to jeopardise his masculine status because it disrupts the social expectations of a man of his age achieving a heterosexual union.

Reflecting on the relationship between historical fiction and the short story, George Green (2011) argues that historical short fictions are not popular or often produced because the spatial limitations of the short story genre are unsuitable for writing historical fiction (63). Due to the novel having a larger 'canvas' upon which to paint the historical scene, there is a much greater freedom in the historical novel than in the historical short story. In analysing the relationship between short fiction and history, then, Green proposes three devices that enable historical short fiction to work: the familiar, the enclosed and the generic (ibid.). In other words, it is by drawing on recent history (familiar), by selecting a smaller canvas or period of history (enclosed), or by engaging with situations that have reoccurred throughout history (generic) that short stories are able to engage with history. It is notable that two of these devices (familiar and generic) both nurture an ability to create close comparisons with the contemporary and therefore facilitate a potentially political narrative.

Moreover, these types of narrative require more work on the part of the reader as they are provided with far less detail and description on this smaller canvas. In the short story, history is not reproduced as an authentic and all-encompassing grand narrative with a clear beginning, middle and end. Instead, as Tremain's short stories illuminate, they engage in a range of chronological disruptions in the process of telling stories from the past.

The historical short fiction 'Wedding Night', from Tremain's collection *The Colonel's Daughter and Other Stories* (1999), illuminates how numerous time periods are brought together through a character's memory and storytelling. In this respect, the short story is not set in the distant, historical past but meanders between the past and present life of a character. 'Wedding Night' centres on the twin brothers Jacques and Paul, and is narrated from the perspective of Jacques. In telling his story Jacques relies heavily on his childhood memories, and the narrative contains numerous flashbacks. As a narrator he demonstrates self-awareness about the act of remembrance. He reflects:

> I have always remembered the details of things, especially of rooms where I've lived. My brother does this too: together, we can reconstruct places, object by object. I think this gift or skill of ours is not really a gift or skill at all, but merely a habit into which, as soon as we could talk, we were obliged to fall: because our father was blind. (47)

It emerges here that Jacques and Paul's gift is caused by their father's disability. As such, Jacques positions himself and his brother in opposition to their father. While their father cannot see (implying he is somehow 'lacking'), Jacques emphasises his own ability to see, own and know and, consequently, assert his authority over his father. Crucially, the word 'habit' suggests an element of repetition to Jacques's act of storytelling, and implies that his identity and authority are *performed* over time. Furthermore, the ability of Jacques and his brother Paul to translate images into stories for their father mimics the very act of storytelling as experienced by the reader.

On the night of their father's second marriage, to Pierette, Jacques and Paul procure a prostitute, in an attempt to become 'real men' by asserting their (hetero)sexuality. It is at this point in the story that the narrative perspective changes. Previously, the narrative voice has appeared distant and reflective because Jacques is drawing on his childhood memories in the fictional present, as an adult. However, in an instant, the point of focalisation changes, the story is submerged into the past, and the narrative voice becomes that of the child Jacques. Lying in their bedroom Jacques announces to Paul that 'I'm going down, . . . to buy us a woman' (57). Once away from his brother and on the street a nervous Jacques loses this dominant voice and, encountering a group of women, stands 'speechless but earnest' (58). Without a voice, or more accurately, with a voice trapped inside his body, the physical body is foregrounded as the women smile and make 'almost identical movements of their hips' (59). Compensating for his failure to perform adequately through speech, the women's bodies become objects to Jacques. Given his earlier assertion of masculine sexual dominance, it is interesting that only Paul has sex with the prostitute, Bettina. Notably, it is following Paul's sexual encounter with Bettina that Jacques refers to Paul as 'the man' (62).

The psychological impact of Jacques' failure to perform sexually is highlighted at the end of the story when he reveals that, in periods of depression, he is haunted by the thoughts of 'Paul making love to Bettina' (62). By connecting Jacques' depression in later life with his adolescent inability to perform sexually, Tremain reveals the powerful interconnection between (hetero)sexuality and gender identity. 'Wedding Night' demonstrates how the struggle to conform to hegemonic masculinity and maintain a sense of a coherent identity is nowhere 'more acute than in the emerging sexuality of boys' (Rutherford 1988: 27). Jacques' emotional response to this sexual encounter exposes one of the problems with the social dominance and cultural normalisation of hegemonic masculinity, in that those who do not achieve it (at the juncture at which boys are supposed to become men) are made to feel inadequate. As such, the predominance of a single hegemonic masculinity overlooks the existence of masculinities. Despite narrating this story as an older, married man, Jacques remains haunted by his earlier failure. The past and the present intersect in this story in order to realise the ways in which sexuality defines a man's sense of his own masculinity. Narrative voice is central to the representation of masculinity offered in this story. While Jacques loses his voice in front of the prostitutes, it is in the act of retelling his story that he asserts his authority by claiming control over his life story.

'The Priest and the Parrot', the opening story of Victoria Hislop's collection *The Last Dance and Other Stories* (2012), features Stavros, a 'spiritual shepherd' of a 'parish comprising a village of no more than four hundred' (3). The first line illuminates the importance of sexuality to understanding Stavros' character and identity: 'Stavros had chosen to be celibate' (ibid.). The fact that this is a 'choice' on his part is clarified by a comparison to all of the other priests that Stavros knew, who were married and had children. Thus, Stavros' dedication to 'the Virgin Mary, the Mother of God' (ibid.) is firmly positioned as a 'free choice', unconstrained by religious doctrine or rulings. Despite his tendency to shy 'away from any contact that might be misconstrued as friendship' (ibid.), Stavros 'benefited from the love and adoration of the local women' (5) who bring him food almost every day. Whenever any of the women in the village were ill 'he would mix them a hot, sweet, comforting potion' (4), and as a result, by the end of his first year in the village the many widows who lived there had decided he had 'remarkable powers' (ibid.).

When an epidemic breaks out at the local school the teacher, Katerina Manakis, is taken ill. After she has been treated by the doctor for ten days, Stavros visits her to give her some of his potion. He visits each day for a week thereafter and prays silently at her bedside. As she recovers, 'Katerina Manakis was sad when she realised that she would no longer hear Papa Stavros' business-like tap on her door' (6). Later, sitting with the elderly ladies from the village, Katerina notices how they 'flush slightly whenever the priest approached' and, with horror, she realises that she does the same (8). While the widows announce how handsome the priest is, Katerina remains silent, 'fondly remembering' the hours she spent with him. For the elder women of the village their status as widows protects them from judgement when it comes to demonstrating affection for the priest; yet the same amorous affection on the part of Katerina provoke feelings of guilt and shame in the younger woman. However, it is not only Katerina that is affected by her encounter with Stavros, as 'in the past few weeks he had been distracted' (10) and he confides in his parrot, Niko, how he cannot stop thinking of Katerina. With a loss of appetite and suffering from insomnia, Stavros finds himself 'pursued by visions of the young teacher and constantly mutter[ing] in his sleep' (ibid.) before waking himself (and Niko) in the morning by calling out her name. Upon visiting the priest to leave him some food, Katerina hears the parrot calling her name and she enters the house. Discovered inside the house by Stavros, she is 'mortified' and frantically explains how she had heard her name being called. Subsequently, it is Stavros who is left trying to find the words to explain to Katerina why the parrot was calling her name, but before he has the chance she 'had already slipped away' (12).

In this brief moment, when Katerina is in his home, Stavros is 'smiling broadly' and realises he felt 'better than I've ever felt before' (ibid.). Despite the initial proclamation that Stavros has freely chosen a life of celibacy at the opening of the story, his growing affection for Katerina undermines this proclamation. Seemingly, a brief moment can have profound consequences and challenge assumed roles and identities. Although Stavros begins to hurry after Katerina he swiftly stops himself, insisting instead: 'I'll return her dish tomorrow' (13). On the one hand these words suggest Stavros has managed to overcome his inability to communicate with the young woman, rectifying his earlier silence when confronted with her presence. However, the fact that these words are spoken directly to his parrot suggests that the priest is still unable to cross the boundary formed by his vow of celibacy and is instead trapped in a state of silent emotional turmoil. It is pertinent that the reason for Katerina being in the house is because of Niko: he is the one who speaks her name, thus inviting her inside. Indeed, the parrot acts as a counterbalance to the priest in this story and, despite his limited language skills, the fact he dares actually to speak Katerina's name in her presence, when the priest does not, illuminates the stranglehold Stavros is in due to religious expectations. The ending of the story signals the future, as Stavros defers action until tomorrow. In actuality, in this final scene it is Niko who is empowered with the ability to act, as he 'puffed out his bright turquoise feathers' (ibid.). In this story it seems that heterosexual desire is a defining feature of masculine identity and one which is revealed to have profound effects on behaviour, character and the actions of individuals. In all of these stories the influence of heterosexuality, in informing masculine identity, is abundantly clear, which in turn reinforces the ongoing interdependence of gender, sex and sexuality in informing sociocultural understandings of identity.

Gender blending? Margaret Thatcher and female masculinity

In my earlier discussion of Tremain's story 'Loves Me, Loves Me Not' I reflected on the ways in which this story engages with the landscape of 1980s Britain through a fleeting reference to Margaret Thatcher. Later in the story, Frank makes a second reference to Thatcher, once again commenting on her appearance. This time 'he turned on the TV and saw Mrs Thatcher, wearing her Pacific blue, addressing some awesome gathering, against a billowing blue backdrop. All the men on the podium behind her were smiling anguished smiles, as though at some adored and disdainful lover' (157). The juxtaposition of 'adored' with 'disdainful' in this passage illuminates the contradictory feelings expressed towards Thatcher, and these emotions also summarise Frank's complex feelings towards Marie. A significant element of Thatcher's ambivalence arises from her gendered identity. As Mark Hussey (2004) states, in a description through which he performs his own version of hegemonic masculinity, Thatcher

> drew her values from a middlebrow culture of exclusive masculinity that maintained the importance of a Victorian separation of spheres in which her own foray into public life could be justified by the attitude that she was surrounded by ninnies, 'wets' as she termed them, who could not shape up to their masculine responsibilities and so had to be rescued by a 'nanny', a schoolmarm. (17)

As the first female prime minister of Britain, Thatcher 'rejected ideas of gender significance or normative gendered behaviour' (Harmes 2013: 56). However, at the same time Thatcher consciously usurped masculine qualities while purposefully drawing attention 'to her appearance and acknowledg[ing] that it was culturally coded' (ibid.). Thus, in positioning herself as the 'schoolmarm' figure that the country needed in order to lead the 'wets', she exploited both masculinity and femininity in her leadership of the country.

The 'gender blending' of Thatcher is nowhere more apparent than in her self-proclaimed identity as an 'Iron Lady'. Marcus Harmes (2013) notes, 'the attributes of iron . . . are traditionally ascribed with male qualities' (57). Thus, the 'Iron Lady' equates with the image of a 'Masculine Lady'. However, the phrase contains wider implications as it resonates with phrases such as the 'Iron Maiden' and the 'Iron Curtain'. The 'Iron Maiden', the well-known example being the 'Iron Maiden of Nuremberg', destroyed in the Second World War, 'was supposedly the image of a woman large enough to hold a man and lined with spikes' (Mannix 2014: 74). Similarly, the 'Iron Curtain' is a term used to describe the fortified boundary that divided Europe after the Second World War, and symbolises the ideological conflict that split Europe as the Soviet Union and its satellite states attempted to disconnect themselves from the West. With the end of the Cold War in 1991, the 'Iron Curtain' was a particularly poignant phrase in the Thatcher era. Thus, the 'Iron Lady' subtly invokes weapons of torture and the politics of war, both discourses being traditionally associated with masculinity and male power.

Similar imagery resides in Hilary Mantel's story 'The Assassination of Margaret Thatcher: August 6th 1983'. While Tremain's narratives allude or make passing reference to Thatcher, Mantel's story, as the title indicates, is entirely focused on this political figure. The story from which the short story collection (2014) takes its name, 'The Assassination of Margaret Thatcher' provoked public outcry when it was first published, and this media 'frenzy' is an interesting textual afterlife of the narrative I will reflect on shortly. The story itself is set in Windsor and sees an unwitting resident admit a stranger into her home; he reveals how he wants to 'get a clear view' of Thatcher leaving the hospital across the road (217). There is a double entendre as this raises the question of 'seeing' and thereby 'knowing' who Margaret Thatcher was, while his desire to see her reflects a frustration of never being able to understand fully her identity and, suggestively, politics. Initially mistaking him for a plumber, the resident then assumes that this stranger is perhaps a photographer hoping to capture a clear image of Thatcher's departure from the hospital. However, there is a dark humour which cuts through the narrative as the title has already revealed to the reader the grim intentions of this stranger; the resident's naivety and lack of awareness place the reader in a privileged position and heighten the reader's anticipation of narrative closure, which becomes synonymous with the expectation of revelation.

However, it is the pointed descriptions and character 'assassinations' of Thatcher in the story which are particularly interesting in the context of masculinity politics. After being in the company of the IRA assassin, the resident and narrative voice (the story is her retelling of events to an implied listener) declares: 'It's the fake femininity I can't stand, and the counterfeit voice', before concluding her tirade with, 'why does she need an eye operation? Is it because she can't cry?' (220). Such statements imply that Thatcher is a man (as determined by sociocultural stereotypes of sex and gender) and that in fact it is her femininity which is performed. Her inability to cry is not a character strength but a weakness, as it assumes she therefore cannot be a woman. Interestingly, this emphasises the delicate relations between masculinity and femininity in which they are placed in stringent opposition and used to define one another mutually. This is strengthened later in the story: 'there's not a tear in her ... she lives on the fumes of whisky and the iron in the blood of her prey' (232). Here it is not merely the connotations of whisky and iron which imply masculinity; this is furthered by an animalistic and violent implication behind the image of Thatcher consuming her 'prey'. With the handbag she carries 'slung like a shield' (242) on her arm throughout, in this narrative the description of Thatcher continually blurs the boundaries between a female body/masculinity and male body/femininity. Poignantly, through such representation, the story illuminates the continuing tendency to equate sex, gender and sexuality, in turn upholding a traditional heteropatriarchal norm.

Such an understanding of Thatcher's gender identity chimes with Judith Halberstam's *Female Masculinity* (1998), a text Halberstam hopes will 'form just one part of a cultural onslaught on the privileged reservation of masculinity for men' (xii). She argues that 'female masculinity actually affords us a glimpse of how masculinity is constructed as masculinity' (1). Further, Halberstam contends that 'the very existence of masculine women forces us to ask why the bond between men and masculinity has remained relatively secure despite the continuous assaults made by feminists, gays, lesbians, and gender-queers on the naturalness of gender' (45). As a public figure, then, Thatcher exemplifies this notion of female masculinity and troubles the accepted affiliation of masculinity with the male body. Accordingly, her prominence in the public domain contributes to an unsettling of traditional gender binary divisions because her performance of masculinity, as and when it is required, challenges the assumption that masculinity is the preserve of men.

While much of the media attention surrounding Mantel's collection's publication (and the book's inclusion on the BBC's 'Book at Bedtime' programme) criticised Mantel's personal views (as the author of the text) on Thatcher's politics, a close reading of the story itself reveals the ways in which the text seeks to trouble the accepted conflation of Thatcher's personal and political identity. In a tense exchange, the assassin turns to the resident and makes it clear why he is carrying out the assassination: 'It's not about her handbag. It's not about her hairdo. It's about Ireland' (229). The political actions of Thatcher are firmly identified as the motivation behind the assassin's actions. This is reinforced by the framing of the story, which opens with a prologue featuring Thatcher on the doorstep of 10 Downing Street, reporting to the world that the Falklands had been recaptured and therefore people should 'rejoice' (206), and concludes with the assassin's words: 'Fucking rejoice' (242). The echoes that ring out at the end of the story ensure that the narrative is framed by the political context. Despite all of the personal criticism of Thatcher, and the gendered discussions that prevail throughout the story, ultimately, the narrative is shaped by a critique of her politics. Arguably this acts as a rebuttal to those negative judgements of Thatcher based on her as a person, or more pertinently, as a woman. While invoking and certainly acknowledging the portrayal of Thatcher's female masculinity, the story questions the relevance of such gendered attacks and instead places the emphasis back on Thatcher's politics.

The intersection between the personal and political arenas transcends this historical moment of Thatcher's time in power as the publication of the short story reignites gendered debates, which, on this occasion, tread the line between the author's personal politics and the textual representation. Thus, Mantel's contemporary short story also provides insight into the way in which, historically, gender and power play a part in representation. Turning to the narrative surrounding Mantel and the response to her story in the media, the language and register are particularly noteworthy. For example, a piece published in the *Daily Mail* in September 2014 takes a fairly neutral tone and refers to the author as 'Dame Hilary Mantel', thereby giving her the full title she has been awarded in recognition of her literary achievements. Conversely, in the *Mail on Sunday* in December 2014 the author is condescendingly named as 'Ms Mantel', and in this more scathing and negative article the author herself is undermined through the language used to introduce her. Finally, the fact that, across a range of articles discussing the author and the short story, the most often quoted statement comes from Lord Tebbit, declaring it a 'sick book' written by a 'sick mind' (Kelly 2014: n. p.), underlines the way in which a textual portrayal has morphed into a personal attack on the author in the present. Crucially, the 'sickness' which characterises the text and the author, for Lord Tebbit, chimes with Victorian depictions of women as hysterical and/or sick when their behaviour goes against patriarchal standards and social norms.

Finally, while my reading is purely based on the short story as a text, this reading is challenged by taking into account Mantel's statements to the media about Thatcher. In an interview with Isaac Chotiner (2014), Mantel refers to Thatcher as a 'male impersonator'. Clarifying this statement, Mantel adds: 'And in order to successfully impersonate men, the woman launched a war [*laughs*].' The laughter at the end of this remark underlines the irony that Mantel identifies at the heart of *her* interpretation of Thatcher. However, while my own personal reading of the story interpreted the framing of the narrative and actions of the assassin as based on political action, not personal identity, Mantel's conflation of the two in this interview complicates my initial reading. Furthermore, this is particularly apparent in the space of a short story as, in its thirty-six pages, there is a much greater requirement on the part of the reader to make a decision for themselves with far less text to guide and inform that decision, compared to a longer narrative. Of course, while on the one hand this empowers the reader to take from the text what she feels most important, a significant limitation, particularly when discussing narratives that are informed by feminist, gender and/or sexual politics, is that the political impetus and ability of the story to act as a political vehicle are arguably diminished and thus more reliant on the reader's politics.

Reflecting on the figure of Thatcher, Mantel discloses that much of the interest in writing a story about her was because of a desire to examine 'why she did arouse such a visceral passion in so many people' (Bentley and Duell, 2014: n. p.). In the shifting perceptions of Thatcher, the 'total construct' (Chotiner 2014: n. p.), from the milk-snatcher and Iron Lady through to the shopkeeper's daughter who would get the nation's accounts in order, the response to her has become a narrative all of its own. In writing a story set in, albeit recent, history ('August 6th 1983'), Mantel presents a particular vision of Thatcher at this point in history, but also challenges the reader to respond to this depiction in the present. Crucially, the political context of the contemporary has a direct impact on the reception of the story at the point of publication as, with the recent death of Thatcher, the reimagining was viewed, by some, as being even more distasteful. The desire to capture the often troubling and ambiguous nature of response, representation and identity in literature, which Mantel articulates here, reminds us of the important role literature plays in understanding society, culture and politics. Equally, as the understandings of Thatcher's identity have continued to morph, literature serves as a reminder that the politics of masculinity and, especially, feminism is never a simple, linear narrative of progress or regression; instead the flux and dialogue of discourses across time and space should always be remembered.

In conclusion, the conceptualisation of female masculinity offers one means of reconsidering the importance of masculinity as a gendered identity and its relationship with the female body. However, as Halberstam argues, it is also important to interrogate the politics of masculinity because 'it so often expresses itself through the desire to destroy others, often women' (1998: 274). Thus, exploring the manifestations, guises and implications of masculinity helps in unravelling the ways and means through which gendered discourses are upheld. Importantly, as with feminism, it is not simply a narrative of linearity – of either progress or demise – but instead it is vital to recognise that masculinity is a sociocultural construct central to the hierarchical and gendered power relations at the heart of society. What these short stories have all illuminated is the fact that, regardless of which period of history they speak from or seek to represent, there is a commonality in the attempt to portray the ways in which masculinity is, and always has been, a sociocultural construct.

In 'Unmaking: Men and Masculinity in Feminist Theory' (2002), Robyn Weigman discusses the differing ways in which masculinity has been an important element of contemporary feminisms, from the second wave's desire to 'remove the generic fallacy, to unveil masculinity as a particularized ontology linked to a normative rendering of a male body' (34), which often resulted in a critique of patriarchy and the ensuing oppression of women, through to 'how feminism's critical interrogations of gender have productively disassembled the normative cultural discourse that weds masculinity to men and thinks about women only in the register of the feminine' (33). While trying to avoid developing a narrative of progress here, Weigman's work does emphasise the relevance of masculinity politics to a discussion of contemporary feminisms. Put another way, it is not merely a development of a recent 'wave' of feminism. The invocation of history in order to critique masculinity, in particular, emphasises the way in which masculinity, as a key site of identity politics, is not a 'new' idea. As the analysis of short stories throughout this chapter has demonstrated, 'masculinity [is] a site for the complex negotiation of feminism's own understanding of identities, bodies, and both political and erotic desire' to play out (ibid.).

Chapter 5

Sexuality

In 2010 there was a plethora of publications debating the current position of contemporary feminism, including Kat Banyard's *The Equality Illusion*, Natasha Walter's *Living Dolls*, and Catherine Redfern and Kristin Aune's *Reclaiming the F Word*. At the heart of these texts, and the feminist politics with which they engage, reside women's bodies and the politics of sexuality, choice and agency. Also in this year, in the *Guardian* Charlotte Raven considered 'how the "new feminism" went wrong', and Kira Cochrane reported that 'feminism is not finished'.[1] Evident in all of these texts is a commentary that responds to a particular feminist zeitgeist, which Raven summarises thus: 'in the 90s – I wince to recall it – when women themselves fell in with the view that feminism was unglamorous and inhibiting' (2010: n. p.). Raven's statement alludes to the times when, amidst the clamour of 1990s 'girl power', as exemplified by the Spice Girls, *The Girlie Show* on Channel Four and even Naomi Wolf's *Fire with Fire*, second-wave feminist politics was rebuked as a necessity of the past, as women's liberation and equality, it was suggested, had been achieved. In many of these notably post-feminist discussions, women's sexual liberation is used as evidence of feminism's success and thereby invoked in order to justify why we are post-feminist now. Sexuality, then, is an important marker in the overarching narrative of feminism and has often been used to exemplify discourses of both feminism's success (and therefore redundancy) and its failure (and therefore necessity). While the 'sex wars' played a key role in feminist debate of the 1970s, in the twenty-first century once again women's sexuality re-emerges at the forefront of feminist discourses. It is unsurprising, then, that since the turn of the millennium there has been a plethora of short stories which engage with the topic of women's sexuality and scrutinise the implications of this in propagating a productive feminist politics.

After some initial reflection on the political significance of sexuality, this chapter engages with how sexuality has been conceptualised and continually repositioned by women short story writers. The section on '"Transgressive" female sexuality' examines sexuality as a site of political resistance for women, and considers how gender and sexual 'norms' shape understandings and responses to female sexuality. Developing this discussion, the notion of choice is central to contemporary feminist debates, and by focusing on the work of Michèle Roberts and Kalbinder Kaur I consider how 'choice' is perceived in relation to women's sexuality, and what this means in different cultural contexts. Finally, this chapter turns to questions of how the politics of queer theory interact with feminisms via the locus of sexuality in the writings of Jackie Kay and Ali Smith, before turning to Janice Galloway's story 'We're Not in This Together' to reflect on the ever-shifting negotiation of feminist politics and female sexuality. Through this chapter's own short story, then, I continually return to the relevance of sexuality for feminism, while illuminating the ways in which sexuality enables feminist critique of wider sociocultural discourses.

In recent years there has been increased critical attention paid to the politics of sexuality, and a notable aspect of this work has focused on the sexualisation of women's bodies. Rosalind Gill's 'The Sexualisation of Culture?' (2012) succinctly summarises this phenomenon:

> The last decade has seen a significant development of interest in what has become known variously as 'the rise of porno chic', the 'pornification' of society or the 'sexualisation of culture' – namely the perception that Western societies are becoming increasingly saturated by representations of sex. What makes the contemporary moment different from previous waves of interest in the sex industry and pornography is the concern with practices and representations that are understood as becoming increasingly normalised, widely dispersed and mainstreamed. (483)

Gill's appraisal is significant in that it establishes a link between increasing representations of sex, a cultural fascination with sexuality and this concept of 'normalisation'. For Gill, the contemporary moment is unique in the relationship it propagates between sex, sexuality and culture. As with the majority of stories of feminism, the notion of waves is invoked in Gill's appraisal in order to perpetuate a narrative of difference. Thus, the contemporary era is ambivalent with regard to how sexuality is positioned. It is viewed as a turning backwards of feminism, a regression; yet it is also embraced as empowering, a turning point to a more feminist sexual future.

Notions of choice and agency have increasingly been invoked in the context of women's sexuality as critics have sought to problematise the simplistic narratives of women's sexual liberation and thus the redundancy of feminism. Eva Chen (2013) notes how the terms 'choice', 'freedom' and 'agency' have been 'liberally appropriated in recent years', especially in the context of women's cultural genres such as chick lit, chick flicks and beauty advertisements (440). However, such unquestioning endorsement of sexuality is problematic because 'while these terms suggest a feminist legacy, they are used not to advance the feminist cause, but to celebrate a rhetoric of individual choice and freedom which often is measured in terms of commodity consumption' (ibid.). This line of argument is an extension of Gill's work on neoliberalism, culture and subjectivity in the context of post(-)feminism, in which she critiques the notions of subjectification and objectification and highlights how in this discourse 'women are presented as not seeking men's approval but as *pleasing themselves*, and, in so doing, they just happen to win men's admiration' (437). The driving force of Gill's analysis leads to one clear conclusion: cultural influence needs to be recognised and it is crucial that all critical engagements with gender politics become involved with 'the complex ways in which we are all entangled in the relation between culture and subjectivity' (443). By taking such an approach it may be possible to avoid perpetuating the sweeping generalisations which result in simplistic binary conclusions of either sexually liberated or sexually objectified.

Choice, then, is a reoccurring feature throughout this chapter, as I discuss short stories which scrutinise women's sexuality from a variety of perspectives and which often illuminate the wider context in which such choices are made. After all, 'just looking at the final choice that was made tells us nothing about how much a woman actually struggled to balance competing imperatives, such as gender equality and sexual pleasure' (Snyder-Hall 2010: 256). Discussing the limits of choice, Shelley Budgeon (2011) questions 'the role that choice is playing in the constitution of emerging gendered subjectivities', and crucially, whether this choice does actually result in women's autonomy (131). Thus, in the context of women's short story writing it is important to acknowledge the story as put forward by the narrative voice, but also to scrutinise the contextual details and descriptions which may complicate the initial narrative. Equally, with the short story's gaps and ambiguities, the tendency to say less rather than more, the reader's own politics arguably exerts great influence in the interpretation of the text's politics.

'Transgressive' female sexuality

Victoria Hislop's 'One Cretan Evening' (2012), set in a village at a time of year when all the tourists have departed, is a commentary on how sexuality can often influence the perceptions and representation of women. The story sees a strange man arrive in a taxi and enter the house of Maria Makrakis, but explains 'no one stirred' in the village as 'they did not feel protective towards it. The concern was no greater than it had been for the woman who lived there' (89). The only person who notices his arrival is Despina, the owner of the village *kafenion* (café). Immediately, the story establishes Maria as a social outcast, raising questions in the reader's mind as to what this woman might have done to deserve such status. Later, when the stranger enters Despina's bar, in a brief exchange, the truth about the former resident – a 'spinster' and 'object of suspicion and derision' (89) – is revealed. Her name was not Maria Makrakis but Sofia Taraviras. While the children of the town were told never to go near her house, because she was a 'witch' (91), this stranger, her brother, reveals that actually 'at the age of sixteen she had a child' and was sent away by her family (ibid.). He adds: 'she was just a woman who made a single mistake. She paid a high price for it, I think' (ibid.). In this moment of realisation Despina reflects on the way that she and the entire community treated this woman, and 'she felt the force of this community's shame' because 'they had never given her a chance' (92). In an act of repentance for this sin, early the next evening Despina and all the men 'who rarely stirred from the *kafenion* went to say prayers for the woman who had died alone' (ibid.). 'One Cretan Evening' raises questions as to how 'a single mistake' can taint a woman's life and result in social ostracism. Indeed, through expulsion from her own identity as 'Sofia', 'One Cretan Evening' critiques the influence that sexuality can have over a woman's body, and indeed life. Over her lifetime Maria/Sofia is positioned as everything from a 'slut' to 'spinster' or 'witch'. All of these labels imply something negative, or non-normative, about her sexual and marital status and carry a sense of judgement. Seemingly, this story challenges the fact that deviating from the traditional route of marriage followed by bearing children is viewed as socially transgressive. With Despina's sympathetic narration the reader is coerced into empathising with Maria/Sofia, and subsequently into reflecting critically on societal norms.

Similarly, Sarah Hall's 'The Beautiful Indifference' (2011) highlights how individuals are socially conditioned to measure and judge their own behaviour through comparisons to one another.

The story's narrator recalls how she recently confided in her friend how she and her lover 'were perfectly capable of having conversations . . . they were not capable of corralling the animal necessity of ruining each other first' (43). Poignantly, her friend, who is busy feeding her child, responds negatively to this confession, which causes the protagonist to reflect on how 'notes of disapproval' had recently taken hold of her friends' responses to this relationship. Their disapproval causes her to question whether 'she was not entitled to the sex after all' (45). In contrast to the increasing disapproval of her female friends, the narrator reveals how men had been 'unnerved' by her sexual behaviour because 'she was not keeping the natural order of things' (ibid.). Again, it is following a conversation with male friends that 'she was left with the dual feeling of being both transgressor and specialist' (ibid.). Yet again it is through the formalistic feature of combining internal and external perspectives in this story that a subtle critique emerges. Subsequently, such critique provokes questions as to the ways in which sexuality, sexual identity and behaviour are mediated by the expectations and 'norms' of society and culture.

The politics of choice also come to bear in the conversation with the female friend, who comments that: 'Anyway. Isn't it what you want, at the moment? Being with him means you can defer all the rest' (44). The sentiment that her casual sexual relationship with the lover is a means of escaping responsibility, 'the hard stuff' like having children (ibid.), emphasises the way in which sexuality interacts with issues of motherhood and women's domestic roles. Seemingly, sexual activity is deemed as being an element of a woman's life prior to the more 'serious' commitments of being a wife and mother. At this stage in her life, at this particular age, having a casual sexual relationship is viewed as non-normative and being a means of rejecting these traditional patterns of life development. The tendency to associate sexuality with the young female body is perceptible here. As the narrator realises later, 'Children? Her friends now assumed what her position was' (49). The word 'assumed' is telling; after all, it is merely assumptions on the part of her friends (who metonymically signify society) which form the basis of such judgements. More broadly, this tension between having a lover versus settling down with children signals a conflict between living in and for the moment against the prioritisation of a longer life trajectory in which fulfilment is measured by cohabitation and procreation. In 'The Beautiful Indifference' the pleasure of experience is foregrounded and there is a beauty in the moment itself through intimacy, pleasure and sexual fulfilment. Thus, the narrative commentary complicates the temporal trajectory often aligned with womanhood and disrupts the linear tendencies which suggest that at a particular age a woman's sexual relationship or her social responsibilities should be of a certain makeup. The indifference projected by the narrator's friends reflects the sentiment of judgement inherent in their responses, while the protagonist's indifference to societal expectations contains a beautiful resonance of its own.

The narrative device of two friends conversing is also used by Nicola Barker in her story 'Skin' (2003). Set in a local pub, it sees Jane and Stephanie meeting after work. With Stephanie already late, Jane reads a book, 'an early Jilly Cooper' (82), and the erotic connotations of this book foreshadow Stephanie's sexual encounter at work, which she is about to reveal to Jane. At work that day (a John Lewis Department Store) Stephanie sees two men 'skins, really tall in puffy green jackets and tight, short jeans and boots' (86), and she suddenly notices one of them shoplifting. However, when she confronts this man she is overcome by 'that feeling . . . when everything feels sort of, strong' (ibid.). Struggling to articulate her emotions, she eventually confesses to kissing the man and to having sex with him subsequently (90). Reflecting on her experience, Stephanie states: 'I've never done anything like this before. It was strange, as though . . . like a compulsion. Inevitable. Dangerous but compulsive. I don't know. I can't understand it myself' (ibid.). The immediacy of narration here illuminates the conflict Stephanie is battling with: the impulsive sexual encounter with a stranger sits uncomfortably alongside her status as a woman in a long-term relationship with boyfriend Chris. Significantly, the narrative device of confessional conversation with best friend Jane positions the reader as a witness. As a result, the reader is forced to process this information at the same time as the textual figure of Jane, thereby creating a sense of affiliation between character and reader.

The position of the reader in relation to the two characters is significant because it is through the awareness of both women's reactions to the situation that the reader's response comes into play. Jane's reaction is uncompromising:

Jane was devastated. She looked at Stephanie and couldn't understand her, she couldn't contain what she had done in the relevant compartments of her brain. She wondered whether Stephanie was now a slag. A slut. Finally she said, 'You behaved like a slut, with some big, ugly skinhead.' (90)

The language here of 'compartments' and 'contain' emphasises the fact that, in Jane's mind, Stephanie's behaviour represents an act of social transgression: she has burst out of the boxes (or departments of the store, if we return to the story's setting) and acted in a sexually deviant manner. Indeed, this behaviour, in Jane's mind, justifies the classification of Stephanie as 'slut', and she uses this language in an attempt to shame her for her actions. However, Stephanie simply shrugs and responds: 'If you mean "slut" in a good way, then yes, I did' (ibid.). The language of this exchange taps into recent feminist activism, such as 'SlutWalk'. The campaign outlines how: 'SlutWalk wants justice for the thousands of rape survivors who were told by the police and courts that they were dressed too provocatively' (Cardiff 2012: n. p.). This deployment of the derogatory term 'slut' as a means of reclaiming public space and women's bodies illuminates a tension in contemporary usage of the term and broader understandings of women's sexuality. The ambivalence in the term, which is both derogatory and affirmative for women, is symbolic of the conflicting tension inherent in discourses of women's sexuality.

Through this exchange, 'Skin' engages with post-feminist debates about women's sexual agency and choice and replicates one of the central tensions to inform the debate in the twenty-first century. It is in this post-feminist context that the phrase 'do-me feminist' was first coined, by Tad Friend (1994) in the men's magazine *Esquire*, and it refers to a woman who promotes individualism over community and often outwardly rejects the sisterly values proffered by second-wave feminists. As Kellie Bean (2007) states, the 'Do-Me feminist presents herself as a provocative political player, a vixen with a whip and a graduate degree', and she attempts to 'achieve social parity through a sexualised submission not only to male fantasy, but to male aggression' (1). As such, 'do-me feminism' is aligned with post-feminist discourses, as it positions society beyond the need for a feminism based on social justice and a collective women's movement. Thus, the sexual activity of Stephanie in 'Skin', and of the narrator of Hall's 'The Beautiful Indifference', can be understood as both speaking to these contemporary issues and offering another means of scrutinising the consequences of such gender discourses for women's bodies and everyday lives.

Post(-)feminisms, sexuality and choice

The focus on sex as an erotic act and on sexual politics is not new with the emergence of post(-)feminist debate. However, in recent years, critics such as Rosalind Gill have scrutinised sexuality in relation to neoliberal discourses and the notion of 'choice'. Thus, while sexuality is another theme upon which feminism has recurrently debated, the notion of choice and what is meant by 'free choice' is an increasing point of focus and one that is pivotal to my discussion here. Sexuality once again reminds us that the development of feminist thought cannot be confined to linear understandings of knowledge. In *Straight Sex* (1994), Lynne Segal reflects on the 1960s milieu and her experiences of the sexual liberation movement. However, she also considers how this period caused women to equate sex with liberation and, subsequently, provoked women into seeking liberated sex (30). By comparison, reflecting on the contemporary context, Angela McRobbie argues that, in a post-feminist era (her usage), there is an

> uncritical relation to the dominant, commercially produced, sexual representations that actively invoke hostility to assumed feminist positions from the past in order to endorse a new regime of sexual meanings based on female consent, equality, participation, and pleasure, free of politics. (34)

This 'uncritical' and therefore normalised assumptions that this is an age in which women can have sex 'free of politics' is problematic. Instead, Gill argues, there is a need to listen to women's stories about their personal choices and 'to contextualise these stories, to situate them, to look at their patterns and variability, to examine their silences and exclusions, and, above all, to locate them in a wider context' (2007: 77). At the heart of contemporary feminist debates about sexuality, therefore, is the question of choice and, in particular, how we understand the implications of 'free choice' in a neoliberal era.

In her 2010 collection *Mud: Stories of Sex and Love*, Michèle Roberts engages directly with the approach to sexuality that is generally categorised as 'post-feminist', and she critiques this 'new regime of sexual meaning based on female consent' by telling stories and situating them, 'their patterns and variability . . . in a wider context' (ibid.). As a result, sex is revealed to be always a choice that must be negotiated within a given set of socioeconomic and cultural parameters. As such, the politics of sexuality are located in the cultural and political moment of the stories' setting. In 'Colette Looks Back', the second story in the collection, Colette reminisces about growing up as 'a girlboy, a boygirl' (12), a description that challenges the essentialist and binary construction of gender. The entire story is narrated from one temporal moment and, through memory, it looks back upon Colette's life. Colette recollects her childhood romance with a local boy, Jean-Luc, and discusses her marriage to Willy, a 'stout, moustachioed, licentious, Parisian' (21). By juxtaposing these two relationships the story begins to encapsulate the tension between sexual politics and women's choice that resides within the short story collection. In positioning these two men as oppositional from the beginning of the narrative, Roberts asks the reader to choose for herself which man is the 'right choice' for Colette.

Jean-Luc is romanticised through his association with childhood and Colette's 'two thick plaits' (9) that wrap around him. This imagery continues as these young children run across meadows and in the barn 'lay on a bed of parched stalks covered with empty flour sacks' (10). On their first walk together, between their parental homes, Colette remembers how 'I didn't want our walk to end' (15), emphasising the sense of pleasure she feels in the company of Jean-Luc. Conversely, her relationship and subsequent marriage to Willy are depicted as a necessity. It is an unavoidable resolution and an 'escape route from my adored, all-possessing, country-goddess mother' (22). Crucially, this opposition of the two men is most pertinent with regard to sex.

Unbeknownst to Willy, the day of his marriage to Colette demarcates an intersect in which these two men are both in Colette's life. On the eve of her wedding Colette leaves her parental home to meet Jean-Luc in secret. What originates as a desire 'to say goodbye' (24) results in the pair making 'a new animal between us' (25), and Colette losing her virginity. Interestingly, the description of this scene is enshrouded in childhood innocence, as they 'played a new game of animals' and Colette unravels her plaited hair and wraps it around the pair of them. The idea of playing a game, here, reverberates with Roberts' earlier collection, *Playing Sardines*. The young lovers 'knew each other so well: no fumbling and no fuss', and Colette describes how a 'warmth concentrated and rose inside me, slowly bloomed like a gold flower' (25). While literally describing the sexual act, this phrase functions metaphorically to reinforce the desire and freedom of Colette as an equal partner within this sexual encounter.

Further, it is not only a temporal crossover that creates an intersection between these two men but Colette's own storytelling as she emphasises the comparison:

> Years later I'd write my girly porno for Willy, about my childhood in the village, the goings-on at school. I'd fake it to please him, I'd work up salacious details, to titillate him, earn my pin-money. Whereas with Jean-Luc it wasn't like that at all. (24)

The language of this passage is infiltrated by ideas of performativity and hypersexuality, hence the use of the words 'fake', 'titillate' and 'salacious', all in a bid to 'earn my pin-money'. Throughout the story Colette's marriage to Willy is positioned as a marriage of convenience rather than one of love, and here Colette's resentment of and compliance with the image of a dutiful wife emerge. Of course, this description also illuminates a social imperative behind Colette's actions because she must behave in this way to survive and earn her keep. The description of Colette and Willy's sexual relationship is in stark contrast to the earlier description of her relationship with Jean-Luc.

The implications of difference between the power dynamic of these two relationships is realised in the one passage that pays significant attention to Willy. Although, on the whole, Colette's narrative tends to minimise his significance, here he becomes a central figure:

> Willy of course believed, given my youth, that I remained an innocent little savage, that my family delivered me up to him as a virgin sacrifice, that I'd never seen a naked man before and certainly not one with an erection. On our wedding night he'd be the teacher and I his docile pupil. I'd prance for him on the stage of our bed, watch my shadow tremble on the wall, watch my dark shape waver as the shadow of his huge cock loomed beside me. Oh oh oh! Oh la la! Blah blah blah and so on and so forth. (22)

As with the previous extract, Colette positions herself as a passive participant in this scene. Reflecting on how Willy perceives her, she becomes the 'little savage', 'virgin sacrifice', 'docile pupil' and, as doubly emphasised here, a 'shadow'. The entire wedding night scene, which centres on the consummation of the marriage, locates Colette as passive. The fact that this narration is her perception of how Willy perceives her reflects the ways in which this patriarchal view of women's sexuality is internalised by Colette. Compared to the scene with Jean-Luc, in which his 'cock felt dry and warm', and Colette describes how she 'pulled him into me as he pushed inside me' (25), here the 'huge cock loomed' and is both repulsive and threatening. Unlike the physically balanced pushing and pulling with Jean-Luc, domination is implicit here. The closing sounds of this passage insert Colette's voice into the story, outside her general storytelling narration, as she mocks both Willy and the performative aspect of sex, revealing her pleasure and desire to be nothing but an act. Crucially, she is imbued with some power, here, as she manipulates patriarchal expectations of women's sexual pleasure through performance. The sarcasm and irony contained within this passage highlight how Colette reclaims some control via the act of storytelling, as she mocks the patriarchal demands placed upon her body.

'Colette Looks Back' offers a nuanced portrayal of women's sexual pleasure in which divergent representations of women's sexuality exist. While the narrative maintains that sex can be a pleasurable erotic act for women, it also highlights how it is not always a 'free choice' to be desired and enjoyed (by women). Reflecting on her relationship with Jean-Luc, Colette describes how, 'once we turned ten years old, however, new rules issued up from nowhere and constructed us, separated us' (10). As she realises that adults name and separate everything (14), she becomes 'mindful of how girls were supposed to behave' (15). In telling this story Roberts emphasises the wider context and the way in which women's sexual behaviour and desires are shaped by sociocultural demands.

Like 'Colette Looks Back', 'Honeymoon Blues' uses memory as a storytelling device, as the widowed Maud remembers how she and Tom had 'such appetite for each other, and for glasses of wine and grapes and peaches in bed, and for shared baths, and then for more sex' (89). Her memory of sex with Tom is bound up with an appetite for food, especially fruit. Thus, sex is represented as desirable, like the juicy sweetness of grapes and peaches. The sensuous potentials of food and sex merge in the story, reflecting Roberts's self-proclaimed fascination with the two themes. Returning to Venice, the location of their honeymoon, throughout the story Maud inhabits the same physical space that she previously shared with Tom. Significantly, sex is always mediated through memory and Maud's personal experience. Having arrived in Venice, Maud

> pads through the darkness, tugging her wheeled bag along. It glides behind her like a memory. Why not just abandon it? Buy different clothes here, assume a new identity, a disguise. Big dark glasses, red wig, leopardskin wrap, stiletto heels. Become transformed. No more a woman who suffers. No more loss no more hunger no more need. (81)

Maud's desire to become someone else reflects her sense of displacement after becoming a widow. The shedding of her old self, symbolically associated with the 'wheeled bag', acknowledges her need to abandon these old memories, to rid herself literally of 'baggage', to move forward. Where Tom's body once was, Maud now closes her arms 'on air. Her open mouth kisses nothing' (92). The loss of her husband is both an emotional and physical loss and results in her losing her appetite for food and sex. Accordingly, sex in 'Honeymoon Blues' is a positive experience for women and it does not involve their sexual exploitation or victimisation.

Contrasting with this portrayal of sex, 'Easy as ABC' offers a harrowing account of an adolescent girl forced into prostitution. The title invokes the innocence of childhood by alluding to children learning the alphabet. This juxtaposition heightens the tension between childhood innocence and sexual exploitation. This story, with its coarse and gritty language, implicitly alludes to contemporary narratives of prostitution that emerged around the millennium; exemplified by the now mainstream success of *Belle de Jour*.[2] With its depiction of sex work, *Belle de Jour* propagates 'free choice' and the 'do-me feminist' who 'rejects the concept of group oppression and subjugation and instead, she favors and valorizes individual effort and choice' (Genz 2010: 107). This post-feminist approach to sex/uality promotes female power and eschews the idea that patriarchal constructs still mediate women's choices. 'Easy as ABC' rebuts this post-feminist position, and the story reveals the power dynamics that regulate sex and women's ability to make autonomous choices, especially when their bodies are abused and they are sold (unwillingly) to others.

Nameless during the majority of the story, Eva, 'the girl', reveals how the 'friends of her cousins in the city', who appropriate the titles of 'auntie' and 'uncle', sell her into a life of prostitution (129). Her 'uncle' takes her to the airport and tells her 'he is sure I will do very well' (131). The oral aspect of this story makes it particularly powerful as the adolescent voice is given an innocence and perspective that suggest childhood naivety and vulnerability; at the same time it describes the sex acts she is forced to carry out with this body part. Opening with 'Nana, let me tell you a story', the narrative plays on the idea of a grandmother telling a granddaughter a bedtime story, or as the narrative opening of 'once upon a time' suggests, a fairytale, except the roles are reversed and the child narrates her own story to her dead grandmother (129). Yet this is not a fairytale of 'Sleeping Beauty' or 'Cinderella'; it is a young girl who *becomes* a doll as she 'sees the men enter her room, one by one. She sees the men enter her, one by one' (131).

This universality of the first person perspective is crucial to the portrayal of Eva, who could be anyone, as this passage suggests:

> In your places, children! I teach my dead their lessons for the day. E
> is for Eva and for Everyone, for Easy, for Empty, for Eternity. E is for
> the ecstasy the drug promises, E is for the end of anxiety, the end of
> terror. (134)

This is the only time an 'authentic' identity, that of Eva, is discussed
in an attempt to be reclaimed. As Eva says, 'I am Eva. Repeat after
me. Tell me you haven't forgotten me. Tell me I am still alive' (135).
Returning to this first quotation, the ambiguity of 'I teach my dead
their lessons' allows for a multiplicity of meanings to reside here. Is it
Eva's former selves or exterior selves, as represented by the Russian
doll analogy used throughout the narrative, talking back to a younger
version of her, or is it Eva forewarning other young girls of the potential danger in the hope they will avoid her fate? While the list of men's
names is given no great emphasis in the story, the narrative play on
the first letter of Eva's name in this passage creates a picture of her
as empty, anxious and terrified. At the same time, with a bitter irony,
the connection between Eva and the word 'Easy' corresponds to accu-
sations levelled against women of 'being Easy', a colloquialism for
sexual promiscuity.

As in 'Colette Looks Back', the language is bound up with performance:

> She nails on a fake name, a fake identity, she screws on a fake mouth
> that squeaks yes please screw me, fake wooden lips that wait two min-
> utes then squeak with pleasure ooh ooh ooh what a lovely screw thank
> you so much. (ibid.)

Eva, hidden behind her fake identities that she performs on demand,
becomes a doll as the words and sounds she subsequently speaks
are only for the satisfaction of men. Like a child she remembers her
manners, but the 'thank you so much' issues from an undercurrent
of subversive irony highlighting the distinct *lack* of pleasure experienced by Eva. Like the use of 'screw' meaning to screw objects
together *and* the colloquial meaning 'to have sex', language becomes
a double-edged sword which subverts expectations around sex and
pleasure.

Eva internalises patriarchal expectations about women's bodies
and, disturbingly, reproduces them in her storytelling as normalised
ideas. When talking about the men who 'ought to control themselves better but they can't', she continues that it's 'not their fault.

By nature they are bursting with seeds and juice and cum and it's the fault of the girls if they go too far' (135). Here, men are viewed as biologically programmed to behave in the manner they do. These lines reveal the harrowing consequences of women's internalisation of such discourses. In this respect, 'Easy as ABC' chimes with the work of the second-wave feminist Andrea Dworkin (1984) and her influential work on women's sexual subjugation. Dworkin argues that sexual 'crimes against women are ultimately viewed as expressions of male normalcy' (56), and that this is one consequence of patriarchy. Furthermore, by drawing on notions of girlhood, 'Easy as ABC' acts as a rejoinder to the discourse of girl power which developed in the 1990s. As a discourse, girl power 'operates to represent feminism as simultaneously self-evident and redundant, thereby silencing feminist voices through a discourse that appears as "pro-feminist"' (Griffin 2004: 33). Thus, through the use of the girl's voices in 'Easy as ABC', the reader is reminded that not every woman has access to the proclamations of 'girl power' as articulated by celebrities and those with social, cultural and economic capital.

What this selection of stories from *Mud* highlights is how the collection more broadly proffers a productive feminism in which the topic of sexuality is continually reworked. Roberts reconnects the thematic concerns often associated with post-feminism and the 'daughter generation' with earlier, second-wave feminist politics. Sisterhood is not a forgotten concept, but one that inhabits a different guise to its previous incarnation: this does not make it any less valuable. Importantly, the ability to publish a range of short stories together in the collection format facilitate this multifaceted engagement with sexual and feminist politics. *Mud*, as a collection, offers a reading of sex that seeks to complicate any singular, simplistic reading: it can be liberating and enjoyed by women but only when combined with the 'freedom to control our bodies and our lives' (Walker 2001: 80). Broadly speaking, although 'the sex wars of the 1980s divided feminists into those who framed sexuality primarily as a site of danger and oppression for women and those who saw sexuality more ambivalently, as also a site of pleasure and liberation' (Cossman 2004: 851), Roberts's short story narratives complicate this either/or binary. Thus, Roberts suggests that greater understanding of the concept of choice and the politics of sex within a contemporary patriarchal society is needed. This reappraisal would allow for women to be acknowledged as 'sexual subjects in their own right'

(Glick 2000: 20) while still recognising the sociocultural framework in which they exist.

Kalbinder Kaur's 'When English Girls Hold Hands', published in *Kin: New Fiction by Black & Asian Women* (2003), is narrated by an unnamed young woman who is acting as 'the tour guide' for her friend Milla (34). The women are currently in India, as suggested by the description of banyan trees and markets where mini Taj Mahals are located (ibid.). While the opening description paints a still-life portrait of these two women, sitting beneath a banyan tree with Milla writing a postcard, the cultural tensions at the heart of the narrative seep to the fore as the narrator, who assumes a sense of belonging and authority in this space, berates her friend 'for wearing shorts' (ibid.). The narrator has clearly lived in the United Kingdom for a considerable period of time, and her diasporic identity is fore-grounded in the story as in India, her 'homeland', with her white, English school friend Milla, she assumes a position of knowledge. In contrast to Milla, who, from the manner in which she behaves and the fact every experience is 'shiny to her, exotic' (35), is clearly a tourist, the narrator appears to claim an 'authentic' connection with the country which is demonstrated through her knowledge of the bus routes and geography of the city. However, the narrator's desire to assert this authority and maintain appearances for Milla is under-cut, and indeed undermined from the reader's perspectives, due to the narrator's unspoken thoughts which pervade the narrative: 'I should [know] but I don't, so I change the subject' (34), 'my speech is clumsy and in the end I speak English' (35). The narrator's iden-tity is constantly under scrutiny and in contention throughout the narrative. By taking up the position of a returned citizen, she uses Milla's position as the cultural 'Other' to assert her identity. On the one hand she appears to feel superior to Milla in this space in which her identity is mistaken by other women who say they knew her mother (due to the colour of her skin and an assumed familiarity), yet on the other hand a critique runs through the narrative which reveals her lack of knowledge about the country and therefore her own 'foreignness'.

Although the narrator celebrates this 'inbetweeness' – 'I am float-ing in the air between nations' (35) – her desire to act as the 'parent' to Milla during this trip has significant consequences. When the young women take a bus back to the hotel the narrator once again takes an assertive stance and insists that Milla sits between two village women while she stands in the overcrowded space, 'trying to slot in the best way I know how' (36). The desire to 'slot in' on the bus is symbolic of the narrator's attempts to fit in to the wider culture, but, as in other situations, this does not progress as anticipated. The narrator's knowledgeable position is cruelly undermined by the fact that on this journey she learns something new: 'I didn't know what a tweak was before, but now I do. It is about mechanics; a twist, not a stroke or an aim at arousal. He tweaked my right nipple' (37). The ensuing narrative describes how the narrator is sexually assaulted on the bus by 'a pair of thick black eyebrows, and heavy eyelashes, that's all I can see even though his whole face is there' (ibid.). The emphasis of the narrative falls on the response this provokes in the narrator and her internal thoughts: 'People have seen, and they are silently watching me, judging me. I am afraid they think I want this' (ibid.). What scares the narrator more than the assault itself is the response of those around her and her fear at being judged, replicating her experience throughout the trip more broadly.

As the women step off the bus the narrator cannot bring herself to look at Milla, who eventually breaks her silence and admits that she saw the assault. The narrator's response is poignant:

> I don't say that I had been protecting her, that knowing she was watching all that time makes me feel sick, that my sacrifice was obviously a mistake. I try to reassert my identity as expert, and say that I hadn't slapped him or made a scene, as I didn't want her to feel uneasy. I didn't say I was so shocked that I couldn't slap him, so shocked I couldn't speak as I bumped against his body, his hands on my hips holding me in place. (37–8)

Yet again the narrator is striving to maintain her 'identity as expert', and her fear of not behaving in the manner expected by others, by society and culture, fuels her fear of speaking out. However, this response also acknowledges the trauma of the experience itself, and, even though she cannot bring herself to admit it to others, her shock at the assault is revealed to the reader. With this description, an element of sympathy for the narrator is created, and the story attempts to illuminate the plethora of reasons why she did not speak out. It therefore offers a scathing critique of sexual assault and the ways in which women who are victims are often silenced, whether because of stigma, fear or any other reason. The assault itself happens quickly, and the narrative detailing it is only a page and half of the short story (which in total is four pages); thus there is a swiftness and immediacy

to the action. In this respect the reader is suddenly confronted with
the realities of the situation, which are made even more vivid given
that throughout the story the narrator has worked to create an aura
of authority, control and power which, here, is overturned.

Finally, Milla's response to her friend is telling and it reveals the
way in which this incident is perceived through a white, Western
lens:

> She tells me I was wise to keep quiet. She tells me that this is common
> here. With the crowded buses, and all. It's the heat. . . . this type of
> weather makes the locals obscene. She says there is nothing that we can
> do. She has heard of men murdering women for much less than a raised
> voice in countries like these. She tells me we'll get used to it, and squeezes
> me hand. (38)

Importantly, the narrative voice reinforces the difference between the
two women (as she sees it) with the repeated usage of the pronoun
'she' throughout this paragraph. Implicitly, Milla's opinion and view
are not the same as the narrator's. However, despite this, Milla's use
of 'we' still infiltrates this narrative and therefore the narrator cannot escape her conflation with Milla, the foreign 'other'. The sexual
assault, then, is still mediated through the lens of 'them' and 'us' and,
in this instance, the narrator's identity is further conflicted as her vic-
tim status seems to mean she can no longer be a citizen or part of this
'other' community. Furthermore, Milla's words of comfort to her
friend also offer a host of stereotypes, from the behaviour of local
men being put down to the weather (a 'scientific' fact she read in a
Western newspaper) to the phrasing of 'we'll get used to it', which
places the emphasis on women adjusting to the sociocultural context
because this is 'normal' behaviour. Importantly, this story, published
in 2003, tragically anticipates similar events which enraged a global
audience in 2012, when a young woman was raped and murdered on
a bus in Delhi. This was not the first time that such an atrocity had
taken place, but the media attention the incident received brought
the issue to the fore of Western consciousness, and there have been
similar incidents subsequently reported by the British media. Synergies between fact and fiction highlight the way in which literature,
the telling of stories, can act as a political vehicle and, while a work
of fiction, can in fact reflect the realities of everyday life. Kaur tells
an important story in 'When English Girls Hold hands', one which
is, sadly, a fabulation of a dark reality.

Queer love

Ali Smith is a contemporary writer whose work engages with gender and sexuality in diverse and subtle ways. While many critics have noted the playful, even postmodern, tendencies of Smith's writing (Germanà and Horton 2013: 6), there has also be a focus on the representation of sexuality. In discussing Smith's 2007 *Girl Meets Boy*, Kaye Mitchell (2013) uses the text to contribute to understandings of queer theory by considering how the motif of metamorphosis is 'a more productive, less fraught way of "queering" identity than the erstwhile critically dominant concept of performativity' (62). The relevance of queer theory is also prevalent in relation to Smith's short stories. In her first collection, *Free Love and Other Stories* (1995), the title story establishes this open-ended narrative trend. 'Free Love' is the story of an unnamed adolescent female and her first sexual encounter with a prostitute, while on holiday in Amsterdam with her friend, and later lover, Jackie. The narrative commences with 'the first time I ever made love with anyone it was with a prostitute in Amsterdam. I was eighteen and her name was Suzi' (1). This opening foregrounds the destabilisation of the linear, chronological plot of beginning, middle and end as the past tense positioning denotes that the 'end' (which itself is a sexual awakening in this story) has already occurred as the story opens. This in itself is not an unusual feature of a short story, but when combined with the playful and fluid approach to sexuality it works to undermine what Judith Roof terms 'heteronarrative'. Roof (1996) argues that 'our very idea of an end is dependent upon a concept of chronological, linear, unidirectional time that positions the end as the cumulative locus of completed knowledge' (7). Therefore, the subversion of a traditional, linear structure in 'Free Love' defies the (re)productive and orgasmic narrative. Following Roof's theorisation, in 'Free Love' there is not a finalising climax because the (narrative) climax has already happened earlier in the story. Significantly, then, it is by exploiting a frequent tendency of the short story (to play with narrative structure), and combining this with a narrative of sexuality, that 'Free Love' challenges the heteronormative understandings of sexuality and narrative.

Critically, it is the content of 'Free Love' that enables the subversion of the 'straight' plot (as conceptualised by Roof), as the final paragraph returns to an image that first appears in the middle of the story:

> I think about it from time to time, and when I do the picture that comes
> first to mind is one of the sun as it breaks apart and coheres on the
> waters of an unknown city, and I'm there, free in the middle of it, high
> on its air and laughing to myself, a smile all over my face, my wallet in
> my pocket still full of clean new notes. (9)

The image of the sun on the water referenced here first appears earlier in the narrative when, after leaving Suzi's flat, the protagonist
walks along the canal and back to the hostel. She 'stopped there and
leaned on the railings and watched the late sun hitting the water,
shimmering apart and coming together again in the same movement,
the same moment' (4). The story's end refers back to and therefore
depends upon the narrative middle of the story for its closure and
thus defies linearity. Instead, through this image the story proffers
an insular and overlapping structure. Returning to the long quotation above, the language and tone of the story's 'end' are imbued
with images of continuance. The protagonist finds she is 'free in the
middle of it' and the money in her wallet is 'new', suggesting revival
and renewal, as opposed to conclusion and climax. As a result, 'Free
Love' replicates Roof's notion that 'orgasm is not the end, though
most of the time we think so' (6).

The title, 'Free Love', contains various meanings and connotations. The phrase refers to 1960s-style non-commitment sex and the
broader climate of anti-authoritarian politics associated with that
period. However, the title also reflects the narrative's move beyond
the binary understanding of sexuality and eschews the dominance
of heterosexuality. Finally, the title is a direct reference to the protagonist having sex with the prostitute, who, when the protagonist
goes to pay her, remarks, 'it's free, . . . the first time should always
be free' (4). However, if the word 'love' is taken to stand not solely
for the erotic act of sex but for desire and sexuality, then 'free love'
celebrates all sexuality and desire uncontrolled by social, heteropatriarchal discourses. Following their return from Amsterdam (the
second time), Jackie and the story's narrator separate. The narrator remembers how the 'first place we really made love was arriving
back home after Amsterdam in the women's toilets at the bus sta-
tion' (8). While she thinks this 'one of the most exciting things I have
ever done in my life', Jackie considers it a 'sordid first experience'
(ibid.). Smith uses this description of sexual acts as sordid to dis-
mantle the exterior perceptions of hetero- and homo-sexuality. When
the protagonist sees Jackie 'heavily kissing the boy who worked on
the Caledonian Canal tourist boats' (ibid.), she thinks it 'remarkably

more sordid' (9). However, she reflects, 'what people think is sordid is relative after all' (ibid.). By juxtaposing these images of hetero- and homo-sexual acts, and referring to them as 'relative', the story asks the reader to think beyond categories and binary understandings of sexuality, because it is all 'free love'.

'A Quick One' follows the story 'Text for the Day' in the collection and it is this story which most notably connects sexuality and narrative. Once again titles are significant and imbued with multiple meanings, as 'A Quick One' is a colloquial reference to having sex as well as referencing the notion of a 'quick story' being told. 'A Quick One' focuses on yet another unnamed narrator/protagonist as she tries 'to remember how long we had of it, the unconditional, uncontextualised sex, and at the same time I'm walking along the pavement avoiding the cracks between the paving stones' (33). As with 'Cold Iron' in the same collection, memory plays a crucial role in the story's structure as the narrative moves between the present and the protagonist's past. The story opens in the past tense with the opening line, 'when we were first together we made love all the time' (31). Starting in the past tense with this previous relationship highlights how, even when relationships have come to an end, they still haunt the present.

However, this movement between tenses also serves to emphasise the importance of the moment. After all, whether in the present or the past this narrative is structured by discrete moments in the narrator's life. The manner in which the opening of the story places such a strong importance on the erotic time spent together, reliving and capturing that moment, exemplifies this. With this focus on time, 'A Quick One' invokes Halberstam's work *In a Queer Time and Place* (2005). While Halberstam's work was published after Smith's short story collection, the theorisation of a specifically queer time is useful. Halberstam suggests that the notion of queer time most notably emerges 'from within those gay communities whose horizons of possibility have been severely diminished by the AIDS epidemic' (2). As a result, the 'constantly diminishing future creates a new emphasis on the here, the present, the now' (ibid.). She continues, 'the urgency of being also expands the potential of the moment and . . . squeezes new possibilities out of the time at hand' (ibid.). The primacy of the moment to the short story has already been outlined throughout the chapters of this book; nonetheless, Halberstam's work offers an alternative means of thinking about the significance of the moment, through a particularly *queer* moment, which is clearly relevant to Smith's employment of time in her narratives.

Throughout 'A Quick One' the narrator repeatedly wanders into the realm of imagination and memory. When the woman in the coffee shop clears the table next to the protagonist and speaks, the protagonist has to 'ask what it was she said again. I was miles away, actually years away now, running old footage in my head' (35). The word 'footage' here signals the importance of photography in the story, as it suggests that the replaying of memories in the mind is akin to watching old video footage. Later in the story, when the narrative is once again in the past tense, the protagonist reminisces about a day not long after meeting her ex-partner (the implied 'you' of the narrative). The protagonist is taking photos on a 'Kodak Instamatic' camera and, with 'one photo left to take', against 'my better judgement I find myself taking one of you, catching you by surprise' (37). Even when the relationship between the narrator and the 'you' of the story is over the photograph still exists. The present moment, therefore, lives on in this object.

The use of photography in 'A Quick One' provokes further reflection on the short story and queer temporality. Julio Cortázar (1994) suggests that the short story resembles the photograph because it is an isolated object which, paradoxically, exploits its fragmentary status to provide 'a dynamic vision that spiritually transcends the space reached by the camera' (246). This imagery reinforces the short story's ability to exist in and of the moment while also pushing beyond these apparent temporal and spatial confines. Echoing Halberstam's work on queer time, Annamarie Jagose argues that at the moment of inauguration queer theory faced 'anxious notings' of its waning (2009: 158). However, this relationship between queer's initiation and demise might usefully be conceptualised as 'queer temporality, a mode of inhabiting time that is attentive to the recursive eddies and back-to-the-future loops that often pass undetected or uncherished beneath the official narrations of the linear sequence' (ibid.). The short story's ability to move vertically, to plunge into moments and to move in alternative directions to the traditional 'linear sequence', corresponds to this notion of queer temporality. The movement of short story narratives in 'loops' and 'eddies' offers an alternative approach to storytelling that, when combined with stories of sexuality, can fruitfully explore queerness in a variety of ways.

The tension between the present and a future time is reinforced by 'A Quick One' concluding with a forward-facing ending that suggests there are events still to come. The protagonist gives her number to the waitress at the coffee shop, leaving the reader to wonder what happens to their relationship in the future, and she plans to 'go to get

[her] photographs developed' (39). Both actions imply a continuation of events after the narrative's closure. Chronologically, the final paragraph ends before the point at which the story itself has opened. Significantly, the opening of the story details an erotic encounter between the protagonist and her ex-partner. She remembers,

> working slowly round the outer edges [of a satsuma] with my thumb and first finger, working in a circular motion, easing the fruit out of the skin, going in splitting and spreading the pieces, and the effort of excitement and self-control as I'd hold back, hold back the biggest segment till last as the taste of you'd burst each time on my tongue. (32)

Here, the metaphor of peeling a satsuma is used to describe the sexual act. However, the 'circular motion' and roundness of the satsuma also reverberate with the non-linearity of the narrative space. Importantly, this scene places orgasm at the start of the narrative and not at the end. By depicting two women together, 'A Quick One' challenges the dominant understanding of sex as defined by male penetration. Although 'it had to stop somewhere' (12), and the relationship does stop, the subsequent narrative illuminates that 'orgasm is not the end, though most of the time we think so' (Roof 1996: 6).

Like Smith, Jackie Kay is a Scottish writer and is often discussed in relation to national identity or the politics of race and sexuality. This is apparent in Kirsty Williams' (2006) summary that: 'The fiction of Ali Smith and Jackie Kay shares common ground. Both use thematic clashes between language and corporeality as a basis for exploring notions of gendered identity. Both depict gender and sexuality as unstable concepts and both negotiate lesbian love within the context of a society still largely constrained by the idea of sexual opposites' (157). While this is a fair appraisal of these two writers, Kay's 'Grace and Rose' (2012), unlike many of Smith's short stories and especially those just discussed, avoids gender or sexual ambiguity in relation to the characters, as the opening line reveals that Rose is about to marry another woman, Grace. The story has two sections, entitled and told from each of the women's perspectives, and overall the tone is that of a poetic love story. The first section, narrated from Rose's point of view, marks a significant moment of 'coming out' as she confesses her surprise at finally having the opportunity to declare their love for one another publicly. Rose is acutely aware of the public nature of this event, which she juxtaposes with the 'private' and 'secretive' nature of their relationship over the years, emphasising how they had always deployed labels such as *'colleagues'*, *'chums'* or '*best pals*' in order to conceal the sexual nature of their relationship (70). Eventually, however, both women reveal the truth to their parents: 'It was a silly thing because we were women in our late and middle forties, still feart o' telling oor mammies the truth!' (70). Two important elements of characterisation emerge here: firstly, that these are middle-aged women (thereby challenging the stereotype of heterosexual marriage in your twenties), and secondly, that they are Scottish. Indeed, Scottish sayings and phrases like this litter the pages of the story and centralise this particular aspect of their identity.

In both women's narratives their identity as inhabitants of the Scottish island of Shetland is foregrounded. With Rose comparing their love to the 'delicate' island, 'a fretwork of rock and heather and water' (71), the imagery of nature here aligns their relationship with the natural world. Moreover, nature reoccurs later in the story with Grace making reference to their wedding day making 'the puffins and the whales and the seals happy' (76), and the story closing with a reference to even the stars looking 'happy for us' (78). With these references weaving through the story, implicitly, the narrative suggests that, contrary to the predominant heteronormative social lens, their love is indeed 'natural'. The significance of Shetland being a small, Scottish island with especially traditional (read: heteronormative) values is recognised by Grace: 'Rose makes me feel like the first woman on the moon. We're no [*sic*] that fair away from being that, actually: being the first women to marry in Shetland is not so different' (74). With this analogy Grace stresses the rarity of publicly acknowledging homosexuality in a small, rural, traditional place like Shetland, thus emphasising the ways in which sexuality is moderated and patrolled in different settings and cultures.

Finally, 'Grace and Rose' utilises a self-conscious mode of storytelling and, as in many of Smith's stories, invokes the second person pronoun to create a teller–listener dynamic. For example, at the beginning of her section Grace states that, 'I can't wait to tell you all aboot it. It's a story, our love', before signalling the focus of her narration: 'Let me tell you aboot our day' (74). The 'you' of the implied listener draws the reader into the act of narration, to the extent that they become another guest at the wedding. Grace's narration delves into the immediacy of the wedding day and details the intricacies of the event, especially the decadent wedding feast, and when the two women kiss and 'everyone cheers' (77) the moment of 'coming out' is cemented. Furthermore, throughout the story there is a gentle mocking of the heterosexual tradition of marriage, with the women questioning 'how on earth have the heterosexual managed all this wedding stuff for years? It could give you a heart attack' (72). Likewise, they take advantage of the traditions of marriage, 'because both sets of parents would have to pay seeing as we are both daughters' (ibid.), and this decadence is particularly notable in the wedding feast.

However, there is a more serious response to the women's marriage, as Rose remarks: 'I never knew that things mattered in the way they matter until we decided to get married' (73). The right to marry, as two women, offers the opportunity to acknowledge their love for one another publicly but it also causes the women, Rose especially, to reflect on their relationship and view their love from an alternative vantage point. Here, the personal response to the event is connected to the broader political context, as the story acts as a reminder that same-sex marriage is a recent development. With the Civil Partnerships Act coming into effect in the United Kingdom in 2005, and same-sex marriage being legally allowed since 2014, 'Grace and Rose' is a timely fabulation of a significant political issue. Importantly, with Kay's short story collection in which this story was first published, *Reality, Reality*, being published in 2012 'Grace and Rose' can be read as a celebration of civil partnership (which is often referred to colloquially as 'gay marriage' even if it does not hold the same legal status). However, I would suggest it can also be seen to offer a utopian possibility, a contemporary fairytale, of what it might mean to same-sex couples who want to have the option of legal marriage. Thus, published before the legalisation of same-sex marriage, and at a time when it was a subject of ferocious debate, 'Grace and Rose' is an example of how contemporary women writers can contribute to public feminist and sexual equality debates through fictional representation.

Conclusion

Divided into two sections, entitled 'Spring 1970' and 'Spring 1973', Galloway's 'We're Not in This Together' (2011) is firmly set in these two temporal moments but, implicitly, through the use of past-tense narration, the reader is acutely aware of being told a story in the present. Published in Granta's anthology *The F Word*, it offers a fictional dialogue between this time in recent history and the contemporary moment. The first part of the story explores a young woman's experience of beginning menstruation and recalls the manner in which this was dealt with by her family. Her mother

responds practically, but also with a sense of awkward shame as she
thrusts the new box of pads at her daughter, hands her a leaflet and
speaks in code about knowing 'what *it* is' (245–6; emphasis added).
Comparatively, her sister rejoices with a sarcastic 'welcome to the
bloody club' and laughter, remarking 'It'll be boys next. Wait and
see. You'll be chasing bloody boys' (248). Switch to 'Spring 1973'
and the focus falls on a young woman and her boyfriend (implicitly
the same unnamed young woman as in the first section) seeking
support from a doctor to access the contraceptive pill, otherwise
known as 'the Princess of Preventives' (249). However, the response
from the doctor (who has a picture of the pope on his office wall)
is that they should abstain, before he swiftly expels them from his
office. This leaves the narrator to reflect on how: 'It remains an odd-
ity that our legitimate attempts to procure synthetic hormones to
avoid pregnancy should have been subject to censure when we went
to the pub illegally every weekend and nobody said boo' (252). The
double standard is striking and the fact that the story is narrated
from a future point in time allows hindsight to act as a vehicle for
emphasising the social patrolling of women's sexuality.

Galloway's story provokes a reappraisal of sexuality, reproduction
and women's rights then and now, but it also serves as a reminder
that women's sexual rights are always a complicated social and political issue. Furthermore, it illuminates the importance of telling stories
about women's sexuality, experiences and, in doing so, the significance
of attempting to speak across historical moments. Rather than perpetuating a narrative of difference between generations, the tone and
style of this story seek to acknowledge that issues have changed for
women (access to the pill does not come with such moral judgement
now); however, as a story, it also remains open and allows the reader
to make comparisons for herself. After all, the religious condemna-
tion of the hormonal contraceptive certainly chimes with the ongoing
religious patrolling of women's bodies in relation to abortion rights.
In this respect, the story is in keeping with Galloway's wider oeuvre
and approach to gender debates. As Carole Jones (2009) summarises:
'her fiction is a rigorous analysis of the continuing influence of traditional conceptions of gender identities and relations. It is a dissec-
tion of women's oppression under patriarchy, but also an account of
escaping the attractions that bind women to a hegemonic femininity'
(63). Perhaps, most importantly of all, 'We're Not in This Together'
is a reminder that it is vital for women to continue to assert their
rights and, to do this, tell stories about their experiences. It is through

these stories that the politics of choice and agency can be scrutinised and that we can explore the ways in which all individuals experience and embody socioeconomic and cultural discourses that continue to inform gender and sexuality politics.

Notes

1. Raven (2010) and Cochrane (2010) emerged as responses to the publications of Banyard, Walter and Redfern and Aune. All of these feminist writers published at the turn of the millennium and their works take a personal, yet culturally holistic approach to popular feminism.
2. *Belle de Jour* (the pseudonym used by Dr Brooke Magnanti) first appeared as a weblog in 2003 and won the *Guardian*'s 'Best British Weblog' award that same year. This blog was subsequently published in book format with two further sequels, before being made into a television series starring Billie Piper in 2007.

Conclusion

In the Introduction to this book I posed a series of questions which have woven throughout the chapters, with shifts in emphasis upon each of these questions at different moments in my own narrative of feminism and women's short story writing. The first of these questions was how do first-, second- and third-wave feminism inform and influence women's short story writing and, subsequently, how are these differing political moments represented within women's short story narratives? An interesting avenue into reflecting on this question comes through reading Helen's Simpson's short story 'The Festival of the Immortals' (2010). Featuring the narrator, Viv Armstrong, and her school friend Phyllis Goodwin, who meet for the first time in fifty years at a book festival, the story explores generational relations and raises questions about what it means to be a woman across the twentieth and twenty-first centuries. Historical boundaries are diminished as the presence of Daniel Defoe, Charlotte Brontë and Virginia Woolf (all of whom are immortal in this tale) is perceived as a normal occurrence. Instead, it is the women's personal histories that become the significant focus of the story as they reminisce about school days and their life trajectories. Notably, it is the figure of Woolf who is responsible for first bringing Phyllis and Viv together: '"The first time I saw you, we were in the canteen," said Phyllis. "You were reading *The Waves* and I thought, Ah, a kindred spirit"' (398–9). It is a shared passion for Woolf's writing that unites these women, and 'The Festival of the Immortals' emphasises how, 'for many readers and writers – and not only Simpson – the figure of Woolf embodies the female author' (Cox 2013a: 155). Later, when Phyllis tells Viv how her daughter Sarah is the 'Artistic Director of the Festival of Immortals', Viv responds with surprise at 'the opportunities there are for girls these days' (401). This generational shift, Viv contends, is down to the fact that their children are 'first generation university' (402), foregrounding broader social, cultural and economic forces as being responsible for their success. Conversely, Phyllis recollects her resentment and anger at having to leave school at fourteen, having 'just missed the 1944 Education Act with its free secondary schooling for everyone' (ibid.).

With its historical perspective, 'The Festival of the Immortals' contextualises the development of feminist thought. From her anger at the lack of free education for women in the 1940s, and through spending much of her life 'bound by domestic ties', Phyllis regards herself as 'still a feminist' (404). Interestingly, when she asks Viv whether she is too, Viv responds: 'Well, I do think women should have the vote so yes, I suppose I am. Because a lot of people don't really, underneath, think women should have the vote, you know' (ibid.). Here, feminism is reflexively critiqued in the narrative. Despite the rise of multiple labels for different types of feminisms, from the do-me feminist and raunch culture to girlie feminism, post(-)feminisms and the third wave, 'The Festival of the Immortals' sweeps aside all of these discourses to return feminism to its fundamental aim: the legal and social equality of all women. Accordingly, Simpson's short story returns us to arguments put forward by Sam McBean (2016), whose work on the queer temporality of feminism repeatedly articulates the ways in which so-called feminist pasts 'might not be left for dead but might instead travel into various feminist presents' (17). In this short story, Simpson creatively conjures an imagined reality in which labels are secondary to the politics and the principles at the heart of feminism.

Barbara A. Graham's 'Next of Kin' (2003) is set in London and is told from the perspective of a young woman, Veronica. Focusing on the life of Veronica and her sister Brenda, it describes the turmoil experienced by the sisters (especially the younger sibling Brenda) in the years following the death of their parents. While it is clear from the beginning of the story that Veronica is much older than Brenda, seventeen years to be precise, there is still an unexpected revelation at the end of the narrative when it becomes clear Veronica is not actually Brenda's sister but her biological mother. Having spent the majority of the narrative reflecting back on the recent past, in the story's conclusion the distant past and the potential future are suddenly brought into focus. Following a telephone conversation with their auntie, the reader is made aware of the fact that after going away to study Veronica 'come back wid baby [sic]' (73). When Veronica confirms to her aunt that she still has not revealed this to Brenda, her aunt encourages her not to 'till she dun study, cah yuh wi mess up de pickini'ed [sic]' (ibid.). The initial suspicion that Veronica is in fact Brenda's mother is confirmed at the story's conclusion when Brenda tells Veronica that she needs her birth certificate in order to apply for a passport and go on a trip as part of her course. Suddenly, her aunt's words come back to haunt Veronica:

> For a short while life had seemed at last to float on the past instead of being weighed down by it. Faced now with a problem neither love nor money could solve, Veronica wondered how she had let this happen. (75–6)

With this closing passage the past, present and future intertwine and the distinct generations and familial relationships are revealed to be a façade which masks very different familial relations. Sisters are in reality mother and daughter and the supposed similarity between them (that they have both lost their parents) no longer stands true. With the unravelling of this narrative, then, there is the unsettling of generational relations which, metaphorically, reflect the complex relationship between feminist politics. While the waves metaphor presupposes a clear sense of generational relationship, and therefore perpetuates traditional linear narratives of progress and/or failure, the focus on moments reveals such an understanding to be overly simplistic. Indeed, the mapping of feminist moments throughout these chapters has highlighted the ongoing dialectic between contemporary feminisms and the way in which, despite labels suggesting distinct breaks and a clear separation between 'waves', feminisms interact across various cultural moments and in a multitude of ways.

Read collectively, these chapters demonstrate the ongoing fictional negotiation of feminist politics by contemporary women writers and show how these writers have mapped the shifting terrain of feminisms in contemporary Britain. By considering the contextual, political landscape of contemporary feminisms in conjunction with the formal features of the short story and the aesthetic choices of the author in question, this book has explored the productive tension created through the fictional interaction between feminist politics and the short story. In the process, significant characteristics and tendencies of the short story and short story collection have been identified as playing a crucial role in the fictional negotiation of feminism. Throughout the chapters, it has become apparent that narrative brevity plays a vital role in shaping the feminist politics which resides in these short stories. With the emphasis on time and space often being used by writers such as Helen Simpson to intensify the sense of constraint experienced by women, and others such as Ali Smith and Sarah Hall exploiting the ambiguous potential cultivated by brevity, the smaller narrative space of the short story enables an element of ambivalence which is central to contemporary feminist approaches. Moreover, it is clear that the multi-vocal and polyphonic nature of the short story collection itself offers great potential for these women writers as they seek to explore the ontological realities of gender and sexual politics in the most diverse ways.

Furthermore, the position and role of the reader in the relation to the text and to feminist politics have been fundamental to many of the discussions. By considering the implications of the reader for the feminist potential of narratives, a key issue to emerge is the potential limitations of literature to propagate a productive politics which can influence and bring about social change when that politics is dependent on a reader's interpretation. Namely, due to the importance of experiential, affective relationships between the reader and the text, much of the feminist potential and indeed fictional negotiation of feminism throughout these short stories is dependent on the reader. Although in all genres of fiction the reader is important, as 'a text can only come to life when it is read' (Iser 1980: 6), in narratives in which context, description, characterisation or even plot details may be omitted or are ambiguous there is even greater reliance placed on the reader.

From Roberts' depiction of the same issue from differing perspectives, which provokes the reader to reflect on the socioculturally constructed discourses that shape the category 'woman', through to Simpson's exploration of women's everyday lives, in which the reader bears witness to the conflict between external pressures and women's internal emotions, the reader is invested and accountable in the story. This is perhaps nowhere more apparent than in Smith's short stories in which the continual reference to a 'you' persona transcends association with a second person and directly addresses the reader. Likewise, in Mantel's 'The Assassination of Margaret Thatcher', the reader is located at a site of privilege in being more aware of the reality of events than the story's narrator. Furthermore, in being privy to the thoughts of both the assassin and the unwitting resident, the reader encounters multiple perspectives on the situation, as well as on the character of Thatcher. Seemingly, in the contexts of feminisms, gender and sexuality, the reader is therefore made to confront her own preconceptions of these discourses and make a judgement, challenge her perceptions and draw her own conclusions. Of course, the feminist potential of narratives is therefore also dependent on the reader approaching the text with a feminist sensibility or an awareness of feminist politics. In the process of writing this book, therefore, I have brought my own response and politics into play as a reader of these texts, and the story I have told of women's short story writing is undoubtedly a subjective act influenced by my own feminist positionality.

Through the body of short stories considered in this book a clear pattern emerges: that feminism is most frequently associated with young, white, Western, female bodies. However, throughout the chapters I have actively sought to readdress this assumption by including stories which, although not necessarily acknowledged in the literary mainstream, are compelling narratives that take into account the politics of race, ethnicity, migration, class and ageing. Likewise, the chapter on masculinity has told a slightly different tale which does not adhere to a wave-based understanding of feminism and instead recognises the historical implications of gendered and sexual relations. In this way I have attempted to tell feminist stories differently and put into practice Hemmings' (2005) approach that 'stresses the links rather than the discontinuities between different theoretical frameworks, as a way of challenging the linear "displacement" of one approach by another' (131). Consequently, this story has attempted to engage with stories about feminism and feminist stories without being confined to the dominant narrative of contemporary feminisms. This has been a complex challenge, and indeed it is something that may never be wholly possible to achieve. Nonetheless, all of the chapters have offered readings which in some way frustrate the traditional linearity applied to feminisms and instead engage with the diverse, multifaceted, contradictory and overlapping nature of contemporary feminisms through thematic readings of short stories. While in the contemporary era it is near impossible to escape the semantics and labels that have shaped the commonplace narrative of feminism, by paying attention to the nuances, complexities, ambiguities and ambivalence inherent in women's feminist short stories, there has been a grain of resistance underpinning this work which has sought to tell a variety of different stories. Crucially, this is why the short story, as a genre of fiction with certain formal features, has been so important. The feminist politics at play in these narratives has spanned a spectrum from subtle to explicit, and it is the short story's tendency towards indirection, suggestion and ambiguity that has often made such politics possible.

Finally, in the Introduction I quoted Lynne Segal and considered the relevance of her jigsaw imagery to the focus of this work. Indeed, the image of a jigsaw functions on a variety of levels. The jigsaw is a resonant motif that visualises the textual construction of the short story collection. In Chapters 2 and 5 I considered the ways in which Roberts and Smith use individual short stories as narrative 'pieces' and place them together in the short story collection to paint a larger picture. However, there are also limitations to this metaphor because the pieces of a jigsaw only ever fit together to complete the puzzle in one way, and this is not true of the short story. Individual short stories can be successfully resituated in anthologies and, as a consequence, are often brought into dialogue with differing discourses. Finally, then, as a reader, I have also participated in the act of completing a jigsaw puzzle by piecing together and attempting 'to map out and assess which different pieces in the jigsaw of feminism get picked up' (Segal 2001: 57) in contemporary British women's short story writing.

While the jigsaw is clearly a useful visual metaphor for reflecting upon short story writing and for thinking about the approach of this book more broadly, in this conclusion there is a final image on which I wish to draw: the looking glass. Returning to an earlier feminist figure, that of Virginia Woolf, the motif of the looking glass is a recognisable trope in much of Woolf's writing. In 'The Lady in the Looking Glass: A Reflection' (2003) Woolf focuses upon Isabella Tyson, 'at this moment' (216), in order to critique the human desire to capture an individual's life in writing. In Woolf's work there is a tension between the impetus to write women's unnarrated lives and a desire to avoid confining women to an identity straitjacket, and this reflects the conflicting feminist politics of her time. For Woolf, 'women have served all these centuries as looking-glasses possessing the magic and delicious power of reflecting the figure of man at twice its natural size' (2008: 45). The looking glass is a patriarchal tool in which women operate 'as surfaces with no depth' (Hanson 1994: 111). However, in the context of contemporary women's writing and feminist politics I suggest that this image of the looking glass, or mirror, is in fact useful for *reflecting* on the short story. Short stories provide snapshots of life; they project an image or experience, a fleeting or passing moment, without ever pretending to reflect life in its totality. Short stories recognise that 'nothing stay[s] the same for two seconds together' (Woolf 2003: 213). Similarly, the polyphonic, multifaceted and dialectic nature of the short story collection offers an opportunity to hold up multiple textual mirrors to the world. The short story collection refuses to prioritise a single narrative or a particular representation and instead offers an affirmative space in which to reflect on, engage with and map the multiple and diverse natures of gender and sexual identities and feminisms. To put it another way, 'the moment, that snapshot of the discursive dissonance that makes up feminist history, might operate instead as a reminder that all histories are selective and motivated histories' (Hemmings 2011: 16), including my own moment in this work.

The anthology format is another means through which the jigsaw motif materialises in relation to women's short story writing. Throughout the chapters I have drawn on short stories published in anthologies, more specifically *Kin: New Fiction by Black & Asian Women* (2003), *The F Word* (2011) and *Refugee Tales* (2015). In the twenty-first century the anthology remains an important literary space and provides publication opportunities for new writers and those who perhaps do not receive mainstream literary acknowledgement. As such, anthologies often contain narratives which tell stories from differing perspectives. However, the anthology is not just a means of celebrating new voices and championing writers; it also provides a space for curating voices from the past. Even in the period of time I have been researching and writing this book there has been an array of short story anthologies published, and two notable multi-volume works. Victoria Hislop's *The Story: Love, Loss & the Lives of Women: 100 Great Short Stories* (2013) was published across three volumes while Philip Hensher edited *The Penguin Book of the British Short Story Vols I & II* (2015). Both of these anthologies were published in hardback format and are hefty collections of stories with a relatively substantial recommended retail price. The emergence of anthologies like these signals the ongoing belief in the short story as a valuable literary medium and showcases the ways in which the past, present and future intersect in the contemporary via the locus of this textual space.

Looking forward

Following on from the first in-depth statistical survey examining the situation of the short story in Britain, by Jenny Brown Associates and Book Marketing Limited, in 2002 the 'Save the Short Story' campaign was launched in the UK.[1] A collaboration between Booktrust, Scottish Booktrust, *Prospect* magazine, NESTA and the Small Wonder Short Story Festival, the campaign launched the National Short Story Prize. With its rebranding as simply 'Story', the campaign shifted its focus from 'saving' to 'celebrating' the short story, a turn that suggests an improvement in the genre's position within British literary culture.[2] However, despite a catalogue of initiatives and campaigns since the new millennium, and particularly since 2002, that have sought to champion the short story it has also faced ongoing threat. Most notably, in 2012

BBC Radio Four announced that from spring 2012 the number of short stories it broadcasts was to be reduced from three to one a week, suggesting the genre remains a site of literary contention.³ Sparked by this announcement the Society of Authors launched a vigorous campaign to reverse the proposed cuts, which included a 'Tweetathon'. Participating in this event, Simon Brett, Neil Gaiman, Joanne Harris, Ian Rankin and Sarah Waters each tweeted the opening line of a story for members of the public to complete. Harnessing the influence of established authors and a relatively new digital platform, the 'Tweethathon' also illuminates the complementary relations between digital publishing and the short story.

When Random House launched 'Storycuts', a digital publishing venture, it claimed in the tagline to this series that 'The Future of the Short Story is Here'. Comprising a total of 150 e-books – 243 individual short stories – with a blend of individual publications and smaller collections, Storycuts signals a new way of publishing, marketing and selling short stories. An internationally renowned, leading, mainstream publisher being behind this venture reaffirms my contestation that the genre is being paid even greater heed in the twenty-first century. Notably, the authors that constitute the publishing list illuminate the strength of contemporary short story writing. From literary authors acclaimed in the academy including A. S. Byatt, Julian Barnes, Susan Hill and Rose Tremain through to bestselling popular authors like Frederick Forsyth, John Grisham and Irvine Welsh, the scope of this publishing list exemplifies the breadth and diversity of the short story today. However, it also signals how many authors become renowned for their novels to the detriment of their short stories. Nonetheless, with this new way of accessing short stories – the ability to purchase them individually, in smaller collections, and therefore to 'dip in' when the fancy takes – Storycuts circumnavigates some of the publishing and dissemination issues previously encountered by the short story and offers a new model of consumption.

Although the move towards digital publishing has been heralded as a response to consumers being increasingly driven by the ability to access content instantaneously and to devour it quickly whilst on the go, this shift also functions to broaden the potential reach of the short story's audience. In 2010 Ether Books was launched as a dedicated digital short story publisher. With Hilary Mantel, Lionel Shriver and Maggie O'Farrell amongst the first authors to be published on the site, Ether Books publishes work that otherwise would only be available if it was commissioned in anthologies, newspapers or magazines, or if authors compiled a collection. Priced competitively – generally stories range from free to £3 sterling – the mobile site and app demonstrate a new model for disseminating short stories amidst the e-book revolution. Furthermore, it is the element of interactivity on the part of the reader that enhances the dynamic of reading short stories digitally and, arguably, makes for a more dialectic process. With the Ether Books mobile site and app, members of the reading community not only download stories but can comment, rate and discuss them with other members. Thus, to a far greater extent than a traditional short story collection, the paratextual features that virtually surround a story generate further interest in the short story. In this respect, then, the short story becomes a self-perpetuating entity as it digitally enhances its own profile. It builds a sense of community online that encourages interest in the genre as users share the app with friends on social network sites. Consequentially, Ether Books highlights how this digital platform can be deployed as a means of disseminating the short story in innovative ways whilst producing broader cultural value.

Equally, digital space has become a key site of feminist activism in the twenty-first century. One such example is 'The Everyday Sexism Project' (https://everydaysexism.com), which encourages the sharing of stories as 'by sharing your story you're showing the world that sexism does exist, it is faced by women every day and it is a valid problem to discuss' (n. p.). While the project, founded by Laura Bates in 2012, initially harnessed the power of the internet and social media to capture women's stories, by 2014 Bates had published a book which collated many of the stories previously shared digitally by women from around the world. Thus, the book is a direct result of digital storytelling and highlights the ways in which feminist activism is evolving, to the extent that the textual artefact of the book is a result, not a catalyst, of feminism. The Everyday Sexism Project should be understood in a broader context of digital feminism which, writing in the *Guardian*, Tracey McVeigh (2013) describes as: 'The F-word is back, with digital-savvy young women joining forces online' (n. p.), before proceeding to offer a survey of the 'best voices in activism' today. A few of the names to be included in this list were Caitlin Moran, a columnist and 'prolific tweeter'; Kat Banyard for her work with UK Feminista; and Yasmeen Hassan, the global director of Equality Now. Equally diverse is the range of digital media being deployed by these women in engaging with feminism. Including websites, blogs, Facebook and Twitter, the digital age has heralded a vibrant new means not only of telling stories about feminism but also of agitating for feminist change.

In terms of women's short story writing and, indeed, the telling of feminist stories, the move to digital publishing and the use of online platforms open up some interesting avenues of enquiry. While literary publishing has undergone certain changes in the light of digital publishing, there has not been the ground-breaking revolution perhaps anticipated a decade ago, especially in the context of the short story. More evolutionary than revolutionary, nonetheless digital publishing has certainly altered the way in which feminist stories are being told. With the rise of digital storytelling using a plethora of platforms, the ability to communicate has certainly diversified; but this has perhaps had a greater impact on non-fictional writings than fictional short stories so far. As such, it is important to re-evaluate the relationship between women's short story writing and feminist politics continually. After all, as Rosi Braidotti (1995) so eloquently states, feminism 'is a tale full of hope and promise and, like all tales, it requires good story-tellers' (56). The exact nature and medium of these stories may change in the coming years, but what does remain vital is that there are a plethora of vibrant voices telling fascinating stories about feminism, in all its guises, today.

Notes

1. Some of the headlines to emerge from this survey were that in 2002, 53.5 per cent of anthologies of short stories were published by independent publishers as opposed to 39.5 per cent by mainstream publishers, with the remaining 6% being published through other channels. Furthermore, while anthologies published by mainstream publishers had increased, single-author collections had declined from 215 in 2000 to 135 in 2002, and single-author collections published by independents had gone from 203 in 2000 to 287 in 2002. The consequence of this latter statistic is that writers receive smaller advances, less publicity and less high street distribution (quoted in March-Russell 2009: 49).
2. The campaign originally hosted a website (www.theshortstory.org.uk) but this was decommissioned and all content is hosted at http://www.booktrust.org.uk/books/adults/short-stories as part of the broader Booktrust project.
3. The full press release is available at: http://www.bbc.co.uk/pressoffice/pressreleases/stories/2011/07_july/10/radio4.shtml

Bibliography

Adolph, Andrea (2009), *Food and Femininity in Twentieth-Century British Women's Fiction*, Farnham: Ashgate.

Allardice, Lisa (2004), 'The Miniaturist', *Guardian*, 7 January, <http://www.guardian.co.uk/books/2006/jan/07/featuresreviews.guardianreview9> (last accessed 3 March 2013).

Anthias, Floya and Nira Yuval-Davis (1983), 'Contextualizing Feminism: Gender, Ethnic and Class Divisions', *Feminist Review*, 15:1, 62–75.

Aristotle (1954), *Rhetoric*, trans. W. Rhys Roberts, and *Poetics*, trans. Ingram Bywater, New York: Modern Library.

Armitt, Lucie (2014), '"The Whispering of Generations Past": Kate Mosse's Languedoc Trilogy', *Contemporary Women's Writing*, 8:2, 154–70.

Atkinson, Kate (2002), *Not the End of the World*, London: Doubleday.

Attwood, Feona (2009), *Mainstreaming Sex: The Sexualisation of Culture*, London: I. B. Tauris.

Baker, Sam (2014), 'The Irresistible Rise of the Short Story', 18 May, <http://www.telegraph.co.uk/culture/books/10831961/The-irresistible-rise-of-the-short-story.html> (last accessed 5 January 2017).

Baldwin, Dean (1993), 'The Tardy Evolution of the British Short Story', *Studies in Short Fiction*, 30:1, 23–33.

Ballaster, Ros, Margaret Beetham, Elizabeth Frazer and Sandra Hebron (1991), *Women's Worlds: Ideology, Femininity and the Woman's Magazine*, Houndmills: Macmillan.

Banyard, Kat (2010), *The Equality Illusion: The Truth about Men and Women Today*, London: Faber and Faber.

Barker, Nicola (2003), *The Three Button Trick*, London: Flamingo.

Bates, H. E. [1941] (1972), *The Modern Short Story: A Critical Survey*, London: Michael Joseph.

Bates, Laura (2014), *Everyday Sexism*, London: Simon and Schuster.

'BBC R4 to Cut Back on Short Stories' (2011), *The Society of Authors*, 29 July, <http://www.societyofauthors.org/soa-news/bbc-radio-4-short-story-cuts> (last accessed 12 March 2012).

Bean, Kellie (2007), *Post-Backlash Feminism: Women and the Media since Reagan-Bush*, Jefferson, NC: McFarland.

Benn, Melissa (1998), *Madonna and Child: Towards a New Politics of Motherhood*, London: Jonathan Cape.

Benn, Melissa (2000), 'Little Women Writ Large', *Guardian*, 3 October, <http://www.guardian.co.uk/world/2000/oct/03/gender.uk> (last accessed 11 January 2017).

Bentley, Paul and Mark Duell (2014), '"We Can't Be Running Away from History": Hilary Mantel Goes On the Offensive as She Attacks Critics of her Fantasy to Assassinate Margaret Thatcher', *MailOnline*, 22 September, <http://www.dailymail.co.uk/news/article-2764520/Hilary-Mantel-unrepentant-backlash-grows-fantasies-assassinating-Margaret-Thatcher.html> (last accessed 16 June 2016).

Beynon, John (2002), *Masculinities and Culture*, Buckingham: Open University Press.

Blain, Virginia, Patricia Clements and Isobel Grundy (1990), *A Feminist Companion to Literature in English: Women Writers from the Middle Ages to the Present*, London: Batsford.

Bly, Robert (1990), *Iron John: A Book About Men*, Boston, MA: Addison-Wesley.

Boddy, Kasia (1996), 'Women Writers and the Short Story', in Lizabeth Goodman (ed.), *Literature and Gender*, London: Routledge, pp. 80–7.

Boddy, Kasia and Ali Smith (2010), 'All There Is: An Interview About the Short Story', *Critical Quarterly*, 52:2, 66–82.

Bowen, Elizabeth (1994), 'The Faber Book of Modern Short Stories', in Charles E. May (ed.), *The New Short Story Theories*, Athens: Ohio University Press, pp. 256–62.

Bradbury, Malcolm [1987] (1988), 'Introduction', in Bradbury (ed.), *The Penguin Book of Modern British Short Stories*, London: Penguin, pp. 11–14.

Braidotti, Rosi (1995), 'Generations of Feminists, or, Is There a Life after Post-Modernism?', *Found Objects*, 6:1, 55–86.

Braithwaite, Ann (2002), 'The Personal, the Political, Third-Wave and Post-feminisms', *Feminist Theory*, 3:3, 335–44.

Brown, Arthur (2003), 'Death and the Reader: James's "The Beast in the Jungle"', in Farhat Iftekharrudin, Joseph Boyden, Joseph Longo and Mary Rohrberger (eds), *Postmodern Approaches to the Short Story*, Westport, CT: Praeger, pp. 39–50.

Brown, Julie (2000), 'Introduction', in Brown (ed.), *American Women Short Story Writers: A Collection of Critical Essays*. New York: Garland, pp. xv–xxx.

Bryson, Valerie (1992), *Feminist Political Theory: An Introduction*, Houndmills: Macmillan.

Budgeon, Shelley (2011), *Third Wave Feminism and the Politics of Gender in Late Modernity*, London: Palgrave Macmillan.

Burton Harrington, Ellen (2008), 'Introduction: Women Writers and the Outlaw Form of the Short Story', in Burton Harrington (ed.), *Scribbling*

Women and the Short Story Form: Approaches by American and British Women Writers, New York: Peter Lang, pp. 1–14.

Bury, Liz (2013), 'All-Woman Shortlist for BBC Short Story Award 2013', *Guardian*. 20 September, <http://www.theguardian.com/books/2013/sep/20/bbc-short-story-shortlist-2013–woman> (last accessed 10 January 2017).

Bury, Liz, Iain Chambers and Ali Smith (2010), 'Ali Smith Reads "A Conversation with My Father" by Grace Paley', *Guardian Podcast Series*, 21 December, <http://www.theguardian.com/books/audio/2010/dec/07/alismith-short-stories> (last accessed 23 September 2013).

Butler, Judith (1994), 'Against Proper Objects', *differences: A Journal of Feminist Cultural Studies*, 6:2, 1–26.

Butler, Judith (2006), 'Imitation and Gender Insubordination', in John Storey (ed.), *Cultural Theory and Popular Culture: A Reader*, Harlow: Pearson Education, pp. 225–70.

Butler, Judith [1990] (2010), *Gender Trouble: Feminism and the Subversion of Identity*, London: Routledge.

Butler, Judith [1993] (2011), *Bodies That Matter: On the Discursive Limits of Sex*, London: Routledge.

Byatt, A. S (2011), 'NO GRLS ALOD, INSEPT MOM', *Granta: The F Word*, 115, 31–6.

Campbell, Beatrix (1984), *Wigan Pier Revisited: Poverty and Politics in the 80s*, London: Virago.

Cardiff, Erin (2012), '"Slutwalkers" Take Protest to Downing Street', *Independent*, 19 September, <http://www.independent.co.uk/news/uk/home-news/slutwalkers-take-protest-to-downing-street-8156006.html> (last accessed 5 January 2017).

Carter, Angela [1974] (1987), *Fireworks*, London: Chatto & Windus.

Carter, Angela (ed.) (1990), *The Virago Book of Fairy Tales*, London: Virago Press.

Carter, Angela (ed.) (1992), *The Second Virago Book of Fairy Tales*, London: Virago Press.

Carter, Angela [1979] (1995), *The Bloody Chamber: And Other Stories*, London: Vintage.

Carter, Angela (ed.) (2004), *Angela Carter's Book of Wayward Girls and Wicked Women*, London: Virago Press.

Chen, Eva (2013), 'Neoliberalism and Popular Women's Culture: Rethinking Choice, Freedom and Agency', *European Journal of Cultural Studies*, 16:4, 440–52.

Chester, Gail (2002), 'The Anthology as a Medium for Feminist Debate in the UK', *Women's Studies International Forum*, 25:2, 193–207.

Chotiner, Isaac (2014), 'Hilary Mantel: Margaret Thatcher "Wrecked This Country"', *New Republic*, 6 October, <https://newrepublic.com/article/119704/hilary-mantel-interview-margaret-thatcher-wrecked-country> (last accessed 16 June 2016).

Christian, Barbara, Ann duCille, Sharon Marcus, Elaine Marks, Nancy K. Miller, Sylvia Schafer and Joan W. Scott (1990), 'Conference Call', *differences: A Journal of Feminist Cultural Studies*, 2:3, 52–108.

Cixous, Hélène [1975] (2001), 'The Laugh of the Medusa', trans. Keith Cohen and Paula Cohen, in Vincent Leitch, William Cain, Laurie Finke, Barbara Johnson, John McGowan and Jeffrey Williams (eds), *The Norton Anthology of Theory and Criticism*, London: W. W. Norton, pp. 2039–56.

Clare, Anthony (2000), *On Men: Masculinity in Crisis*, London: Chatto and Windus.

Clark, Alex (2000), 'Battery Mums', *Guardian*, 7 October, <http://www.guardian.co.uk/books/2000/oct/07/fiction.reviews1> (last accessed 5 January 2017).

Cochrane, Kira (2010), 'Feminism Is Not Finished', *Guardian*, 24 July, <http://www.guardian.co.uk/lifeandstyle/2010/jul/24/feminism-not-finished-not-uncool> (last accessed 11 November 2016).

Condon, Judith (1990), 'The Women's Weekend: The Beginning of a Movement', *Women: A Cultural Review*, 1:1, 25–8.

Connell, R. W (1982), 'Class, Patriarchy, and Sartre's Theory of Practice,' *Theory and Society*, 11:3, 305–20.

Connell, R. W. (1983), *Which Way Is Up? Essays on Sex, Class and Culture*, Sydney: Allen & Unwin.

Connell, R. W. [1995] (2005), *Masculinities*, Berkeley: University of California Press.

Connell, R. W. and James W. Messerschmidt (2005), 'Hegemonic Masculinity: Rethinking the Concept', *Gender & Society*, 19, 829–59.

Connell, R. W., D. J. Ashenden, S. Kessler and G. W. Dowsett (1982), *Making the Difference: Schools, Families and Social Division*, Sydney: Allen & Unwin.

Cooper, Katherine (2012), 'Things Slipping Between Past and Present: Feminism and the Gothic in Kate Mosse's *Sepulchre*', in Cooper and Emma Short (eds), *The Female Figure in Contemporary Historical Fiction*, Houndmills: Palgrave Macmillan, pp. 153–70.

Coote, Anna and Jacob Mohun Himmelweit (2013), 'The Problem that has No Name: Work, Care and Time', *Soundings: A Journal of Politics and Culture*, 54, 90–103.

Cortázar, Julio (1994), 'Some Aspects of the Short Story', in Charles E. May (ed.), *The New Short Story Theories*, Athens: Ohio University Press, pp. 246–7.

Cossman, Brenda (2004), 'Sexuality, Queer Theory and "Feminism After": Reading and Rereading the Sexual Subject', *McGill Law Journal*, 49, 847–76.

Cox, Ailsa (2008), 'Helen Simpson's "Opera"', *Journal of the Short Story in English*, 51, 1–8.

Cox, Ailsa (2013a), 'Loose Canons: Readers, Authors and Consumption in Helen Simpson's "The Festival of the Immortals"', *Journal of the Short Story in English*, 60, 147–56.

Cox, Ailsa (2013b), 'Walking in Circles: Helen Simpson's *Constitutional* as Short Story Cycle', *Short Fiction in Theory & Practice*, 3:2, 211–20.

De Beauvoir, Simone [1949] (1999), *The Second Sex*, trans. H. M. Parshley, London: Vintage.

De Lauretis, Teresa (1991), 'Queer Theory: Lesbian and Gay Sexualities: An Introduction', *differences: A Journal of Feminist Cultural Studies*, 3:2, iiix–viii.

DiQuinzio, Patrice (1999), *The Impossibility of Motherhood: Feminism, Individualism and the Problem of Mothering*, London: Routledge.

Drewery, Claire (2011), *Modernist Short Fiction by Women: The Liminal in Katherine Mansfield, Dorothy Richardson, May Sinclair and Virginia Woolf*, Farnham: Ashgate.

Duffy, Stella (2014), 'Why Short Stories are Like Great Paintings', *BBC Arts*, <http://www.bbc.co.uk/programmes/articles/58zwwjR0yzf2WDCc0Rz2Sst/why-short-stories-are-like-great-paintings> (last accessed 10 June 2017).

DuPlessis, Rachel Blau (1985), *Writing Beyond the Ending: Narrative Strategies of Twentieth-Century Women Writers*, Bloomington: Indiana University Press.

Durham, Carolyn A. (2002), 'Falling into Fiction(s): Intertextual Travel and Translation in Rose Tremain's *The Way I Found Her*', *Contemporary Literature*, 43:3, 461–87.

Dworkin, Andrea [1981] (1984), *Pornography: Men Possessing Women*, London: Women's Press.

Eagleton, Mary (1989), 'Gender and Genre', in Clare Hanson (ed.), *Re-Reading the Short Story*, Houndmills: Macmillan, pp. 55–68.

Easthope, Anthony (1992), *What a Man's Gotta Do: The Masculine Myth in Popular Culture*, London: Routledge.

Edwards, Tim (2006), *Cultures of Masculinity*, London: Routledge.

Everyday Sexism Project (n.d.), <http://everydaysexism.com/> (last accessed 11 January 2017).

Fairbairns, Zoë (1978), 'Introduction', in Fairbairns, Sara Maitland, Valerie Miner, Michèle Roberts and Michelene Wandor (eds), *Tales I Tell My Mother: A Collection of Feminist Short Stories*, London: Journeyman Press, pp. 1–6.

Falcus, Sarah (2007), *Michèle Roberts: Myths, Mothers and Memories*, Oxford: Peter Lang.

Falcus, Sarah (2013), 'Addressing Age in Michèle Roberts's *Reader, I Married Him*', *Contemporary Women's Writing*, 7:1, 18–34.

Faludi, Susan [1991] (1993), *Backlash: The Undeclared War Against Women*, London: Vintage.

Faludi, Susan [1999] (2000), *Stiffed: The Betrayal of Modern Man*, London: Vintage.

Ferguson, Ann (1997), 'On Conceiving Motherhood and Sexuality: A Feminist Materialist Approach', in Diana Tietjens Meyers (ed.), *Feminist Socialist Thought: A Reader*, Abingdon: Routledge, pp. 38–63.

Ferguson, Suzanne C. (1982), 'Defining the Short Story: Impression and Form', *Modern Fiction Studies*, 28, 13–24.

Ferrebe, Alice (2005), *Masculinity in the Male-Authored Novel 1950–2000: Keeping it Up*, Houndmills: Palgrave Macmillan.

Findlen, Barbara (ed.) (1995), *Listen Up: Voices from the Next Feminist Generation*, New York: Seal Press.

Firestone, Shulamith [1970] (1973), *The Dialectic of Sex: The Case for Feminist Revolution*, St Albans: Paladin.

Fixmer, Natalie and Julia T. Wood (2005), 'The Personal is *Still* Political: Embodied Politics in Third Wave Feminism', *Women's Studies in Communication*, 28:2, 235–57.

Flood, Alison (2009), 'Bespoke Short Stories Commissioned for London's Royal Parks', *Guardian*, 17 February, <http://www.guardian.co.uk/books/2009/feb/17/royal-parks-stories-will-self> (last accessed 14 March 2015).

Forna, Aminatta (2010), 'Haywards Heath', in James Naughtie (ed.), *The BBC National Short Story Award 2010*, Manchester: Comma Press, pp. 9–18.

Foucault, Michel [1975] (1991), *Discipline and Punish: The Birth of the Prison*, trans. Alan Sheridan, London: Penguin.

Foucault, Michel [1984] (1992), *The History of Sexuality, Vol. 2: The Use of Pleasure*, trans. Robert Hurley, London: Penguin.

Frampton, Edith (2006), '"This Milky Fullness": Breastfeeding Narratives and Michèle Roberts', *Textual Practice*, 20:4, 655–78.

Friedan, Betty (1993), *The Fountain of Age*, London: Simon and Schuster.

Friedan, Betty [1963] (2010), *The Feminine Mystique*, London: Penguin.

Friend, Tad (1994), '"Yes!" (Feminist Women who Like Sex)', *Esquire*, 121:2, 48–56.

Gallop, Jane (1992), *Around 1981: Academic Feminist Literary Theory*, London: Routledge.

Galloway, Janice (2011), 'We're Not in This Together', *Granta: The F Word*, 115, 243–52.

Gamble, Sarah (2001), 'Postfeminism', in Gamble (ed.), *The Routledge Companion to Feminism and Postfeminism*, London: Routledge, pp. 43–54.

Gamble, Sarah (2006), '(In)Between Location: Space, Time and the Female Subject in Michèle Roberts' *In the Red Kitchen*', *Feminist Theory*, 7, 7–26.

Gambles, Richenda (2010), 'Going Public? Articulations of the Personal and Political on Mumsnet.com', in Nick Mahony, Janet Newman and

Clive Barnett (eds), *Rethinking the Public: Innovations in Research, Theory and Politics*, Bristol: Policy Press, pp. 29–42.

Gamson, Joshua (1995), 'Must Identity Movements Self-Destruct? A Queer Dilemma', *Social Problems*, 42:3, 390–407.

Gardiner, Judith Kegan (2002), 'Introduction', in Gardiner (ed.), *Masculinity Studies and Feminist Theory*, New York: Columbia University Press, pp. 1–29.

Gavin, Adrienne (2003), 'Living in a World of Make-Believe: Fantasy, Female Identity, and Modern Short Stories by Women in the British Tradition', in Farhat Iftekharrudin, Joseph Boyden, Joseph Longo and Mary Rohrberger (eds), *Postmodern Approaches to the Short Story*, Westport, CT: Praeger, pp. 121–32.

Genz, Stéphanie (2010), 'Singled Out: Postfeminism's "New Woman" and the Dilemma of Having It All', *Journal of Popular Culture*, 43:1, 97–119.

Genz, Stéphanie and Benjamin A. Brabon (2009), *Postfeminism: Cultural Texts and Theories*, Edinburgh: Edinburgh University Press.

Geraghty, Christine [1991] (1992), *Women and Soap Opera: A Study of Prime Time Soaps*, Cambridge: Polity.

Germanà, Monica (2010) *Scottish Women's Gothic and Fantastic Writing: Fiction since 1978*, Edinburgh: Edinburgh University Press.

Germanà, Monica and Emily Horton (2013), 'Introduction', in Germanà and Horton (eds), *Ali Smith: Contemporary Critical Perspectives*, London: Bloomsbury, pp. 1–8.

Gharraie, Jonathan (2012), 'Helen Simpson on *In-Flight Entertainment*', *Paris Review*, 28 February, <http://www.theparisreview.org/blog/2012/02/28/helen-simpson-on-%E2%80%98in-flightentertainment%E2%80%99/> (last accessed 8 January 2013).

Gifford, Douglas (1997), 'Contemporary Fiction I: Tradition and Continuity', in Gifford and Dorothy McMillan (eds), *A History of Scottish Women's Writing*, Edinburgh: Edinburgh University Press, pp. 579–603.

Gilbert, Sandra M. and Susan Gubar [1979] (2000), *The Madwoman in the Attic: The Woman Writer and the Nineteenth-Century Literary Imagination*, New Haven, CT: Yale University Press.

Gill, Rosalind (2007), 'Critical Respect: The Difficulties and Dilemmas of Agency and "Choice" for Feminism: A Reply to Duits and van Zoonen', *European Journal of Women's Studies*, 14:1, 69–80.

Gill, Rosalind (2012), 'The Sexualisation of Culture?', *Social and Personality Psychology Compass*, 6:7, 483–98.

Gillis, Stacy, Gillian Howie and Rebecca Munford (2007), 'Introduction', in Gillis, Howie and Munford (eds), *Third Wave Feminism: A Critical Exploration*, Houndmills: Palgrave Macmillan, pp. xi–xxiv.

Glick, Elisa (2000), 'Sex Positive: Feminism, Queer Theory, and the Politics of Transgression', *Feminist Review*, 64, 19–45.

Gonda, Caroline (1995), 'An Other Country? Mapping Scottish/Lesbian/Writing', in Christopher Whyte (ed.), *Gendering the Nation: Studies in Scottish Modern Literature*, Edinburgh: Edinburgh University Press, pp. 1–24.

Gordimer, Nadine (1968), 'The International Symposium on the Short Story: South Africa', *Kenyon Review*, 30:4, 457–63.

Graham, Barbara A. (2003), 'Next of Kin', in Karen McCarthy (ed.), *Kin: New Fiction by Black & Asian Women*, London: Serpent's Tail, pp. 57–76.

Green, George (2011), 'Orcs on Mars: Historical Fiction and the Short Story', *Short Fiction in Theory and Practice*, 1:1, 59–69.

Greer, Germaine [1991] (1992), *The Change: Women, Ageing and the Menopause*, London: Penguin.

Greer, Germaine [1970] (2006), *The Female Eunuch*, London: HarperCollins.

Griffin, Christine (2004), 'Good Girls, Bad Girls: Anglocentrism and Diversity in the Constitution of Contemporary Girlhood', in Anita Harris (ed.), *All About the Girl: Cultures, Power and Identity*, New York: Routledge, pp. 29–43.

Grogan, S. (1999), *Body Image: Understanding Body Dissatisfaction in Men, Women and Children*, London: Routledge.

Hadley, Tessa (2006), 'Her Proper Duties', *London Review of Books*, 28:1, <http://www.lrb.co.uk/v28/n01/tessa-hadley/her-proper-duties> (last accessed 12 December 2016).

Halberstam, Judith (1998), *Female Masculinity*, Durham, NC: Duke University Press.

Halberstam, Judith (2005), *In a Queer Time and Place: Transgender Bodies, Subcultural Lives*, New York: New York University Press.

Halberstam, Judith (2011), *The Queer Art of Failure*, Durham, NC: Duke University Press.

Hall, Donald (2003), *Queer Theories*, Houndmills: Palgrave Macmillan.

Hall, Sarah (2011), *The Beautiful Indifference*, London: Faber and Faber.

Halperin, David (1995), *Saint Foucault: Towards a Gay Hagiography*, Oxford: Oxford University Press.

Hanisch, Carol (2013), 'The Personal is Political', 25 August, <http://www.carolhanisch.org/CHwritings/PIP.html> (last accessed 17 March 2015).

Hanson, Clare (1985), *Short Stories and Short Fictions, 1880–1980*, Houndmills: Macmillan.

Hanson, Clare (1989a), 'Introduction', in Hanson (ed.), *Re-Reading the Short Story*, Houndmills: Macmillan, pp. 1–9.

Hanson, Clare (1989b), '"Things out of Words": Towards a Poetics of Short Fiction', in Hanson (ed.), *Re-Reading the Short Story*. Houndmills: Macmillan, pp. 22–33.

Hanson, Clare (1994), *Virginia Woolf*, Houndmills: Macmillan.

Hanson, Clare (1996), 'The Lifted Veil: Women and Short Fiction in the 1880s and 1890s', *Yearbook of English Studies*, 26, 135–42.

Hanson, Clare (2000), 'During Mother's Absence: The Fiction of Michèle Roberts', in Abby H. P. Werlock (ed.), *British Women Writing Fiction*, Tuscaloosa: University of Alabama Press, pp. 229–47.

Harde, Roxanne (ed.) (2007), *Narratives of Community: Women's Short Story Sequences*, Newcastle: Cambridge Scholars.

Harmes, Marcus K. (2013), 'A Creature Not Quite of This World: Adaptations of Margaret Thatcher on 1980s British Television', *Journal of Popular Television*, 1, 53–68.

Harris, Amanthi (2003), 'Red Sari', in Karen McCarthy (ed.), *Kin: New Fiction by Black & Asian Women*, London: Serpent's Tail, pp. 101–11.

Hastings, Chris (2014), 'Thatcher "Murder" is BBC's Book at Bedtime: Radio 4 Ignores Protests to Give Author's "Sick and Perverted" Fantasy a Coveted Broadcast Slot', *MailOnline*, 13 December, < http://www.dailymail.co.uk/news/article-2873006/Thatcher-murder-BBC-s-Book-Bedtime-Radio-4-ignores-protests-author-s-sick-perverted-fantasy-coveted-broadcast-slot.html> (last accessed 10 June 2016).

Head, Dominic [1992] (1994), *The Modernist Short Story: A Study in Theory and Practice*, Cambridge: Cambridge University Press.

Hekman, Susan (2000), 'Beyond Identity: Feminism, Identity and Identity Politics', *Feminist Theory*, 1:3, 289–308.

Hemmings, Clare (2005), 'Telling Feminist Stories', *Feminist Theory*, 6:2, 115–39.

Hemmings, Clare (2011), *Why Stories Matter: The Political Grammar of Feminist Theory*, Durham, NC: Duke University Press.

Henry, Astrid (2004), *Not My Mother's Sister: Generational Conflict and Third-Wave Feminism*, Bloomington: Indiana University Press.

Hensher, Philip (ed.) (2015), *The Penguin Book of the British Short Story, Vols I and II*, London: Penguin.

Herd, David and Anna Pincus (ed.) (2016), *Refugee Tales*, Manchester: Comma Press, e-book.

Hernández, Daisy and Bushra Rehman (eds) (2002), *Colonize This! Young Women of Color on Today's Feminism*, New York: Seal Press.

Heywood, Leslie and Jennifer Drake (1997), 'Introduction', in Heywood and Drake (eds), *Third Wave Agenda: Being Feminist, Doing Feminism*, Minneapolis: University of Minnesota Press, pp. 1–20.

Hill, Susan (ed.) (1990), *The Penguin Book of Modern Women's Short Stories*, London: Penguin.

Hill, Susan (ed.) (1995), *The Penguin Book of Contemporary Women's Short Stories*, London: Penguin.

Hill, Susan (ed.) [1988] (1997), *The Second Penguin Book of Modern Women's Short Stories*, London: Penguin.

Hill Collins, Patricia (2000), *Black Feminist Thought: Knowledge, Consciousness, and the Politics of Empowerment*, New York: Routledge.

Hinds, Hilary and Jackie Stacey (2001), 'Imaging Feminism, Imaging Femininity: The Bra-Burner, Diana, and the Woman Who Kills', *Feminist Media Studies*, 1:2, 153–77.

Hislop, Victoria (2012), *The Last Dance and Other Stories*, London: Headline.

Hislop, Victoria (2013), *The Story: Love, Loss & the Lives of Women: 100 Great Short Stories*, London: Head of Zeus.

Hollows, Joanne (2000), *Feminism, Femininity and Popular Culture*, Manchester: Manchester University Press.

Horton, Emily (2013), 'Contemporary Space and Affective Ethics in Ali Smith's Short Stories', in Monica Germanà and Horton (eds), *Ali Smith: Contemporary Critical Perspectives*, London: Bloomsbury, pp. 9–22.

Humm, Maggie (1994), *A Reader's Guide to Contemporary Feminist Criticism*, Hemel Hempstead: Harvest Wheatsheaf.

Hunter, Adrian (2007), *The Cambridge Introduction to the Short Story in English*, Cambridge: Cambridge University Press.

Hunter, Margaret (2005), *Race, Gender and the Politics of Skin Tone*, London: Routledge.

Hurley, Ursula (2011), 'Look Back in Wonder: How the Endings of Short Stories Can Be Their Most Powerful and Effective Distinguishing Features', *Short Fiction in Theory and Practice*, 1:1, 25–35.

Hussey, Mark (2004), 'Mrs. Thatcher and Mrs. Woolf', *MFS Modern Fiction Studies*, 50, 8–30.

Iser, Wolfgang (1980), *The Act of Reading: A Theory of Aesthetic Response*, Baltimore: Johns Hopkins University Press.

Jackson, Stevi (2006), 'Heterosexuality, Sexuality and Gender: Re-Thinking the Intersections', in Diane Richardson, Janice McLaughlin and Mark E. Casey (eds), *Intersections Between Feminist and Queer Theory*, Houndmills: Palgrave Macmillan, pp. 38–58.

Jagger, Alison M. (1983), *Feminist Politics and Human Nature*, Oxford: Rowman & Littlefield.

Jagose, Annamarie (1996), *Queer Theory*, Victoria: Melbourne University Press.

Jagose, Annamarie (2009), 'Feminism's Queer Theory', *Feminism and Psychology*, 19:2, 157–74.

Jeffreys, Sheila (2003), *Unpacking Queer Politics: A Lesbian Feminist Perspective*, Cambridge: Polity.

Jones, Adele (2009/2010), 'A Feminist Act of Adaptation: Identities and Discourses in Michèle Roberts's *In the Red Kitchen*', *Neo-Victorian Studies*, 2:2, 86–108.

Jones, Carole (2009), *Disappearing Men: Gender Disorientation in Scottish Fiction, 1979–1999*, Amsterdam: Rodopi.

Jones, Carole (2015), '"Femininity in crisis": The Troubled Trajectory of Feminism in Laura Hird's *Born Free* and Jenni Fagan's *The Panopticon*', *Contemporary Women's Writing*, 9:3, 385–400.

Kaur, Kalbinder (2003), 'When English Girls Hold Hands', in Karen McCarthy (ed.), *Kin: New Fiction by Black & Asian Women*, London: Serpent's Tail, pp. 57–76.

Kay, Jackie (2012), *Reality, Reality*, London: Picador.

Kellaway, Kate (2000), 'Life is What You Had Before Kids', *Observer*, 8 October, <http://www.guardian.co.uk/books/2000/oct/08/fiction. reviews> (last accessed 3 March 2013).

Kelly, Adam (2014), '"It's a Sick Book Being Promoted by a Sick Broadcasting Corporation": Lord Tebbit Leads Fury at BBC Choosing Story about Margaret Thatcher Being Murdered as Book at Bedtime', *Daily Mail*, 14 December, <http://www.dailymail.co.uk/news/article-2873842/ It-s-sick-book-promoted-sick-broadcasting-corporation-Lord-Tebbit-leads-fury-BBC-choosing-story-Margaret-Thatcher-murdered-Book-Bedtime.html> (last accessed 15 June 2016).

Kim, Rina (2012), 'Introduction: Cross-Gendered Literary Voices', in Kim and Claire Westall (eds), *Cross-Gendered Literary Voices: Appropriating, Resisting, Embracing*, Houndmills: Palgrave Macmillan, pp. 1–11.

Kimmel, Michael (2002), 'Foreword', in Judith Gardiner (ed.), *Masculinity Studies and Feminist Theory*, New York: Columbia University Press, pp. ix–xi.

King, Jeannette (2013), *Discourses of Ageing in Fiction and Feminism: The Invisible Woman*, Houndmills: Palgrave Macmillan.

Knight, Damon (1997), *Creating Short Fiction*, New York: St Martin's Griffin.

Kooistra, Lorraine Janzen and Dennis Denisoff (2012), 'Introduction to the Yellow Nineties', in Denisoff and Kooistra (eds), *The Yellow Nineties Online*, Ryerson University, <http://www.1890s.ca/HTML. aspx?s=Intro_Y90s.html> (last accessed 11 December 2013).

Kristeva, Julia (1981), 'Women's Time', trans. Alice Jardine and Harry Blake, *Signs*, 7:1, 13–35.

Lanser, Susan S. (1996), 'Queering Narratology', in Kathy Mezei (ed.), *Ambiguous Discourse: Feminist Narratology and British Women Writers*, Chapel Hill, NC: University of North Carolina Press, pp. 250–61.

Ledger, Sally (1997), *The New Woman: Fiction and Feminism at the Fin de Siècle*, Manchester: Manchester University Press.

Lee, Hermione [1978] (1993), 'Introduction', in Lee (ed.), *The Secret Self 2: Short Stories by Women*, London: Everyman.

Lee, Hermione [1987] (1995), 'Introduction', in Lee (ed.), *The Secret Self: A Century of Short Stories by Women*, Weidenfeld: Phoenix Giants.

Levy, Andrea (2014), *Six Stories & an Essay*, London: Headline.

Lezard, Nicholas (2011), 'Mum's Rush', *Guardian*, 30 June, <http://www. guardian.co.uk/books/2001/jun/30/fiction.reviews3> (last accessed 3 March 2013).

Lezard, Nicholas (2012), 'A Bunch of Fives by Helen Simpson: Review', *Guardian*, 22 May, <http://www.guardian.co.uk/books/2012/may/22/ bunch-of-fives-helen-simpson-review> (last accessed 3 March 2013).

Liggins, Emma, Andrew Maunder and Ruth Robbins (2010), *British Short Story*, Houndmills: Palgrave Macmillan.

Lister, Rachel (2007), 'Female Expansion and Masculine Immobilization in the Short Story Cycle', *Journal of the Short Story in English*, 48, 43–58.

Lohafer, Susan and Jo Elleyn Clarey (eds) (1989), *Short Story Theory and a Crossroads*, Baton Rouge: Louisiana State University Press.

Lopez-Ropero, Lourdes (2016), 'Searching for a "Different Kind of Freedom": Postcoloniality and Postfeminist Subjecthood in Zadie Smith's *NW*', *Journal of the Spanish Association of Anglo-American Studies*, 38:2, 123–39.

Lounsberry, Barbara, Susan Lohafer, Mary Rohrberger, Stephen Pett and R. C. Feddersen (eds) (1998), *The Tales We Tell: Perspectives on the Short Story*, Westport, CT: Greenwood Press.

Lumsden, Alison (2000), 'Scottish Women's Short Stories: "Repositories of Life Swiftly Apprehended"', in Aileen Christianson and Lumsden (eds), *Contemporary Scottish Women Writers*, Edinburgh: Edinburgh University Press, pp. 156–69.

Luscher, Robert M. (1989), 'The Short Story Sequence: An Open Book', in Susan Lohafer and Jo Elleyn Clarey (eds), *Short Story Theory at a Crossroads*, Baton Rouge: Louisiana State University Press, pp. 148–67.

McBean, Sam (2016), *Feminism's Queer Temporalities*, Abingdon: Routledge.

McCarthy, Karen (ed.) (2003), *Kin: New Fiction by Black & Asian Women*, London: Serpent's Tail.

McClave, Heather (ed.) (1980), *Women Writers of the Short Story*, Englewood Cliffs, NJ: Prentice Hall.

McDermott, Sinead (2006), 'Kate Atkinson's Family Romance: Missing Mothers and Hidden Histories in *Behind the Scenes at the Museum*', *Critical Survey*, 18:2, 67–78.

McInnes, John (1998), *The End of Masculinity: The Confusion of Sexual Genesis and Sexual Difference in Modern Society*, Buckingham: Open University Press.

McLaughlin, Janice, Mark E. Casey and Diane Richardson (2006), 'Introduction', in Richardson, McLaughlin and Casey (eds), *Intersections Between Feminist and Queer Theory*, Houndmills: Palgrave Macmillan, pp. 1–18.

McRobbie, Angela (2007), 'Postfeminism and Popular Culture: Bridget Jones and the New Gender Regime', in Yvonne Tasker and Diane Negra (eds), *Interrogating Postfeminism*, Durham, NC: Duke University Press, pp. 27–39.

McVeigh, Tracey (2013), 'Meet the New Wave of Activists Making Feminism Thrive in a Digital Age', *Guardian*, 1 June, <https://www.theguardian.com/world/2013/jun/01/activists-feminism-digital> (last accessed 20 December 2016).

Malcolm, David (2007), *The British and Irish Short Story Handbook*, Chichester: Wiley-Blackwell.

Mannix, Daniel [1963] (2014), *The History of Torture*, Lake Oswego, OR: eNet Press.

Mantel, Hilary (2014), *The Assassination of Margaret Thatcher and Other Stories*, London: Fourth Estate.

March-Russell, Paul (2009), *The Short Story: An Introduction*, Edinburgh: Edinburgh University Press.

Marcus, Sharon (2005), 'Queer Theory for Everyone: A Review Essay', *Signs*, 31, 191–218.

Marinucci, Mimi (2010), *Feminism is Queer: The Intimate Connection Between Queer and Feminist Theory*, London: Zed Books.

Marsh, Nicky (2007), 'Taking the Maggie: Money, Sovereignty, and Masculinity in British Fiction of the Eighties', *MFS Modern Fiction Studies*, 53:4, 845–66.

Mars-Jones, Adam (2006), 'Brief Lives', *Observer*, 8 January, <http://www.guardian.co.uk/books/2006/jan/08/fiction.features3> (last accessed 7 June 2016).

Martin, Biddy, (1994), 'Sexualities without Gender and Other Queer Utopias', *Diacritics*, 24:2–3, 104–21.

Matthews, Brander (1994), 'The Philosophy of the Short-Story', in Charles E. May (ed.), *The New Short Story Theories*, Athens: Ohio University Press, pp. 73–80.

May, Charles E. (1994), 'The Nature of Knowledge in Short Fiction', in May (ed.), *The New Short Story Theories*, Athens: Ohio University Press, pp. 131–43.

Meyer, Michael (2008), 'Feminist Voices: Women's Short Fiction After 1945', in Cheryl Alexander Malcolm and David Malcolm (eds), *A Companion to the British and Irish Short Story*, Oxford: Blackwell, pp. 342–54.

Miller, Lucasta (2007), 'Take Risks: An Interview with Michèle Roberts', *Guardian*, 14 July, <http://www.guardian.co.uk/books/2007/jul/14/fiction.women> (last accessed 9 July 2013).

Millett, Kate [1970] (1977), *Sexual Politics*, London: Virago.

Miner, Valerie (1978), 'Feminist Fiction and Politics', in Zoë Fairbairns, Sara Maitland, Miner, Michèle Roberts and Michelene Wandor (eds), *Tales I Tell My Mother: A Collection of Feminist Short Stories*, London: Journeyman Press, pp. 61–3.

Mitchell, Juliet and Ann Oakley (eds) (1986), *What is Feminism?*, New York: Pantheon.

Mitchell, Kaye (2013), 'Queer Metamorphoses: *Girl Meets Boy* and the Futures of Queer Fiction', in Monica Germanà and Emily Horton (eds), *Ali Smith: Contemporary Critical Perspectives*, London: Bloomsbury, pp. 61–74.

Modleski, Tania [1982] (1994), *Loving with a Vengeance: Mass-Produced Fantasies for Women*, London: Routledge.

Mohanty, Chandra Talpade (1984), 'Under Western Eyes: Feminist Scholarship and Colonial Discourses', *Boundary 2*, 12:3, 333–58.

Moi, Toril (2002), *Sexual/Textual Politics: Feminist Literary Theory*, London: Routledge.

Monaghan, David (2001), 'Margaret Thatcher, and the Struggle for Working-Class Identity', *JPF&T: Journal of Popular Film and Television*, 29, 2–13.

Mosse, Kate (2013), *The Mistletoe Bride and Other Haunting Tales*, London: Orion.

Mullan, John (2006), 'Limited Lives', *Guardian*, 8 April, <http://www.guardian.co.uk/books/2006/apr/08/featuresreviews.guardianreview4> (last accessed 3 March 2013).

Mundler, Helen E. (2009), 'Apocalypse and the Resurgence of the Creative Imagination in *Not the End of the World* by Kate Atkinson', *Journal of the Short Story in English*, 52, 195–206.

Munford, Rebecca (2007), '"Wake up and smell the lipgloss": Gender, Generation and the (A)Politics of Girl Power', in Stacy Gillis, Gillian Howie and Rebecca Munford (eds), *Third Wave Feminism: A Critical Exploration*, Houndmills: Palgrave Macmillan, pp. 266–79.

Murphy, Meghan (2014), 'Kicking Against our Foremothers: Does Feminism have an Ageism Problem?', *New Statesman*, 26 February, <http://www.newstatesman.com/2014/02/kicking-against-our-foremothers-does-feminism-have-ageism-problem> (last accessed 7 March 2014).

Nestle, Joan (ed.) (1987), *A Restricted Country: Essays and Short Stories*, London: Sheba Feminist.

Newman, Jenny (2003), 'An Interview with Michèle Roberts', *Cercles*, <http://www.cercles.com/interviews/roberts.html> (last accessed 12 May 2015).

Nissen, Axel (2004), 'The Queer Short Story', in Per Winther, Jakobe Lothe and Hans H. Skei (eds), *Art of Brevity: Excursion in Short Fiction Theory and Analysis*, Columbia: University of South Carolina Press, pp. 181–90.

Noble, Jean Bobby (2003), *Masculinities without Men? Female Masculinity in Twentieth-Century Fictions*, Vancouver: University of British Columbia Press.

Nochimson, Martha (1992), *No End to Her: Soap Opera and the Female Subject*, Berkeley: University of California Press.

Oakley, Ann [1974] (1990), *Housewife*, London: Penguin.

O'Connor, Frank (1963), *The Lonely Voice*, London: Macmillan.

Orel, Harold (1986), *The Victorian Short Story: Development and Triumph of a Literary Genre*, Cambridge: Cambridge University Press.

Orr, Katherine (2011), 'Overturning the Narrative: An Interview with Helen Simpson', *Short Fiction in Theory and Practice*, 1, 109–18.

Parker, Emma (2007), 'The Real Thing: Transsexuality and Manhood in Rose Tremain's *Sacred Country*', *Women: A Cultural Review*, 18:3, 303–26.

Patea, Viorica (2012), 'The Short Story: An Overview of the History and Evolution of the Genre', in Patea (ed.), *Short Story Theories: A Twenty-First-Century Perspective*, Amsterdam: Rodopi, pp. 1–25.

Pearce, Sharyn (2000), 'Performance Anxiety: The Interaction of Gender and Power in *The Full Monty*', *Australian Feminist Studies*, 15:32, 227–36.

Pickering, Jean (1989), 'Time and the Short Story', in Clare Hanson (ed.), *Re-Reading the Short Story*, Houndmills: Macmillan, pp. 45–54.

Pilcher, Jane (1999), *Women in Contemporary Britain: An Introduction*, London: Routledge.

Pratt, Mary Louise [1981] (1994), 'The Short Story: The Long and the Short of It', in Charles E. May (ed.), *The New Short Story Theories*, Athens: Ohio University Press, pp. 91–113.

Quinsey, Katherine M. (1996), 'Introduction', in Quinsey (ed.), *Broken Boundaries: Women and Feminism in Restoration Drama*, Lexington: University of Kentucky Press, pp. 1–12.

Radicalesbians (1970), 'The Woman-Identified Women', in *The Women's Liberation Movement: An On-Line Archival Collection*, Special Collections Library: Duke University, <http://library.duke.edu/rubenstein/scriptorium/wlm/womid/> (last accessed 2 July 2014).

Raven, Charlotte (2010), 'How the "New Feminism" went Wrong', *Guardian*, 6 March, <http://www.guardian.co.uk/books/2010/mar/06/charlotte-raven-feminism-madonna-price> (last accessed 9 July 2014).

Redfern, Catherine and Kristin Aune (2010), *Reclaiming the F Word: The New Feminist Movement*, London: Zed Books.

Reid, Ian (1977), *The Short Story*, London: Methuen.

Reynolds, Margaret (ed.) [1990] (1998), *Erotica: Women's Writing from Sappho to Margaret Atwood*, New York: Ballantine Books.

Rich, Adrienne (1972), 'When We Dead Awaken: Writing as Re-Vision', *College English*, 34:2, 18–30.

Rich, Adrienne (1980), 'Compulsory Heterosexuality and Lesbian Existence', *Signs*, 5:4, 631–60.

Rich, Adrienne [1976] (1992), *Of Woman Born: Motherhood as Experience and Institution*, London: Virago.

Richardson, Diane (2000), *Rethinking Heterosexuality*, London: Sage.

Richardson, Diane (2006), 'Bordering Theory', in Richardson, Janice McLaughlin and Mark E. Casey (eds), *Intersections Between Feminist and Queer Theory*, Houndmills: Palgrave Macmillan, pp. 19–37.

Riley, Sarah C. E. and Christina Scharff (2012), 'Feminism versus Femininity? Exploring Feminist Dilemmas through Cooperative Inquiry Research', *Feminism & Psychology*, 23:2, 207–23.

Roberts, Michèle (1983), 'Questions and Answers', in Michelene Wandor (ed.), *On Gender and Writing*, London: Pandora Press, pp. 62–8.

Roberts, Michèle [1993] (1994a), *During Mother's Absence*, London: Virago.

Roberts, Michèle (1994b), 'Yellow Scarf Dreams: *Evangelista's Fan* by Rose Tremain', *Independent*, 16 July, <http://www.independent.co.uk/

arts-entertainment/books/book-review--yellow-scarf-dreams-evangelis-
tas-fan--rose-tremain-sinclairstevenson-1499-pounds-michele-roberts-
considers-the-refined-clarity-and-historical-fervour-of-rose-tremains-
short-stories-1414222.html> (last accessed 14 March 2013).

Roberts, Michèle (1998), *Food, Sex & God: On Inspiration and Writing*, London: Virago.

Roberts, Michèle (1999), 'Taking the P', *Guardian*, 11 October, <http://www.guardian.co.uk/world/1999/oct/11/gender.uk1> (last accessed 9 April 2013).

Roberts, Michèle (2001), *Playing Sardines*, London: Virago.

Roberts, Michèle (2010), *Mud: Stories of Sex and Love*, London: Virago.

Rogers, Jane (2012), *Hitting Trees with Sticks*, Manchester: Comma Press, e-book.

Roiphe, Kate (1993), *The Morning After: Sex, Fear, and Feminism*, London: Hamish Hamilton.

Roof, Judith (1996), *Come as You Are: Sexuality and Narrative*, New York: Columbia University Press.

Rowbotham, Sheila (1973), *Hidden from History: 300 Years of Women's Oppression and the Fight Against It*, London: Pluto Press.

Rowbotham, Sheila [1972] (1990), 'The Beginnings of Women's Liberation in Britain', in Michelene Wandor (ed.), *Once a Feminist: Stories of a Generation*, London: Virago, pp. 14–27.

Rowbotham, Sheila (1992), *Women in Movement: Feminism and Social Action*, New York: Routledge.

Rowland, Susan (1999), 'Michèle Roberts' Virgins: Contesting Gender in Fictions, Re-Writing Jungian Theory and Christian Myth', *Journal of Gender Studies*, 8:1, 35–42.

Rushdie, Salman [1991] (1992), 'Imaginary Homelands', in Rushdie (ed.), *Imaginary Homelands: Essays and Criticism 1981–91*, London: Granta.

Rutherford, Jonathan (1988), 'Who's that Man?', in Rowena Chapman and Rutherford (eds), *Male Order: Unwrapping Masculinity*, London: Lawrence and Wishart, pp. 21–67.

Sanger, Nadia (2009), 'New Women, Old Messages? Constructions of Femininities, Race and Hypersexualised Bodies in Selected South African Magazines, 2003–2006', *Social Dynamics: A Journal of African Studies*, 35:1, 137–48.

Sceats, Sarah (2005), 'Appetite, Desire and Belonging in the Novels of Rose Tremain', in James Acheson and Sarah C. E. Ross (eds), *The Contemporary British Novel Since 1980*, Edinburgh: Edinburgh University Press, pp. 165–76.

Sedgwick, Eve Kosofsky (1990), *Epistemology of the Closet*, Berkeley: University of California Press.

Sedgwick, Eve Kosofsky (1993), *Between Men: English Literature and Male Homosocial Desire*, New York: Columbia Press.

Sedgwick, Eve Kosofsky (1998), *Tendencies*, London: Routledge.

Segal, Lynne (1994), *Straight Sex: The Politics of Pleasure*, London: Virago.

Segal, Lynne (2001), 'Only Contradictions on Offer: Anglophone Feminism at the Millennium', in Marianne DeKoven (ed.), *Feminist Locations: Global and Local, Theory and Practice*, New Brunswick, NJ: Rutgers University Press, pp. 37–59.

Shaw, Valerie (1983), *The Short Story: A Critical Introduction*, London: Longman.

Sheba Collective (ed.) (1989), *Serious Pleasure: Lesbian Erotic Stories and Poetry*, London: Sheba Feminist.

Sheba Collective (ed.) (1990), *More Serious Pleasure: Lesbian Erotic Stories and Poetry*, London: Sheba Feminist.

Showalter, Elaine [1977] (1984), *A Literature of Their Own: British Novelists from Brontë to Lessing*, London: Virago.

Showalter, Elaine (1993), 'Introduction', in Showalter (ed.), *Daughters of Decadence: Women Writers of the Fin-de-Siècle*, London: Virago, pp. vii–xx.

Shriver, Lionel (2010), 'Introduction', in Betty Friedan, *The Feminine Mystique*, London: Penguin, pp. v–xi.

Siegel, Deborah L. (1997a), 'The Legacy of the Personal: Generating Theory in Feminism's Third Wave', *Hypatia*, 12:3, 46–75.

Siegel, Deborah L. (1997b), 'Reading Between the Waves: Feminist Historiography in a "Postfeminist" Moment', in Leslie Heywood and Jennifer Drake (eds), *Third Wave Agenda: Being Feminist, Doing Feminism*, Minneapolis: University of Minnesota Press, pp. 55–82.

Simpson, Helen [1990] (1991), *Four Bare Legs in a Bed*, London: Minerva.

Simpson, Helen [1995] (2001a), *Dear George*, London: Vintage.

Simpson, Helen [2000] (2001b), *Hey Yeah Right Get a Life*, London: Vintage.

Simpson, Helen (2003), 'Introduction', in Susan Dick (ed.), *Virginia Woolf: A Haunted House: The Complete Shorter Fiction*, London: Vintage, pp. vii–xiv.

Simpson, Helen [2005] (2006a), *Constitutional*, London: Vintage.

Simpson, Helen (2006b), 'With Child', *Guardian*, 22 April, <http://www.guardian.co.uk/books/2006/apr/22/featuresreviews.guardianreview3> (last accessed 3 March 2013).

Simpson, Helen (2010), *In-Flight Entertainment*, London: Jonathan Cape.

Simpson, Helen (2012), *A Bunch of Fives: Selected Stories*, London: Vintage.

Simpson, Helen (2014), 'Re: Textual Allusion', email message to Emma Young, 7 July.

Sinclair, Peter (1987), 'Foreword', in Zoë Fairburns, Sara Maitland, Valerie Miner, Michèle Roberts and Michelene Wandor (eds), *More Tales I Tell My Mother*, London: Journeyman Press, pp. vii–viii.

Skelton, Felicity (2013), 'Echo Writes Back: The Figure of the Author in "True Short Story" by Ali Smith', *Short Fiction in Theory and Practice*, 2:1–2, 99–111.

Smith, Ali (1995), *Free Love and Other Stories*, London: Virago.

Smith, Ali (1996), 'The Preconception Game', in Lizabeth Goodman (ed.), *Literature and Gender*, London: Routledge, pp. 4–9.

Smith, Ali [1999] (2004a), *Other Stories and Other Stories*, London: Penguin.

Smith, Ali [2003] (2004b), *The Whole Story and Other Stories*, London: Penguin.

Smith, Ali (2008), *The First Person and Other Stories*, London: Hamish Hamilton.

Smith, Ali (2009), 'The Definite Article', in *Park Stories*, London: The Royal Parks.

Smith, Ali (2012), 'Short Story Report', *The Bridport Prize 2009*, 12 March, <http://www.bridportprize.org.uk/alismith report.htm> (last accessed 23 June 2016).

Smith, Ali (2015), 'The Detainee's Tale', *Guardian*, 15 June, <https://www.theguardian.com/books/2015/jun/27/ali-smith-so-far-the-detainees-tale-extract> (last accessed 5 January 2017).

Smith, Barbara (1982), 'Toward a Black Feminist Criticism', in Gloria T. Hull, Patricia Bell Scott and Smith (eds), *But Some of Us Are Brave*, Old Westbury, NY: Feminist Press, pp. 157–75.

Smith, Zadie (2013), *The Embassy of Cambodia*, London: Hamish Hamilton.

Smith, Zadie (2016), 'Two Men Arrive in a Village', *New Yorker*, 6 and 13 June, <http://www.newyorker.com/magazine/2016/06/06/two-men-arrive-in-a-village-by-zadie-smith> (last accessed 15 October 2016).

Snyder-Hall, Claire (2010), 'Third-Wave Feminism and the Defence of "Choice"', *Symposium: Women's Choices and the Future of Feminism*, 8, 255–61.

Spivak Gayatri Chakravorty (1988), 'Can the Subaltern Speak?', in Cary Nelson and Lawrence Grossberg (eds), *Marxism and the Interpretation of Culture*, London: Macmillan, pp. 271–313.

Spivak, Gayatri Chakravorty [1987] (2006), *In Other Worlds: Essays in Cultural Politics*, New York: Routledge.

Steffens, Daneet (2007), 'Interview: Helen Simpson', *Mslexia*, 35:1, <http://www.mslexia.co.uk/magazine/interviews/interview_35.php> (last accessed 3 March 2013).

Sullivan, Nikki (2003), *A Critical Introduction to Queer Theory*, Edinburgh: Edinburgh University Press.

Tate, Shirley Anne (2009), *Black Beauty: Aesthetics, Stylizations, Politics*, Farnham: Ashgate.

Taylor, Anthea (2003), 'What's So New About "The New Femininity?"': Feminism, Femininity and the Discourse of the New', *Hecate: An Interdisciplinary Journal of Women's Liberation*, 29:2, 182–98.

Third World Woman's Alliance (1973), 'The Black's Woman's Manifesto', in *The Women's Liberation Movement: An On-Line Archival Collection*, Special Collections Library: Duke University, <http://library.duke.edu/rubenstein/scriptorium/wlm/blkmanif/> (last accessed 8 July 2013).

Thomas, Calvin (2000), *Straight with a Twist: Queer Theory and the Subject of Heterosexuality*, Champaign: University of Illinois Press.

Thornham, Sue (2001), 'Second Wave Feminism', in Sarah Gamble (ed.), *The Routledge Companion to Feminism and Postfeminism*, London: Routledge, pp. 29–42.

Tolan, Fiona (2009), '"Everyone has left something here": The Storyteller-Historian in Kate Atkinson's *Behind the Scenes at the Museum*', *Critique Studies in Contemporary Fiction*, 50, 275–90.

Tremain, Rose [1987] (1988), *The Garden of Villa Mollini and Other Stories*, London: Sceptre.

Tremain, Rose [1994] (1995), *Evangelista's Fan and Other Stories*, London: Minerva.

Tremain, Rose [1983] (1999), *The Colonel's Daughter and Other Stories*, London: Vintage.

Tremain, Rose [1999] (2006), *The Darkness of Wallis Simpson and Other Stories*, London: Vintage.

Tremain, Rose (2010a), 'Still Lives', *Guardian*, 26 June, <http://www.guardian.co.uk/culture/2010/jun/26/rose-tremain-portraits-and-writing> (last accessed 18 January 2013).

Tremain, Rose (2010b), 'Wallis Simpson: Just Who Did She Think She Was?', *Telegraph*, 14 December, <http://www.telegraph.co.uk/culture/tvandradio/8202340/Wallis-Simpson-Just-who-did-she-think-she-was.html> (last accessed 9 July 2015).

Tremain, Rose (2012), 'The Art of Not Winning Literary Prizes', *Guardian*, 8 November, <http://www.guardian.co.uk/books/2012/nov/08/art-of-not-winning-literary-prizes> (last accessed 18 January 2013).

Trussler, Michael (1996), 'Suspended Narratives: The Short Story and Temporality', *Studies in Short Fiction*, 33:4, 557–77.

Tuttle Hansen, Elaine (1997), *Mother without Child: Contemporary Fiction and the Crisis of Motherhood*, Berkeley: University of California Press.

Umansky, Lauri (1996), *Motherhood Reconceived: Feminism and the Legacies of the Sixties*, New York: New York University Press.

Viner, Katherine (1990), 'The Personal is Still Political', in Natasha Walter (ed.), *On the Move: Feminism for a New Generation*, London: Virago, pp. 10–26.

Vowler, Tom (2013), 'An Interview with Michèle Roberts', *Short Fiction: The Visual Literary Journal*, 3 April, <http://www.shortfictionjournal.co.uk/ ?page_id=355> (last accessed 7 October 2014).

Walker, Rebecca (ed.) (1995), *To Be Real: Telling the Truth and Changing the Face of Feminism*, New York: Anchor.

Walker, Rebecca (2001), 'I Am the Third Wave', in Barbara Ryan (ed.), *Identity Politics in the Women's Movement*, New York: New York University Press, pp. 78–80.

Walter, Natasha (ed.) (1999a), *On the Move: Feminism for a New Generation*, London: Virago.

Walter, Natasha [1998] (1999b), *The New Feminism*, London: Virago.

Walter, Natasha [2010] (2011), *Living Dolls: The Return of Sexism*, London: Virago.

Wandor, Michelene (ed.) (1972), *The Body Politic: Women's Liberation in Britain, 1969–1972*, London: Stage 1.

Wandor, Michelene (ed.) (1983), *On Gender and Writing*, Kitchener, ON: Pandora Press.

Wandor, Michelene (ed.) (1990), *Once a Feminist: Stories of a Generation*, London: Virago.

Warner, Michael (1993), 'Introduction', in Warner (ed.), *Fear of a Queer Planet: Queer Politics and Social Theory*, Minneapolis: University of Minnesota Press, pp. vii–xxxi.

Wassermann, Steve (2012), 'Short Story Masterclass with Michèle Robert', *THRESHOLDS*, <http://blogs.chi.ac.uk/shortstoryforum/wp-content/uploads/2012/12/Short-Story-Masterclass-with-Michele-Roberts.mp3> (last accessed 2 March 2014).

Weeks, Karen (2003), 'Postmodernism in Women's Short Story Cycles: Lorrie Moore's *Anagrams*', in Farhat Iftekharruddin, Joseph Boyden, Mary Rohrberger and Jai Claudet (eds), *The Postmodern Short Story: Forms and Issues*, Westport, CT: Praeger, pp. 94–106.

Weigman, Robyn (2002), 'Unmaking: Men and Masculinity in Feminist Theory', in Judith Kegan Gardiner (ed.), *Masculinity Studies and Feminist Theory*, New York: Columbia University Press, pp. 31–59.

Wesely, J. K. (2002), 'Growing up Sexualized: Issues of Power and Violence in the Lives of Female Exotic Dancers', *Violence against Women*, 8:10, 1182–1207.

Westall, Claire (2012), 'Conclusion: Crossings and Re-Crossings', in Rina Kim and Westall (eds), *Cross-Gendered Literary Voices: Appropriating, Resisting, Embracing*, Houndmills: Palgrave Macmillan, pp. 222–37.

Whelehan, Imelda (1995), *Modern Feminist Thought: From Second Wave to 'Post-Feminism'*, Edinburgh: Edinburgh University Press.

Whelehan, Imelda (2000), *Overloaded: Popular Culture and the Future of Feminism*, London: Women's Press.

White, Rosie (2003), 'Permeable Borders, Possible Worlds: History and Identity in the Novels of Michèle Roberts', *Studies in the Literary Imagination*, 36:2, 71–90.

White, Rosie (2004), 'Visions and Re-Visions: Women and Time in Michèle Roberts' *In the Red Kitchen*', *Women: A Cultural Review*, 15:2, 180–91.

Whitehead, Stephen M. (2002), *Men and Masculinities: Key Themes and New Directions*, Chichester: Wiley.

Williams, Kirsty (2006), '"A Different Kind of Natural": The Fiction of Jackie Kay and Ali Smith', in James McGonigal and Kirsten Stirling (eds), *Ethically Speaking: Voice and Values in Modern Scottish Writing*, Amsterdam: Rodopi, pp. 157–78.

Winther, Per, Michael Trussler, Michael Toolan, Charles E. May and Susan Lohafer (2012), 'Introduction', *Narrative: Journal for the International Society for the Study of Narrative*, 20:2, 135–70.

Wittig, Monique (1992), *The Straight Mind and Other Essays*, Boston: Beacon Press.

Wolf, Naomi (1993), *Fire with Fire: The New Female Power and How it Will Challenge the 21st Century*, London: Vintage.

Woolf, Virginia (1976), 'A Sketch of the Past', in Jeanne Schulkind (ed.), *Moments of Being: Unpublished Autobiographical Writings*, London: Sussex University Press, pp. 61–138.

Woolf, Virginia (2003), *A Haunted House: The Complete Shorter Fiction*, Susan Dick (ed.), London: Vintage.

Woolf, Virginia [1992] (2008), *A Room of One's Own and Three Guineas*, Morag Shiach (ed.), Oxford: Oxford University Press.

XLondonCallGirl (2010), 'Can Prostitution be Empowering?', 26 October, <http://xlondoncallgirl.blogspot.co.uk/2012/10/can-prostitution-be-empowering.html> (last accessed 1 July 2014).

Young, Emma (2015), 'Feminist F(r)iction: Short Stories and Postfeminist Politics at the Millennial Moment', in Young and James Bailey (eds), *British Women Short Story Writers: The New Woman to Now*, Edinburgh: Edinburgh University Press, pp. 133–47.

Young, Iris Marion (1997), 'Gender as Seriality: Thinking About Women as a Social Collective', in Linda Nicholson and Steven Seidman (eds), *Social Postmodernism: Beyond Identity Politics*, Cambridge: Cambridge University Press, pp. 157–68.

Young, Robert (2003), *Postcolonialism: A Very Short Introduction*, Oxford: Oxford University Press.

Young, Tory (2014), 'You-niversal Love: Intimacy and the Second Person in Ali Smith's Short Fiction', in Antonio Venezia and Bianca Leggett (eds), *21st-Century British Writing*, Canterbury: Glyphi, pp. 293–312.

Yu, Su-Lin (2011), 'Reclaiming the Personal: Personal Narratives of Third-Wave Feminists', *Women's Studies*, 40, 873–89.

Index